THIS IS NO LONGER THE PROPERTY
OF THE SEATTLE PUBLIC LIBRARY

WALL STREET WARS

WALL STREET WARS

THE EPIC BATTLES WITH
WASHINGTON THAT CREATED
THE MODERN FINANCIAL SYSTEM

RICHARD E. FARLEY

Regan Arts.

NEW YORK

TO JOSEPH, CONOR, JAMES, AND CHELE

(in order of appearance)

Regan Arts.

65 Bleecker Street
New York, NY 10012

Copyright © 2015 by Richard E. Farley

All rights reserved, including the right to reproduce this book or portions thereof in any form whatsoever. For information address Regan Arts Subsidiary Rights Department, 65 Bleecker Street, New York, NY 10012.

Photo credits, which constitute an extension of this copyright page, appear on page 284.

First Regan Arts hardcover edition, May 2015.

Library of Congress Control Number: 2014955525

ISBN 978-1-941393-00-0

Interior design by Kris Tobiassen of Matchbook Digital
Jacket design by Richard Ljoenes
Jacket art by © Bettmann/CORBIS (top); The National Archives/Franklin D. Roosevelt Library (left); © Corbis (middle left); © Bettmann/CORBIS (middle right); The Library of Congress (right)

Printed in the United States of America

10 9 8 7 6 5 4 3 2 1

The past is never dead. It isn't even past.

—*William Faulkner*

TABLE OF CONTENTS

CAST OF CHARACTERS

(Positions Held at Times Relevant Herein)

IN THE EXECUTIVE BRANCH

At the White House:

Franklin D. Roosevelt, 32nd President of the United States

Eleanor Roosevelt, First Lady

Raymond Moley, Roosevelt adviser, member of the "brain trust"; nominally, an
    Assistant Secretary of State

Louis McHenry Howe, Roosevelt's Chief of Staff

At the Treasury Department:

William H. Woodin, Secretary of the Treasury (1933)

Henry J. Morgenthau Jr., Secretary of the Treasury (1934–1945)

F. Gloyd Awalt, Acting Comptroller of the Currency

J.F.T. O'Connor, Comptroller of the Currency

Dean G. Acheson, Undersecretary of the Treasury

Tom K. Smith, Special Assistant to Treasury Secretary Woodin

At the Federal Trade Commission:

James M. Landis, Commissioner (previously, Harvard Law School professor; and
later, Commissioner, Securities and Exchange Commission)

Huston Thompson, Former Commissioner; Special Adviser

At the Commerce Department:

Daniel C. Roper, Secretary of Commerce

John Dickinson, Assistant Secretary of Commerce (former partner, Sullivan &
Cromwell)

At the Reconstruction Finance Corporation:

Jesse Jones, President

Thomas "Tommy the Cork" Corcoran, Assistant General Counsel

At the Post Office Department:

James A. Farley, Postmaster General; also Chairman of the Democratic National
Committee

At the Securities and Exchange Commission:

Joseph P. Kennedy, Chairman

George C. Mathews, Commissioner

Robert E. Healy, Commissioner

John J. Burns, General Counsel and Director of the Legal Division

David Saperstein, Director of the Trading and Exchange Division

Baldwin Bane, Executive Administrator; later, Director of the Registration
Division

Donald Montgomery, Director of the Registration Division

James A. Fayne, Director of the Regional Administration Division

William O. Douglas, Director of the Protective Committee Study

Abe Fortas, Assistant Director of the Protective Committee Study

Edward Moore, Personal Assistant to the Chairman

In Congress

At the United States Senate:

Carter Glass, Senator from Virginia

Huey P. Long, Senator from Louisiana

Duncan U. Fletcher, Senator from Florida; Chairman, Banking and Currency
Committee

Joseph T. Robinson, Senator from Arkansas; Senate Majority Leader

Key Pittman, Senator from Nevada; Chairman, Foreign Relations Committee

Hiram W. Johnson, Senator from California

Arthur H. Vandenberg, Senator from Michigan

Ferdinand Pecora, Chief Counsel, Subcommittee on Stock Exchange Practices,
Banking and Currency Committee; later, Commissioner, Securities and
Exchange Commission

At the House of Representatives:

Samuel "Sam" T. Rayburn, Representative from Texas; Chairman, Interstate and
Foreign Commerce Committee

Henry B. Steagall, Representative from Alabama; Chairman, Banking and Currency
Committee

Henry T. Rainey, Representative from Illinois; Speaker of the House of
Representatives

Fred Bitten, Representative from Illinois

Middleton G. Beaman, Legislative Counsel

On Wall Street

At the New York Stock Exchange:

Richard Whitney, President; Chairman, Richard Whitney & Co.

Edward A. Pierce, Member; Leader of the "customers' men" broker faction;
Chairman, E.A. Pierce & Co.

Charles R. Gay, President (succeeding Richard Whitney)

Frank Altschul, Chairman, Listing Committee; Partner, Lazard Frères & Company

Paul V. Shields, Member; Chairman, Shields & Co.; Leading Democrat among
NYSE Members

At J.P. Morgan & Co.:
J.P. Morgan Jr., Managing Partner
George Whitney Jr., Partner
Russell C. Leffingwell, Partner
Thomas W. Lamont, Partner
S. Parker Gilbert, Partner

At National City Bank:
Charles E. Mitchell, Chairman
Gordon Rentschler, President
Hugh Baker, President of National City Company, National City Bank's
    Securities Affiliate

At Chase National Bank:
Albert H. Wiggin, Former Chairman

At Kuhn, Loeb & Company:
Otto H. Kahn, Senior Partner
Elisha Walker, Partner
George W. Bovenizer, Partner

At Dillon, Read & Co.:
Clarence Dillon (Born Clarence Lapowski), Chairman

At M.J. Meehan & Co.:
Michael J. Meehan, Chairman

At W.E. Hutton & Company:
Bernard E. "Sell 'Em Ben" Smith, Partner

At Sullivan & Cromwell:
Arthur H. Dean, Partner
John Foster Dulles, Partner
Eustace Seligman, Partner

At Davis Polk & Wardwell:
John W. Davis, Partner

At Cravath, DeGersdorff, Swaine & Wood:
Alexander Henderson, Partner

At Carter Ledyard & Milburn:
Roland L. Redmond, Partner

At the Investment Bankers Association:
Frank M. Gordon, President

IN THE PRESS
William Randolph Hearst, Publisher, Hearst Newspapers
Arthur B. Krock, *The New York Times,* Washington Correspondent and Bureau
    Chief
John T. Flynn, writer; contributor to *The New Republic* and *Harper's Magazine;*
    investigator for Ferdinand Pecora

REFORMERS IN THE PRIVATE SECTOR
Felix Frankfurter, Professor, Harvard Law School
Benjamin V. Cohen, attorney, private practice
Samuel Untermyer, attorney, private practice
Edward A. Filene, department store magnate; philanthropist; founder, Twentieth
    Century Fund

BROTHER, CAN YOU SPARE A DIME?

In March 1933, the United States economy was in a shambles. The nationwide unemployment rate stood at 25 percent. In certain areas of the country, the rate was twice that—this in an era when single income households were the norm.[1] Gross domestic product had fallen by more than 45 percent since October 1929, when the stock market crash tripped the wire that sent the economy into free fall.[2] The Dow Jones Industrial Average had fallen 85 percent from its 1929 high and stood at 59 as 1933 began.[3] The nation's financial system, the lifeblood of the economy, had ceased functioning, and banks were failing at an astounding rate.

In New York City, things were so desperate that Parks Commissioner Robert Moses ordered the sheep removed from the Central Park Zoo and relocated to Prospect Park in Brooklyn, where they could be securely protected from hungry residents of a nearby "Hooverville" who had taken to stealing the sheep and cooking them on open trash can fires.[4] Winter 1933 would prove to be the cruelest season of an economic depression that Lionel Robbins from the London School of Economics named "Great," and curiously the label took.[5]

Four months earlier, the incumbent president, Herbert Hoover, had been voted out of office by a lopsided margin. Contrary to later conventional belief, the election of Franklin Roosevelt in November 1932 did not give birth to a widespread feeling of optimism about the country's economic future. In fact, it made things worse. His election was more a personal repudiation of Hoover than it was an endorsement of Roosevelt's economic plan, which was, to put it kindly, not fully formed. The change Roosevelt promised was to use the full power of federal government to combat the Great Depression and reform the financial system. Few—not even the president-elect himself—could fully foresee and comprehend what course the application of that awesome power would take. Fewer still believed it would effect a quick end to the suffering. Roosevelt's campaign song, "Happy Days Are Here Again," from the MGM film *Chasing Rainbows,*[6] famously captured the candidate's unbridled optimism and self-confidence. Few of his fellow citizens found his optimism contagious.

That winter, Bing Crosby had a number-one hit song with "Brother, Can You Spare a Dime?" capturing the mood of disillusionment and despair that enveloped the nation between Roosevelt's election and inauguration:

They used to tell me I was building a dream
And so I followed the mob
When there was earth to plow or guns to bear,
I was always there, right on the job
They used to tell me I was building a dream
With peace and glory ahead—
Why should I be standing in line, just waiting for bread?

Once I built a railroad, I made it run
Made it race against time
Once I built a railroad, now it's done
Brother, can you spare a dime?[7]

Out of the anger and despair came the popular support for Roosevelt's efforts to reform the rules governing financial markets. Beneath his cheery exterior, Roosevelt possessed a steel will and cunning determination not to waste the nation's anger but to channel it for his political advantage. And

Roosevelt possessed that most important and elusive quality in a leader: luck. Time and again, a serendipity of events would nudge outcomes in Roosevelt's favor—and he seemed so often to have the right men in the right positions at the right times. Roosevelt was elected on a promise to use the power of the federal government to end the Great Depression. He made good on that promise, though there would be many ideological course changes and a frustrating trial-and-error approach to policy. And there would also be embarrassing missteps. What follows is the story of the battles of the first two and a half years of his administration that remade the country's decimated and corrupt financial system—and how, from this crisis, the modern financial system was born.

During that brief period, the Roosevelt administration enacted the Emergency Banking Act of 1933, instituting a nationwide shutdown and massive bailout of the nation's banks; the Banking Act of 1933, commonly referred to as Glass-Steagall, establishing national deposit insurance and separating commercial banking from investment banking; the Securities Act of 1933, mandating full and fair disclosure in the issuance of securities; and the Securities Exchange Act of 1934, regulating the trading of securities and the exchanges they are traded on and creating a national securities regulator, the Securities and Exchange Commission, which would become the most effective and long lasting of any of the New Deal agencies.

This is the story of that remarkable period and the remarkable men who made the modern American financial system.

It is a story of conflicts—Republicans battling Democrats; rural America competing against urban America; hard-money men versus inflationists; ideological reformers fighting free market bankers, brokers, and traders; old-line investment banks competing against upstart commercial banks; youthful New Deal reformers versus old Wilsonian progressives; and brokers competing against traders. And just underneath the surface of these conflicts were the class, ethnic, and religious rivalries that fueled them. Wall Street and Washington were forever changed by these battles.

ONE

CRASH
AND BURN

With the benefit of hindsight, the onset of every financial bubble appears blindingly obvious, every collapse is inevitable and preventable. How could they not have seen it coming? The indispensable ingredient for a bubble, however, is plausibility. There could not have been a subprime mortgage collapse in 2007 if it were not "plausible" that interest rates and unemployment would remain low indefinitely, qualified borrowers would continue to increase in number, home prices would continue to rise, and the mortgage refinancing market would remain robust. Plausibility was the Kool-Aid that washed down the adjustable-rate mortgages, the "no down payment" mortgages, the "no document" mortgages, and the synthetic credit default swaps.

The stock market crash of October 1929 had its own narrative of plausibility. A revolution in consumer technology had launched a "new era" of economic prosperity. Commercial aviation, "talkie" movies, affordable refrigerators, air conditioners, washers and dryers, and many other new applications of electrical motors and internal combustion engines were creating new markets and enormous wealth. Why *shouldn't* the Dow Jones Industrial Average have nearly doubled between January 1928 and August 1929?[1]

But as summer turned to fall in 1929, a nervous disquiet had overtaken Wall Street. On September 5, a financial adviser named Roger Babson (founder of Babson College) gave a not-too-important speech at a luncheon for the not terribly influential financial community of Wellesley, Massachusetts. Babson said a major stock market correction was coming. The Dow Jones newswire picked up his speech, and without any logical explanation, his remarks caused a frantic last hour of trading, sending prices tumbling. It would later be dubbed "Babson's break."[2] On September 24, there was a similar sharp stock market decline, this one without any obvious explanation. Prices held in early October, but market insiders took no comfort from this, as the number of margin loans taken from the "call money" market—where banks and corporations loaned excess cash at high interest rates overnight to stock market and commodities market speculators—was increasing. Normally, in a healthy, functioning market, this rush of debt-financed liquidity into the equity market would be accompanied by a rise in stock prices. Prices, however, remained stagnant.

During a Saturday morning trading session on October 19, the market dropped sharply on heavy volume. On Monday, October 21, the margin calls began and a chain reaction—a downward spiral in prices—followed. As stock price decreases led to margin calls that were met not with more cash deposited in brokerage accounts but with sell orders, prices declined further, leading to even more margin calls—and even more sell orders. Prices rebounded slightly the following day, but on Wednesday, October 23, the Dow dropped 7 percent on heavy volume.[3]

On Thursday morning, the market continued its free fall.

In the past, when corrections veered toward something worse, toward panic, the market looked for protection and leadership not from Washington, not from the New York Stock Exchange, but from the bank that bore the name of a father and son who were thought to hold nearly godlike powers over the world of finance. Across the street from the New York Stock Exchange, on the southeast corner of Wall Street and Broad Street in lower Manhattan, stood the most important edifice in the history of American finance: 23 Wall Street, the office of J.P. Morgan & Co., known simply as "The Corner." At J.P. Morgan & Co. that Thursday morning, the nation's most prominent bankers were summoned by J.P. Morgan Jr. to devise a plan to bail out the stock market. Morgan's crisis working group was comprised of Thomas Lamont and George Whitney of J.P. Morgan & Co., Albert Wiggin of Chase National Bank,

Charles Mitchell of National City Bank, and Richard Whitney, George's brother, the acting president of the New York Stock Exchange and a floor broker for the House of Morgan.[4]

The course of action agreed upon by Morgan and the rest of the bankers' consortium that day would propel Richard Whitney on a ten-year course of triumph and disgrace unparalleled in American financial history. Whitney started life perfectly credentialed for leadership in the American WASP aristocracy. His family came over on the *Arbella*, the first ship to land in the Massachusetts Bay Colony following the *Mayflower*. Born in Boston in 1888, the son of a bank president and nephew of a Morgan partner, he attended the Groton School, where he was a favorite of headmaster Reverend Endicott Peabody and captain of the baseball team. At Harvard, he was asked to join the Porcellian Club and rowed varsity crew. After a year at a brokerage firm in Boston, he went to Wall Street, buying a seat on the New York Stock Exchange in 1912 and forming his own firm, Richard Whitney & Company. He married Gertrude Sheldon, the daughter of George Sheldon, a business associate of J.P. Morgan Sr. and president of the elite Union League Club in New York City. And when Richard's brother George became a J.P. Morgan & Co. partner in 1919, the Whitney brothers became the brightest young stars among Wall Street royalty.[5]

Indicative of the respective power and influence of the two institutions on Wall Street at the time, the Federal Reserve Board also met that morning in Washington, D.C., to receive word from J.P. Morgan & Co. as to what action it should take in response to the emerging crisis. The bankers' consortium put together a pool of $240,000,000 to stabilize the market and sent Richard Whitney back across the street to the New York Stock Exchange with instructions to buy stock. Whitney marched onto the trading floor, went straight to post No. 2, and placed the single most celebrated order in stock market history, bidding $205 for 10,000 shares of U.S. Steel—even though the market price was below $200 per share and falling fast. Word of Whitney's bid spread quickly and the mood of the market brightened, with traders believing that Morgan would be able to stop the collapse as his father had done in the Panic of 1907. The next day newspaper headlines declared that Richard Whitney had halted the stock panic. Whitney's status as the hero of Black Thursday propelled him to the presidency of the New York Stock Exchange in 1930. But the reprieve was short-lived.[6]

On Tuesday, October 29—Black Tuesday—the Dow Jones Industrial Average lost 11.75 percent on record volume of 16.4 million shares.[7] There would be no Morgan bailout this time. The capital of the private sector banks was exposed to be a drop in the bucket as an ocean of leverage drained from the market. By the market's close, the Dow stood at 230, having lost 40 percent of its value from its peak of 381 earlier in the year.[8] It would ultimately bottom out at 41 during the summer of 1932.[9] Unlike his father in the Panic of 1907, J.P. Morgan Jr. in 1929 could not save the day.

It is difficult to comprehend today what a psychic shock it was to Wall Street in 1929 when J.P. Morgan & Co. proved impotent in preventing the Crash. The defusing of the Panic of 1907 by Morgan the Elder was the template that all of Wall Street had believed would solve any future crisis. It was during the 1907 crisis that J.P. Morgan & Co., already the dominant bank in America, established itself as effectively the nation's central bank. By the turn of the century J.P. Morgan & Co., under the iron-fisted control and leadership of John Pierpont Morgan, Sr., was the preeminent banking firm for mergers, acquisitions, and restructurings for the railroad, steel, and banking industries. As the lender and adviser of choice to industrial corporate America during this period of rapid growth, Morgan Sr. was arguably more powerful in economic matters than the president. His son, J.P. Morgan Jr., joined the firm after graduating from Harvard in 1886 and was close at hand when his father saved the financial system in 1907.[10]

The Panic of 1907 began with the San Francisco earthquake of 1906. The huge insurance payouts in the disaster's aftermath resulted in insurance companies liquidating investments and withdrawing deposits, which depressed asset prices and strained the available currency supply, particularly on the West Coast. There was no central bank in the United States then—the Federal Reserve system would not be created until 1914—so a nationwide, coordinated control of the money supply in such emergencies was impossible. But it was the disastrous attempt by Augustus and Otto Heinze to corner the market in shares of their own firm, United Copper Company, while the system was stressed that precipitated the panic, resulting in both their financial ruin and the insolvency of the banks that financed their scheme. This failure set off a run on the already cash-strapped banks.[11]

On November 2, 1907, as the crisis escalated with bank runs and rumors of bank runs, J.P. Morgan Sr. summoned to his Manhattan residence more than forty senior executives from the nation's largest banks to orchestrate a bailout plan: the strongest institutions would acquire the weakest, with others being provided liquidity by solvent banks such as J.P. Morgan & Co. The banks were thus saved.[12] Morgan Sr. was convinced by the experience that a formal central banking apparatus was needed to avoid future crises, and he encouraged the federal government to develop one.

To prevent future liquidity crises and panics, in May 1908, Congress passed the Aldrich-Vreeland Act, authorizing national banks in groups of ten or more, with at least aggregate capital of $5,000,000, to form currency associations approved by the Comptroller of the Currency and issue emergency currency backed by obligations and securities. The emergency currency was issued only once—during the panic arising from the outbreak of World War I in 1914.[13]

But more important, the Aldrich-Vreeland Act also established the National Monetary Commission, chaired by Republican senator Nelson Aldrich, to study banking and monetary systems around the world and make legislative recommendations to improve the nation's banking system and eliminate future financial panics. The report was submitted to Congress on January 9, 1912, and formed the foundation of the Federal Reserve Act of 1913, save one critical feature: the "Aldrich Plan" contemplated a central banking system under the control of private bankers as opposed to the federal government.

The Aldrich Plan was conceived at a secret "Skull & Bones"–type conference that could have been scripted by a conspiracy theorist (and indeed has fascinated conspiracy theorists ever since). In November 1910, Senator Aldrich invited to the gathering five of the country's leading bankers—Henry P. Davison and Benjamin Strong, senior partners of J.P. Morgan & Co.; Frank Vanderlip, president of National City Bank; Charles D. Norton, president of First National Bank of New York; and Paul Warburg, senior partner of the Kuhn, Loeb & Company banking house. The men met on a train platform in Hoboken, New Jersey, dressed as duck hunters supposedly on their way to a hunting trip and departed in a private, sealed railcar. Two days later, they disembarked in Brunswick, Georgia, where they boarded a boat to a private resort on Jekyll Island, owned by J.P. Morgan, Sr. Throughout the train journey, the men only referred to one another by their first names in order to maximize the secrecy of their mission. The "First Names Club," as they called themselves, met for nine days, emerging with what became the Aldrich Plan—a National Reserve Association with fifteen regional banks, its directors chosen by geographic region by private bankers. The National Reserve Association would have been given the power to print money and make loans to member banks and otherwise function as a traditional central bank but for its private ownership and control.[14]

But in May 1912, the Aldrich Plan ran head on into a wave of anti–Wall Street sentiment stirred by hearings conducted by a U.S. House of Representatives Committee on Banking and Currency subcommittee, chaired by Louisiana Democrat Arsene Pujo, to investigate whether an illegal cartel controlled credit in America. Under the direction of lead counsel Samuel Untermyer, the Pujo Committee revealed the enormous influence of banks such as J.P. Morgan & Co., but found no conclusive violations of law.

Untermyer's star witness was J.P. Morgan, Sr., who made his first and only appearance before a congressional committee. His defiant, condescending lecturing of Untermyer reinforced the public perception of him as an imperious, overbearing figure:

> "There is no way in which one man could obtain a money monopoly. . . .
> Commercial credit is based primarily on character. Money cannot buy
> it. . . . A man I do not trust could not get money from me on all the bonds in
> Christendom. . . . I have known men to come into my office and I have given
> them a check for $1,000,000 when I know they had not a cent in the world."[15]

Untermyer's investigation was materially hampered by a lack of cooperation from the administration of Republican president William Howard Taft. Taft instructed his Comptroller of the Currency to block Untermyer's attempts to access any records of national banks. Despite its inability to prove violations of the law, the Pujo Committee did make a number of recommendations for new legislation to improve the financial system.

With the election of Woodrow Wilson in 1912, the Democrats advanced their own plan for a central banking system under the control of a public entity, the Federal Reserve Board, to be appointed by the president and confirmed by the Senate. The legislation was sponsored by Virginia representative Carter Glass and Oklahoma senator Robert Latham Owen. The Glass-Owen bill passed the House on December 22, 1913, and the Senate on the following day. It created twelve regional Federal Reserve Banks, from which all nationally chartered banks—and state-chartered banks that became members of the Federal Reserve System—could borrow money in times of stress and in a single national currency, the Federal Reserve Note.[16]

Both Wall Street and the reformers were hopeful that the creation of the Federal Reserve System marked the end of financial panics in the United States. Oversight by the Federal Reserve Board would modernize American banking and end bank failures. It proved to be an overly optimistic belief. The problems with American banking weren't limited to those arising by the absence of a central bank. The uniquely American invention of unit banking—the laws of many states prohibiting a single banking company from owning more than one bank or a few bank branches—born of the fear of consolidation of financial control in the large Wall Street banks, emerged from the Pujo Committee hearings stronger than ever. The quaint, naive American love affair with the small-town *It's a Wonderful Life*-type bank perpetuated an outdated, fragmented banking system that was overbanked with too many small, thinly capitalized mom-and-pop operations scattered throughout the heartland. And these small banks, because of their size and the lack of sophisticated controls and operating procedures, were not eligible (or willing to change to become eligible) to be members of the Federal Reserve System, which had minimum asset and governance criteria for membership. Accordingly, in times of stress, these banks could not access the Fed discount window for liquidity.

But despite the creation of the Federal Reserve System, all wasn't well with the banking system long before the 1929 Crash. An average of more than 600 banks a year failed between 1921 and 1929, ten times the rate of failure during the preceding decade.[17] Most of the failed banks in the 1920s were small institutions in rural areas, leading many on Wall Street to conclude that the collapses were caused by mismanagement. Whatever the cause, these bank failures had caused the insolvency of the state deposit insurance funds (there was no federal deposit insurance then).

After the Crash, the illusion of a financial safety net anchored by J.P. Morgan & Co. and the Federal Reserve vanished, and the number of failures and the size of the failed banks and depositor losses increased dramatically. In 1929, 659 banks failed that had in the aggregate $230,643,000 of deposits, losing depositors $76,959,000. In 1930, 1,350 banks failed, holding deposits of $837,096,000, with depositor losses of a staggering $237,359,000.[18]

The largest bank to fail in 1930—what was then the largest bank failure in U.S. history—was the Bank of the United States in New York, with over $286,000,000 in deposits. The bank had been chartered by two unscrupulous garment dealers, Bernard Marcus and Saul Singer. They granted $2,578,932 in uncollateralized loans to themselves and their cronies on the bank's board of directors. When the New York State Commissioner of Banks shut the Bank of the United States—a purposely misleading name designed to imply a government connection—on December 11, 1930, more than 440,000 depositors, mostly Jewish immigrants like the bank owners, lost their savings. They would only recover about half of their account balances. Marcus and Singer were convicted of fraud and sentenced to prison terms in Sing Sing.[19]

With Wall Street incapable of containing the economic collapse, the nation looked to Washington. It is untrue that President Herbert Hoover declined to take action to try to stop the economic slide, but different and much more dramatic action was required to stop the hemorrhaging of economic output and jobs. Hoover's support of the disastrous Smoot-Hawley Tariff Act in 1930 accelerated the decline in international trade at precisely the moment when barriers needed to be eliminated. But Hoover had engaged in a large public works spending program and had successfully negotiated a one-year international moratorium on the repayment of World War I reparations in 1931, helping to slow the decline in international trade. He also attempted to coordinate private sector efforts to strengthen the financial system. On October 4, 1931, the president summoned a group of bankers to the Washington, D.C., home of his secretary of the Treasury, Andrew Mellon, to obtain pledges for a $500,000,000 credit pool to bail out weak and failing banks. This pool, named the National Credit Corporation, turned out to be a futile half measure, lasting only a few weeks and dispersing a paltry $20,000,000. The funding banks, mostly large New York City institutions, had no desire to risk larger sums.[20]

In December 1931, at the urging of Federal Reserve chairman Eugene Meyer, plans were drawn up for a publicly funded federal agency to stem bank failures. On January 22, 1932, President Hoover signed the law creating the Reconstruction Finance Corporation (RFC), with banker Charles G. Dawes as its president. The RFC was funded by the issuance of $2,000,000,000 of government bonds, an unprecedented debt raise by a government-sponsored entity then. By the end of 1932, it had authorized loans of almost $900,000,000 to more than 4,000 banks, though its effectiveness was significantly hampered by political squabbling over its operations.[21]

The principal squabbler was Senator Huey P. Long of Louisiana, who sought to use the RFC as his personal piggy bank to promote his "Share the Wealth" populist, socialist agenda, in order to advance his presidential ambitions. Long called Fed chairman Meyer, a member of the RFC board, and demanded immediate loans for his favored banks in Louisiana. When Meyer explained that the RFC had procedures that needed to be followed, including approval of loans the size Long was requesting by the full board of the RFC, Long threatened to take the next train out of Washington, D.C., and close all the banks in Louisiana, Mississippi, and Arkansas. Meyer wished him safe travels and hung up the phone. Senator Long would be a colorful, infuriating force to be reckoned with throughout Roosevelt's drive to regulate the financial markets, and his relentless advocacy for small banks and "Main Street" financial interests left an indelible mark on financial regulation.[22]

Long's life story is so outlandish, his antics so outrageous, that only the truth about him can do him justice. Hugh Pierce Long Jr. was born in Winn Parish, Louisiana, the seventh of nine children born to Hugh and Caledonia Long. Inexplicably, his mother thought he should be a Baptist preacher. Huey thought maybe he should become a lawyer, and with $100 dollars in his pocket set out for law school at the University of Oklahoma. En route to Norman, Oklahoma, he happened upon a casino, promptly lost the $100, and, without money to pay tuition, thought a career in sales might be a wiser choice. In 1913, he married Rose McConnell, the winner of a baking contest he staged to promote a vegetable shortening he was selling.[23]

In 1914, he enrolled in Tulane University Law School. Not interested in further studying after his first year, he nevertheless convinced the Louisiana Bar Association to let him take the bar exam. He passed. In 1918, Long ran for the Louisiana State Railroad Commission and won, becoming the commission's chairman by 1922. In 1924, he ran for governor, finishing third in the Democratic primary. He ran again in 1928 and won.[24]

Long was an extraordinary campaigner, equally popular with the downstate Catholics as with upstate Baptists. He often told the story of how on Sunday mornings he would wake up early and hitch the horse to the wagon and take his Baptist grandparents to 7:00 a.m. service, hurrying home to take his

Catholic grandparents to 9:00 a.m. Mass. When an aide mentioned he never knew Long had Catholic grandparents, the governor answered, "Don't be a damn fool, we didn't even have a horse."[25] He railed against the anti-Catholic bigotry expressed against Al Smith, the Democratic presidential nominee that year, while in the next breath declaring that Herbert Hoover was unfit to be president because he was a Quaker.[26]

After his election, Long proceeded to shock even the rather jaded Louisiana political class with his aggressive patronage spending, often joking that every one of his relatives was on the state payroll except those in federal prison. He didn't like the governor's mansion and soon after being sworn in requested the public works department build him a new one. When an official correctly pointed out that funds for the project would require legislative approval, Long had a friend in the demolition business level the mansion in the middle of the night. The next morning he called the official and suggested they start cleanup and construction on a new mansion.[27] After a year in office, Long was impeached by the Louisiana House of Representatives, but he had the support of the Senate, which dropped the case. Long appeared invincible. They started calling him the "Kingfish."

In March of 1930, Long launched his own newspaper, funded with "voluntary" subscriptions from all state workers—none declined to subscribe. Later that year, he announced he was running for U.S. Senate and, if elected, would continue to hold the governorship as well. He won—and kept his promise.

During Long's Senate campaign, the Bank of Lafayette and Trust Company experienced a run, and if it opened for business the following day, it would not be able to meet withdrawals. They called Governor Long. Long showed up at the bank at dawn, making sure he would be first in line when the bank opened. About an hour before opening time, nervous customers gathered, withdrawal slips in hand, shocked to see the governor also in line. When the bank opened on time, as Long had directed, he gathered all the customers in the lobby and informed them that he had in his hand a withdrawal slip for $260,000, the entire amount the State of Louisiana had on deposit at the bank—and far more than the cash the bank had available. Accordingly, they could leave their money in the bank, as Long was prepared to do. If not, Long would withdraw all the state's cash and declare the bank insolvent right then. With no alternative, the customers left. And the bank was saved.[28]

By the spring of 1932, bank failures had spread to money center cities. Charles Dawes resigned as president of the RFC and returned to Chicago in order to save his own family bank, the Central Republic National Bank. By June, bank runs had closed fifteen smaller banks in Chicago and twenty-five more in the suburbs. Central Republic had lost $239,000,000 in deposits over the prior year, and Dawes concluded that the bank could not be saved. Melvin Traylor, president of the First National Bank of Chicago, Chicago's largest bank, feared that if Central Republic failed, First National would soon follow, and appealed to President Hoover and Dawes's successor at the RFC, Jesse Jones, for a bailout. The Democratic National Convention was being held in Chicago when this banking crisis was erupting, and Hoover thought it would be a political disaster for the biggest banks in the nation's second largest city to collapse with the national press in town. Saving Central Republic became Hoover's top priority. The RFC agreed to loan the bank $90,000,000 and the crisis was temporarily averted.[29]

It was later revealed by Dawes that Central Republic had loaned amounts equal to nearly 90 percent of its deposits to companies in the highly leveraged utility conglomerate of Samuel Insull, the bankrupt Chicago magnate whose byzantine holding company structures allowed him to control a $500,000,000 empire with only $27,000,000 in equity.[30] The Insull and Central Republic disasters were the impetus for the Public Utility Holding Company Act of 1935.

Despite the fact that Jesse Jones and Melvin Traylor were both Democrats, Hoover's intercession on behalf of Republican Dawes's family bank became a political football, with congressional Democrats alleging partisan favoritism. The Speaker of the House, Texas Democrat John Nance Garner, pushed through an amendment to the RFC enabling legislation requiring full disclosure of all RFC loans.

Thereafter, banks feared that if it was publicly disclosed that they had received a loan from the RFC, that alone might trigger a run on the bank. The result, of course, was that weak banks were afraid to access the liquidity they desperately needed. (It was this failure of the RFC that Treasury secretary Hank Paulson and Federal Reserve chairman Ben Bernanke sought to avoid when requiring the nine largest American banks to take TARP equity investments from the Treasury in October 2008—whether or not they needed or wanted the equity capital.)

Nonetheless, the efforts of the RFC contributed to a reduction in bank failures in 1932, as compared with 1931. In 1932, 1,453 banks failed (as compared with 2,293 in 1931) that had deposits of $706,187,000 and depositor losses of $168,302,000 (as compared with deposits of $1,640,232,000 and losses of $340,476,000, respectively, in 1931).[31]

The leader of the RFC's elite legal corps was a jovial, brilliant 32-year-old Irish American corporate lawyer from Pawtucket, Rhode Island, named Thomas Corcoran, whom an adoring Franklin Roosevelt would nickname "Tommy the Cork."

Corcoran had ended up at the RFC by accident. After catching the eye of Professor Felix Frankfurter while working on the *Harvard Law Review,* Corcoran, together with eight of the other gifted students in his graduating class, was selected to join the Harvard Law School faculty as a teaching fellow. Frankfurter would make Corcoran his most nurtured mentee and was determined to protect and promote his extraordinarily gifted—but sensitive— protégé. "He is struggling hard with the burden of inferiority imposed on him because of his Irish Catholicism, by his experiences at Brown, in Providence, and in Boston," Frankfurter wrote. After his teaching fellowship ended in 1926, Frankfurter arranged for Corcoran to clerk with Supreme Court Justice Oliver Wendell Holmes and arranged a permanent job for Corcoran with the Wall Street firm of Cotton & Franklin (predecessor to today's Cahill Gordon & Reindel LLP), predicting correctly that Joseph Cotton, a Newport native, would take a liking to the fellow Rhode Islander.[32]

By 1932, the Great Depression had ravaged the corporate law business. Wall Street law firms were slashing the salaries of even top-performing associates like Corcoran. When Federal Reserve Board chairman Meyer set out to create the RFC, he asked George Franklin, the other name partner of Cotton & Franklin, to serve as the new agency's general counsel. Franklin agreed to take the position, but when Joseph Cotton was tragically killed in a car accident, Franklin concluded he could not leave his law firm without both name partners. Instead, he recommended to Martin Bogue, who was chosen as general counsel, that he offer Tommy Corcoran the assistant general counsel position. Corcoran accepted the offer and rented a house in Georgetown with Edward Foley Jr., another young Irish American lawyer who came to Washington, D.C., from Syracuse, New York, to help start the RFC. Their house would become a boarding house and clubhouse for the youthful New Deal legal elite.[33]

While the private Wall Street banks no longer had balance sheets capable of bailing out a financial system that had grown so large since 1907, certainly the Federal Reserve Banks did. But the Federal Reserve Board had done far too little, far too late, to stem the financial meltdown. As stock prices soared in 1928 and 1929, the Fed grew alarmed that Federal Reserve Bank loans were being loaned by member banks—and by corporate and industrial borrowers from member banks—to brokers financing purchases of stock on margin by brokerage customers. In response, the Fed raised the discount rate from 3.5 percent to 5 percent. It also reduced liquidity through open-market securities sales. While loans to brokers and loans by brokers to their customers turned out to be remarkably safe (broker loans of more than $4,000,000,000 made in the "call money" market were liquidated between October 1, 1929, and December 1, 1929, without the loss of a penny to a single lender), consequences to the purchasers of the securities on margin and to the economy were catastrophic. Easy money pouring into equity markets from the Federal Reserve Banks had created a financial bubble. In many ways, the ease with which the bubble could be burst and the inflated assets liquidated on publicly traded equity markets, while advantageous for the margin lenders, intensified the shock and panic to the economy.[34]

Rather than flooding the system with emergency liquidity after the Crash, the Fed acted timidly, as if repenting for the past sins of its easy-money policies that fueled the boom before the bust. This was due in part to an institutional belief that its responsibility was principally to protect its member banks, which were mostly safe and solvent at the time, and not to shore up equity values or the economy at large.[35] New York Federal Reserve Bank president and former J.P. Morgan & Co. banker Benjamin Strong, who had served since the creation of the Federal Reserve System in 1914 and had the confidence of all Federal Reserve Bank directors, died on October 16, 1928. His successor, George L. Harrison, was Strong's general counsel, and although able, Harrison could not take command of the situation and demand decisive action from his colleagues as Strong could have.[36]

After the Crash, the Federal Reserve Board acted, but moderately, lowering the discount rate progressively from 5⅛ percent to 1⅞ percent by the end of 1930 and increasing its open-market purchases. But banks used these funds not to make loans but to bolster reserves and maintain their liquidity in fear of bank runs.[37]

Throughout 1931, another crisis was looming for the Fed. Fearful of both inflationary government policies and the safety of the American banking system, foreigners began large-scale withdrawals from U.S. banks and demanded payment in gold, to which they were entitled. These withdrawals accelerated after England went off gold standard in September 1931, with fears growing that America would be next. Dollars leaving the Federal Reserve System in massive amounts created problems that moving money between U.S. banks did not. Under law, each Federal Reserve Bank had to hold gold or short-term commercial paper with an aggregate value at least equal to the Federal Reserve Notes they issued, and at least 40 percent of that amount was required to be gold. Given the collapse in economic activity, there was a sharp decline in short-term commercial paper issued by businesses and held by banks. Since banks needed currency to stave off bank runs and satisfy withdrawals, that left only gold to backstop the currency. And there was not enough gold available.

On January 27, 1932, Hoover summoned Senator Carter Glass, the leading Democrat on the Banking and Currency Committee, to the White House and asked him to introduce legislation expanding the eligible collateral for Federal Reserve Notes to include U.S. government bonds and expanding the eligible collateral for the Federal Reserve Bank's loans to their member banks. Glass was reluctant to support such an inflationary measure, but as the banking system weakened, he relented. The measure passed both houses of Congress by a voice vote on February 26 and was signed by President Hoover the next day.[38]

The Federal Reserve Banks also undertook massive open-market purchases over the next six months, doubling the size of the Fed's balance sheet. But bank lending did not increase, and business activity and prices of securities and commodities declined. The money that didn't go under people's mattresses stayed in bank vaults or went overseas.[39]

Hoover made efforts to counteract the currency hoarding. On March 6, 1932, he announced a program whereby the secretary of the Treasury would issue one-year Treasury certificates at 2 percent interest in small denominations—$50, $100, and $500—to encourage hoarders who did not trust the banks to leave their money with the federal government, and thereby get that currency back in circulation. There were few takers—only $35,000,000 of these so-called Baby Bonds were issued.[40] In addition, on July 21, 1932,

Hoover signed the Emergency Relief and Reconstruction Act, which for the first time allowed the Federal Reserve Banks to lend to non-banking entities, including individuals, if no bank would lend to them, so long as high-quality collateral (short-term commercial paper or government securities) was pledged.[41]

Hoover also took action to attempt to help homeowners unable to meet their mortgages. Like in the 2008 crisis, the financial system was weighed down by defaults on mortgages obtained in an easy-money environment based on values inflated by a housing bubble. On July 22, 1932, Hoover signed the Federal Home Loan Bank Act, establishing twelve Federal Home Loan Banks supervised by the Federal Home Loan Bank Board to buy troubled mortgages from banks and thereafter favorably modify their terms for homeowners. The problem with the legislation was that it required that any mortgage purchased not have unpaid principal in excess of two-thirds of the current value of the home (in other words, requiring a 33⅓ percent equity cushion). Few troubled mortgages fit that profile, and the banks did not want to part with those that did. The program was totally ineffective. (Roosevelt would take the idea and retool it with the Home Owners' Loan Act, enacted on June 13, 1933, creating the Home Owners' Loan Corporation, which was authorized to acquire and readjust the terms of mortgages, but with eligibility requirements that allowed unpaid principal of up to 80 percent of the value of the home. This program was a success, refinancing nearly 10 percent of all nonfarm mortgages in the country, and with the Home Owners' Loan Corporation ultimately netting the U.S. taxpayers a small profit.)

By the fall of 1932, time had run out for Herbert Hoover. There would be no recovery to save him from electoral defeat. Franklin Roosevelt would be the next president. But his economic program, set out piecemeal in his campaign speeches that fall, was skeletal. He had few Wall Street supporters and only a handful of advisers with Wall Street experience. The one who appeared to be closest to him was a young, lone-wolf Irish American banker from Boston.

On October 1, 1932, the Roosevelt campaign train arrived for a one-day visit to Chicago, where the candidate was to give a speech at the Hotel Stevens. On the train with Roosevelt was his friend from Boston Joseph P. Kennedy, who had made his first fortune in 1920s Hollywood restructuring failing movie companies. Kennedy had contributed generously to Roosevelt's campaign and had been extraordinarily helpful at the nominating convention in Chicago, but many in the Roosevelt inner circle were leery of him because of his Wall Street ties and rumors of his participation in bear pools. That day of campaigning also coincided with the third game of the World Series between the New York Yankees and the Chicago Cubs, with the Yankees ahead two games to none. Joe Kennedy, to everyone's amazement, arranged a block of tickets large enough for everyone on Roosevelt's campaign train to attend the game.[42]

In the top of the fifth inning, with the bases empty and the score tied four to four, Babe Ruth came to the plate against Cubs left-hander Charlie Root. Ruth had homered against Root in the first inning. With a zero-to-two count, Ruth lifted his bat, pointing it toward the center field stands. Root delivered a curve ball that Ruth demolished, launching a towering home run well over the 440-foot mark in the deepest part of Wrigley Field. Reporter Joe Williams for *The New York World-Telegram* wrote the headline "Ruth Calls Shot," naming the most famous home run in World Series history.[43]

Kennedy had a knack for being at the right place at the right time with the right people. This talent would later prove invaluable for Roosevelt's program of market reform.

The landslide election of Franklin Roosevelt on November 8, 1932, did little to calm the nation's depositors. Roosevelt's 22,800,000 popular votes to Hoover's 15,750,000 resulted in an Electoral College rout of 472 to 59, but this was more a vote of no confidence in Hoover than an endorsement of Roosevelt.[44] Many feared that Roosevelt would devalue the dollar and otherwise implement inflationary policies in order to stimulate exports and economic growth. This fear led to increased gold withdrawals from the Federal Reserve System, particularly by foreigners, further limiting the amount of gold-backed currency the Federal Reserve Banks could issue.

The first bank holiday of the Great Depression was announced by the lieutenant governor of Nevada on October 31, 1932. The Nevada banking system was dominated by one man, George Wingfield, who controlled twelve of the state's twenty-six banks. Wingfield was Nevada's Republican national committeeman, and his lawyer was the Democratic national committeeman. Local journalists would joke that Wingfield's Reno National Bank building was the real capital of the state.[45]

In the 1930s, Nevada's economy was dominated by mining and ranching, and with the collapse in commodity prices, most loans were substantially underwater. Wingfield's banks had foreclosed on loans to 150 ranches, which owned 70 percent of the cattle and sheep in Nevada. He loaned on sheep at $8 per head but only realized $0.25 per head in foreclosure sales.[46]

Four months later, a public-private consortium bailed out the Nevada banks by merging all of Wingfield's properties into a new, recapitalized Bank of Nevada, with supportive loans from the RFC and California investors.

Nevada's banking holiday had little effect on the national banking system. The state had a small population and was surprisingly self-contained. Its banks had almost no ties outside Nevada. The optimists hoped the bank failures had been contained.

The 1932 presidential election would be the last one with a four-month interregnum before the swearing-in of the president and new Congress. On March 2, 1932, Congress approved an amendment to the Constitution moving the inauguration from March 4 to January 20, but the required thirty-six states did not ratify the amendment until February 9, 1933. This left a long-lived lame-duck president at precisely the time when vigorous, mandated leadership was essential. Nevada would prove to be only the beginning, and Washington was adrift.

Bank runs started occurring regularly in December 1932, mostly in rural areas. The RFC stepped in to save banks in Wisconsin, Pennsylvania, Minnesota, and Tennessee. In January 1933, panics were narrowly averted in Cleveland, St. Louis, Little Rock, Mobile, Chattanooga, and Memphis. By early February 1933, inter-city interbank lending had all but stopped.[47] The warning lights were flashing bright red.

On Friday, February 3, 1933, Huey Long's Louisiana became the second state to announce a bank holiday, but being Louisiana, it was accomplished creatively. On that day, the Hibernia Bank and Trust Company of New Orleans, the state's third largest bank, informed state officials that it could not make another day's withdrawals. Senator Huey Long came to the bank's rescue. Needing no convincing of the gravity of the situation this time, the RFC approved a loan and told Long that it would be negotiated over the course of the weekend and funded on Monday, February 6. On Sunday, the banks were closed. This left the problem of Saturday, February 4. Needing only a one-day reprieve—and a Saturday no less—Long and Louisiana governor Oscar Allen wanted to avoid declaring a banking holiday. Late Friday night, Long had the New Orleans City librarian roused from his bed with instructions to find a historical event that had occurred on February 4 that might justify a state holiday. The best the librarian could come up with was that on February 3, 1917, the United States had severed diplomatic relations with Germany. That was good enough for Long. In the early morning hours, Long and Governor Allen gathered a bleary-eyed and confused local press corps and proclaimed that February 4 would thereafter be "Break with Germany Day" in Louisiana, the state's newest holiday. Long laid it on good and thick, praising the wisdom of President Wilson in severing diplomatic relations with the Imperial German Government: "More than 16 years have intervened before the American people have turned their eyes back to the lofty ideals of human uplift and new freedom as propounded by Woodrow Wilson. . . . It is now fitting that due recognition by the great State of Louisiana in line with the far-reaching principles enunciated by that illustrious Southerner who sought to break the fetters of humankind throughout the world be given."[48] The local German consul, outraged, lodged a formal protest. When a Baton Rouge newspaper printed an early edition revealing the true reason for the holiday, Long ordered the state militia to seize all copies at the printing press and to occupy the newspaper's facilities.[49]

On Sunday morning, officials of Hibernia Bank announced the $20,000,000 RFC bailout. On Monday morning, the first person in line at Hibernia's New Orleans branch was none other than Huey P. Long, accompanied by a pack of reporters. Long deposited $20,000 in cash, declaring, "I can't think of a safer place to put the money than right here." The panic was over.[50]

The critical juncture in the banking crisis occurred on St. Valentine's Day 1933 in Detroit. At the center of the disaster was Edsel Ford, the hapless only child of automobile magnate Henry Ford.

To carve out his own identity, separate from that of his tyrannical father, Edsel had invested heavily in the Union Guardian Trust Company of Detroit, a bank started by his brother-in-law. The bank was very successful, in large part due to the exclusive loans it provided to Ford dealers for the financing of automobile purchases. By 1933, the collapse in auto sales had decimated Union Guardian, which needed a bailout from the RFC. Edsel, unable to bear his father's wrath, did not tell him of the extent of the deteriorating financial condition of the bank. When Henry found out, he became so enraged that Edsel fell into a deep depression from which he never fully recovered. While Henry bailed out Edsel personally, he refused to bail out the bank. Had Henry Ford agreed to leave Ford Motor Company deposits in Union Guardian, it's quite possible the banking crisis could have been contained and worked out by the RFC without catastrophe. But when told that Union Guardian would fail without his assistance, possibly triggering a crash of the national banking system, the seventy-year-old Henry Ford replied, "If a crash has to come, let the crash come. I still feel young." Union Guardian's failure prompted Michigan governor William Comstock to declare an eight-day banking holiday, closing all 550 national and state banks in Michigan. This set off an irreversible chain reaction of bank closings across the nation.[51]

The anatomy of a bank run is relatively simple. When there is concern over the solvency of a bank, merchants refuse to accept payment on checks drawn on that bank and depositors rush to withdraw their money, fearing that there will not be enough liquid assets to be converted into cash to cover all deposits. To meet anticipated withdrawals, the bank stops making loans, liquidates whatever assets it can, and withdraws its reserves from either its Federal Reserve Bank (if it's a member) or the large private bank at which it deposits its reserves. If there are enough banks doing this all concurrently in a particular region, the Federal Reserve Bank for that region will itself need to borrow reserves from other Federal Reserve Banks to provide the currency necessary to meet the withdrawals of its member banks. Large banks holding reserves for non–Federal Reserve member banks will, in turn, need to withdraw their deposits from their Federal Reserve Bank to meet their liquidity needs as well. When the bank in trouble runs out of assets to pledge as collateral to the applicable Federal Reserve Bank and large private banks, the cash spigot is shut off and the bank fails. When things are very, very bad, Federal Reserve Banks, worried about the liquidity and solvency of other Federal Reserve Banks, refuse to lend to each other.

This has only happened once.

What occurred after St. Valentine's Day through to Inauguration Day on March 4, 1933, was essentially a run on the entire Federal Reserve System.

During the nine days preceding Inauguration Day, $422,000,000 in deposits and $384,000,000 in gold were withdrawn from the Federal Reserve System. Foreigners converting dollar deposits into bullion accounted for $300,000,000 of the gold withdrawn, and this gold left the country.[52] In addition, during this period, the Federal Reserve Banks assisted member banks by making $347,000,000 of open-market purchases of securities and direct loans of $1,015,000,000. From the week of the Michigan bank holiday through the week of the inauguration, currency in circulation ballooned from $5,470,000,000 to $7,250,000,000, the result of widespread panicked cash hoarding.[53]

As the banking crisis was unfolding, the nation, even President Hoover, looked to President-elect Roosevelt for guidance, some public statement as to how he was going to avert a meltdown. But Roosevelt stayed aloof, vacationing aboard Vincent Astor's 283-foot yacht, the *Nourmahal*, in the Caribbean. In his absence, Roosevelt had delegated to top aides Raymond Moley and Louis M. Howe the task of vetting the candidates for the critical cabinet post of secretary of the Treasury. Word of the man Roosevelt would choose for that position, the field general to confront the crisis, was eagerly awaited by Congress, the press, and the public. Roosevelt's first choice was Virginia senator Carter Glass, who as a fiscal and monetary conservative and former secretary of the Treasury could help calm the panicked markets. But which of Glass's demands could Roosevelt live with?[54]

Carter Glass was, to put it mildly, a difficult man. He was ill-tempered, racist, and often in poor health, physically and mentally, suffering frequent nervous breakdowns and hospitalizations. He was so arrogant that he thought it beneath him to campaign for election. He had never held a job in a private sector financial institution, and what limited formal education he had ended when he was fourteen. He is also the single most important lawmaker in the history of American finance. He drafted and shepherded through Congress the legislation creating the Federal Reserve System and later served as President Wilson's secretary of the Treasury.[55]

Glass was the last man born in the antebellum South to serve in the U.S. Senate. By his own admission, he was an "unreconstructed rebel." He was one of twelve children fathered by Robert Glass, a Lynchburg, Virginia, newspaperman. It was common practice in the mid-nineteenth-century American South for those feeling aggrieved by a newspaper's editorial position to challenge the editor to a duel. Robert Glass was involved in many such duels, and Carter Glass would recall how his father once lost an eye in a shoot-out with three disgruntled readers.[56]

Carter Glass became a newspaperman himself, acquiring ownership of the *Lynchburg News* in 1888, when he was thirty. In 1889, he was elected to the Virginia State Senate. As a delegate to the Virginia Constitutional Convention of 1901–1902, he was author of a plan to institute a voting literacy test for the express purpose of disenfranchising African American voters, including from voting on ratification of the new Constitution itself. "For my part," he said, "no Constitution can be framed by this Convention so obnoxious to my sense of right that I would desire to wield a cudgel against its fate to 146,000 Negro voters. No other member of this body should be willing to appeal to that depraved suffrage to defeat any part of the work of this Convention which may not suit him."[57]

Glass was elected to the U.S. Congress in 1902, becoming chairman of the House Banking Committee in 1913, when he authored the Glass-Owen bill. After serving as Wilson's Treasury secretary for fifteen months, he was appointed to fill the vacant U.S. Senate seat after the death of Senator Thomas Martin on February 20, 1920. While Duncan Fletcher of Florida was the ranking Democrat by seniority on the Senate Banking and Currency Committee, Carter Glass was far and away the Committee's most influential member.

Glass told Moley he had two conditions in agreeing to become Roosevelt's secretary of the Treasury: he wanted J.P. Morgan & Co. partner Russell Leffingwell as his undersecretary and a commitment from Roosevelt that he would take a strong anti-inflation policy position. Roosevelt made it clear that, in the current environment, there was no way he would accept a J.P. Morgan partner as undersecretary nor would he commit to an anti-inflation platform. "If the old boy doesn't want to go along, I wouldn't press it," he said.[58] The old boy didn't go along, withdrawing himself from consideration for "reasons of health." Howe and Moley cabled the news to Roosevelt aboard the *Nourmahal*, using code in case any reporter might intercept the radiogram: "PREFER A WOODEN ROOF TO A GLASS ROOF OVER SWIMMING POOL. LUHOWRAY."[59]

The "wooden roof" was William Hartman Woodin, president of the American Car & Foundry Co., then the largest railroad equipment manufacturer in the world and, like most perfect second choices, a man objectionable to practically no one. But Willie Woodin was no Carter Glass as far as the financial community was concerned, and his appointment did nothing to calm the panic. Woodin, a moderate Republican who backed Democrat Alfred E. Smith for president in 1928 because of his anti-Prohibition stance, had been a director of the Federal Reserve Bank of New York since 1927. Under ordinary circumstances, Woodin would have been the safest of choices for Roosevelt— a member of the big-business establishment, with no discernible ideological views on matters of financial policy. But there was nothing ordinary about March 1933. Woodin's chances for nomination were not hurt by the fact that he contributed $50,000 to the Roosevelt campaign, more than any other business executive.[60]

He was also a man of impeccable manners and politeness. Despite being one of Roosevelt's largest financial contributors, he had once been barred entry from Roosevelt headquarters at the Biltmore Hotel in New York by a security guard who did not recognize him. Rather than confront the guard, Woodin went to a pay phone and called James Farley, Roosevelt's campaign manager, and asked him if he could please have the doorman let him in.[61] He was extraordinarily clubbable, belonging to New York's Union Club, Union League Club, Racquet and Tennis Club, Metropolitan Club, and Lotus Club, among others.[62] He was also a composer of music, both classical (his compositions were performed by Henry Hadley's Manhattan Orchestra) and popular (he wrote *Raggedy Ann's Sunny Songs* with children's book author Johnny Gruelle; one of Gruelle's songs, "Little Wooden Willie,"[63] is believed to be named after him). He composed the theme song for the Inaugural Parade—the "Franklin D. Roosevelt March," and another of his compositions, "The Covered Wagon," was among the songs selected to be played by the National Symphony Orchestra at the pre-inaugural concert.[64] Woodin certainly was in line with Roosevelt's cheery optimism.

Needless to say, Woodin's appointment was not universally praised. Arthur Krock of *The New York Times*, the dean of Washington journalists, wrote, "Knowing of Mr. Woodin only as a successful businessman who freely admitted that he knew nothing of the Treasury and its problems, many important people here, aware of the storm about to swirl about his head, were frankly uneasy." Woodin's amiability was itself viewed with suspicion, according to Krock. "One of the curiosities of the new Secretary's personal and official triumph is that he is one of those men who laugh constantly, and who is generally photographed in that mood. The experience of the observers of Washington affairs is that steady smilers or chucklers who seem to find something agreeable or amusing in all situations are shams or stuffed shirts of a gentler species."[65] Contrary to all predictions, in his too short tenure, William Woodin would prove to be the boldest, most activist secretary of the Treasury since Alexander Hamilton.

There was one notable backer of Roosevelt who was left out of the action in the scramble for positions in the incoming administration. He secretly harbored the unrealistic ambition that he might be appointed secretary of the Treasury—and actually thought he deserved it. But if a J.P. Morgan & Co. partner could not be undersecretary of the Treasury, there was no chance that Joe Kennedy would get the top position. He was a speculator. He was also an Irish Catholic, and Roosevelt already had chosen one of those for his cabinet—James Farley, as postmaster general. In February 1933, Kennedy felt very far away from where he felt he deserved to be.

Following Roosevelt's election, Kennedy awaited a call that never came. Throughout the pre-inauguration period, Kennedy waited and seethed as high-ranking New Deal positions were populated by those who he felt had done less for—and offered less to—the new president. Kennedy's call would come, and his service as first federal securities regulator would be as critical to the creation of the modern financial system as that of Senator Glass or Secretary Woodin. But he would have to wait.

In the weeks before his inauguration, Roosevelt was asked numerous times by Hoover to make a joint statement to calm financial markets and a banking system veering toward outright collapse. He repeatedly refused. Relations between the two men were as poor, and perhaps worse, as between any incoming and outgoing president in history. Hoover refused to extend the customary pre-inaugural White House dinner to his successor, grudgingly agreeing to only a brief afternoon tea. After the inauguration, the two men would never see or speak to each other again.[66]

In the eleven days before the inauguration, as the banking crisis grew and more holidays were declared, seemingly out of nowhere, testimony in a U.S. Senate hearing room would shock and outrage the nation. The hearings held in that room, pitting the titans of banking against a theretofore unknown son of Italian immigrants, put Wall Street on trial before the American people. The verdict would be guilty, the sentence a tangle of new laws and regulations.

TWO

SUNSHINE CHARLIE AND THE SICILIAN

On January 30, 1933, Ferdinand Pecora, former assistant district attorney of New York County, began his work as chief counsel for a subcommittee of the Senate Banking and Currency Committee investigating stock market practices. To the relatively few interested observers paying close attention to the subcommittee's hearings to date, the task ahead of Pecora had all the makings of a debacle—for him. Nearly eleven months into its work, the stock market practices subcommittee had uncovered little of note and had only until March 4, 1933—five weeks away—to report its findings to the full Senate. What was most noteworthy about the chief counsel's job was that no one seemed to want it. Pecora was the fifth attorney in less than a year to fill the position, and his immediate predecessor, Irving Ben Cooper, had resigned in protest only a week after he was hired, claiming that the committee chairman, South Dakota Republican senator Peter Norbeck, failed to give him a free hand in the investigation.[1]

New York Stock Exchange president Richard Whitney was an early witness, appearing before the subcommittee in the fall of 1932. His testimony would be better characterized as a lecture to the assembled senators rather than an interrogation.[2] So ineffectual was questioning of witnesses that Carter Glass publicly admitted that the hearings were going nowhere. The only memorable moment of the first round of hearings was the testimony of New York congressman Fiorello La Guardia. The feisty La Guardia produced evidence that a public relations man named Newton Plummer had paid nearly $300,000 over a ten-year period to various business journalists in exchange for flattering articles about companies whose stocks his clients had invested in. Plummer often wrote the planted stories himself, simply paying journalists to submit the stories under their bylines.[3]

When the hearings adjourned for the 1932 election season, no one thought they would amount to much. Indeed, they were a non-issue during the campaign.

Pecora acted quickly to try to establish that there was a new sheriff in town. As his first official act, he issued a subpoena to Charles E. Mitchell, chairman of the board of directors of National City Bank (predecessor of today's Citigroup), summoning him to appear before the subcommittee on February 21, 1933.[4] Two other National City Bank officials were also subpoenaed—Gordon Rentschler, president of National City Bank, and Horace Sylvester, vice president of National City Company, the securities affiliate of National City Bank. Mitchell, who had previously testified before the subcommittee in June 1932 and escaped unscathed, was more annoyed than concerned. This would prove to be an epic misjudgment by Mitchell.

There was little about the fifty-one-year-old Ferdinand Pecora that concerned senior executives of the nation's largest commercial bank. While a talented prosecutor in New York City, rising to the number two position in the Manhattan district attorney's office under Joab Banton, he was passed over for the top job and had spent the previous three years with an undistinguished record in private practice at the relatively obscure firm of Hartman, Sheridan & Tekulsky.[5] What was interesting about Pecora was that he, of unmistakable Italian ancestry, had studied to be an Episcopal priest, his father having been one of the few successful converts of Protestant missionaries in Sicily during the 1880s. Religion aside, Pecora's journey was a familiar one among the upwardly mobile children of southern and eastern European immigrants of New York. He attended public schools in the Chelsea section of Manhattan and went to college at the Episcopal Seminary School of St. Stephen's College (since renamed Bard College), but dropped out in 1897 when his father became incapacitated as a result of an industrial accident. He took a job as a law clerk with a sole practitioner, J. Baldwin Hands, and worked his way through New York Law School, passing the bar in 1908. He got involved with politics, first with the Progressive "Bull Moose" Party in 1912 and later with the Tammany Hall Democrats in 1916. It was his Tammany connections that landed him the assistant district attorney job two years later.[6]

Few Italian Americans in the 1930s held professional jobs on Wall Street, and even fewer held jobs as attorneys at Wall Street law firms. Many at the time were doubtful that an Italian American like Pecora had the "background" or experience to understand how Wall Street banks operated. But his former boss, New York district attorney Banton, praised Pecora as "the best qualified lawyer in the country" to head the stock market practices subcommittee investigation. Few others agreed. Senator Norbeck offered him the job principally because Cooper's abrupt resignation had left him in a desperate bind. Other, better qualified lawyers, such as Samuel Untermyer, chief counsel in the Pujo's Committee hearings twenty years earlier, either expressed no interest or were waiting to see what, if anything, the new Congress and president would do with the investigation of Wall Street after the inauguration.

As Pecora prepared for the questioning of Mitchell, the drama between President Hoover and President-elect Roosevelt intensified. On Saturday, February 18, at the annual Inner Circle banquet in New York City at the Hotel Astor, a lighthearted dinner where members of the New York press corps would perform skits lampooning New York and national politicians, Hoover sent a Secret Service agent over to Roosevelt's table to deliver a handwritten letter asking that Roosevelt give prompt public assurance that he would balance the budget and maintain an anti-inflation monetary policy. He also requested that Roosevelt publicly name his secretary of the Treasury, who could liaise with the outgoing Hoover administration on responding to the growing banking crisis. Roosevelt read the letter, passed it to his close adviser Raymond Moley and went back to enjoying the dinner. He had no intention to jump aboard Hoover's sinking ship. Roosevelt believed the banks would collapse no matter what he said, and interjecting himself into the crisis would only dissipate his own prestige.[7]

On February 21, Charles Mitchell sat at the center of a long mahogany table in Room 30 of the Senate Office Building, directly across from Ferdinand Pecora and Senator Norbeck. To his left and right sat a phalanx of high-priced lawyers from the Wall Street firm of Shearman & Sterling and the Washington firm of Covington & Burling.[8] Mitchell had no sense that by the end of that day's testimony, his career in banking would be finished.

What changed that day was the public's perception of who was responsible for the Crash and Depression. Before Pecora's first round of hearings, most of the blame was assigned to the political leaders of the country (Hoover in particular) and renegade Wall Street pool operators and short sellers. Remarkably, the nation's banking establishment had successfully avoided the worst of the public's wrath. Prior to 10:00 a.m. on February 21, the most severe criticism levied at Charles Mitchell was that he was too optimistic in the early days of the Crash, when he assured the public that market conditions would soon return to normal. For this, he was derisively nicknamed "Sunshine Charlie."

Mitchell's life story was, in its own way, as uniquely American as Pecora's. A high-achieving son of middle-class parents from the Boston suburb Chelsea, Mitchell graduated from Amherst College in 1899, going on to work for the Western Electric Company in Chicago. In 1907, he took a job on Wall Street with the Trust Company of New York, before striking out on his own as a bond salesman. In 1916, National City Bank hired him to improve their bond underwriting capabilities. Mitchell soon rose to become president of National City Company. In 1921, as the post–World War recession battered the banks, National City's board selected Mitchell as president when James Stillman Jr. was forced out over ill-advised loans (representing 80 percent of the bank's capital) to the Cuban sugar industry during the wartime commodities boom, when sugar was trading at 20 cents a pound. It had since fallen to less than 5 cents a pound and most of the loans were in default. Mitchell's plan for the bad sugar loans was one familiar to many traders with a losing book: double down. National City took controlling equity stakes in the struggling sugar companies and restructured the debt with new loans, keeping the ship afloat until, hopefully, sugar prices rebounded. Most important, the "kick the can down the road" strategy kept bank examiners at bay and avoided writing down the loans to true value, which would have resulted in a gigantic capital hit to the bank.[9]

Mitchell's gambit worked, and over the course of the 1920s, National City was transformed into a "one-stop-shop, financial supermarket" for the burgeoning American middle class. While it competed successfully in the bond and loan origination business with the industry's historical leaders—the gilt-edged private investment banks J.P. Morgan & Co.; Kuhn, Loeb; and Dillon, Read—National City's real competitive strength lay with its vast distribution network, where bond salesmen from the National City Company sat cheek by jowl with National City Bank tellers in sixty-nine offices in fifty-one American cities by 1929, as well as in Canada, London, Amsterdam, Geneva, Tokyo, and Shanghai. It became not only the largest bank in the country but one of the largest corporations of any kind.

Mitchell's wealth and stature rose along with the bank's. He lived extravagantly and spent lavishly. He owned a Fifth Avenue mansion (now home to the French consulate), a summer home in Southampton, and a weekend home in the elite upstate enclave of Tuxedo Park, the latter residence upsetting the town's conservative old guard with its gaudy, massive size. Although his money was welcome at New York City's prestigious cultural institutions, he was considered crass and nouveau riche by the old-money class that ran New York society. He did not reduce the price of his social ascent when he quipped to reporters that the opera was a good place "to catch up a couple hours' sleep."[10] And he had a reputation for being mean-spirited. One day at the bank, a young clerk interrupted Mitchell during a presentation he was giving and asked him to step outside the room for a moment. The young clerk pointed out that Mitchell's trousers were unbuttoned. Mitchell had the clerk fired later that day.[11] It would be his personal greed and insensitivity to propriety and appearances that would be his undoing.

Charlie Mitchell did not like paying taxes. When Pecora questioned Mitchell about whether he'd sold any National City stock during the market meltdown of 1929 (he had), Mitchell was rightly concerned that he would be pilloried for playing "Sunshine Charlie" for public consumption while at the same time privately dumping his National City stock. Mitchell had a benign—so he thought—explanation for his sale of 18,300 shares: "I sold this stock, frankly, for tax purposes." He realized a loss of $2,800,000 ($37,500,000 in today's dollars) on the sale. In early 1930, he repurchased the 18,300 shares at the same price, from the person he had sold the stock to—his wife. He then testified that this "loss" enabled him to avoid paying any federal income tax for 1929, even though he was paid bonuses from the bank and securities affiliate totaling more than $1,100,000 ($14,800,000 in today's dollars) in a disastrous year for the bank's shareholders.[12] The average annual family income in 1933 was $1,500, for those lucky enough to even have a job.

Mitchell's personal tax avoidance strategy had nothing to do with the factors that led to the Crash or the lending decisions that were causing banks to fail in such large numbers. In fact, his bank was among the most financially sound and solvent. It didn't matter. The press, the politicians, and the public were convinced that Charles Mitchell was a crook. And more than that, they were now convinced that the Wall Street establishment was every bit as crooked as the short sellers and pool operators. Mitchell cheated on his taxes, just like Al Capone. A new term was coined: "bankster." Carter Glass took to telling a crudely racist joke: "A banker in my town nearly got lynched. He tried to marry a white woman." The *Nation* magazine wrote, "If you steal $25, you're a thief. If you steal $250,000, you're an embezzler. If you steal $2,500,000, you're a financier."[13]

By the weekend, Mitchell had resigned from National City Bank and was under investigation for tax evasion by the IRS, while the U.S. Department of Justice and New York State attorney general both initiated criminal tax evasion investigations. He was indicted and tried by assistant U.S. attorney, future Republican governor of New York, and 1948 presidential nominee Thomas E. Dewey, but was found not guilty. The IRS ultimately settled a civil case against him for $1,000,000.[14] When enacted the following year, the Securities Exchange Act of 1934 would require public disclosure by executive officers and directors of purchases and sales of company stock.

Mitchell's testimony that day also revealed practices that were very disturbing from the perspective of sound banking, even if they were overshadowed in the headlines by his greed. Ironically, they related to the Cuban sugar loans that had caused the premature departure of his predecessor and paved the way for his own ascent. Though cheating the government out of taxes might have been a pardonable crime to the investor class, misleading your shareholders with bogus prospectus disclosures was not. By 1927, with sugar prices still depressed, National City's bank examiners were pushing management to write down the loans to the General Sugar Corporation, the company formed by

Mitchell when he restructured the failing Cuban sugar industry years earlier. To solve its Cuban problem once and for all, Mitchell had National City Bank undertake a stock offering of 250,000 shares for $200 per share. Half of the proceeds, $25,000,000, was allocated to National City Company, the securities affiliate. National City Company then used the $25,000,000 to acquire the stock of General Sugar Corporation from National City Bank for a nominal price, investing the bulk of the proceeds as a capital contribution to General Sugar Corporation. General Sugar Corporation then used $21,000,000 of the cash, together with the issuance of $11,000,000 of its five-year 8 percent secured notes, to repay all of its outstanding loans owed to National City Bank.[15]

Investors in the National City stock offering were led to believe that the proceeds allocated to National City Company would be used to grow its business. It was not disclosed in the offering's prospectus that these proceeds would be "round-tripped" back to the bank, effectively moving troubled loans off its books to satisfy the bank examiners.

When asked by Pecora about the need for disclosing to the investors the use of their investment funds, Mitchell responded, "I hardly think there was any necessity for it." (When it was enacted later that year, the Securities Act of 1933 required that every prospectus disclose the uses of proceeds received by the issuer of the securities being sold.[16])

On the second day of hearings, Pecora questioned Gordon Rentschler, the forty-seven-year-old president of National City Bank. Rentschler had been Mitchell's point man on the Cuban sugar crisis, and the tall, jovial former Princeton class president had earned the trust and respect of Mitchell, becoming his heir apparent. By day's end, Rentschler had lost any of the trust or respect of his employees that remained, because it was revealed that they, like the government and the investors, had been royally screwed by National City senior management.

Rentschler was questioned about a loan program initiated by the board of directors of National City Bank on November 13, 1929. At precisely the same time the bank was selling out accounts of ordinary customers who had bought securities on margin, it came to the assistance of its one hundred most highly compensated senior executives who were overextended in the market. National City Bank made loans in the hundreds of millions in today's dollars to its executives, interest free and most without security, in order to "protect such officers in the present emergency and thereby sustaining the morale of the organization."[17] At the time of the hearing, 95 percent of those loans had not been repaid, and just like the bad Cuban sugar loans, the loans had been transferred off the bank's books and on to those of the securities affiliate, National City Company. Edward F. Barrett, vice president of National City Bank, borrowed $296,000 and repaid only $11,000. Lee Olwell, another senior banker, borrowed $345,000 and repaid nothing. No enforcement proceedings were taken against any of the senior officers.[18] (The Glass-Steagall Banking Act of 1933, which would become law in June, prohibited officers of Federal Reserve member banks from borrowing money from their own banks.)

As the National City Bank stock price continued to slide in the fall of 1929, the board of directors, in an effort to absorb some of the selling pressure, instituted an employee stock purchase plan whereby low-level bank employees were encouraged to buy stock in four-year installments, with payment automatically deducted monthly from the employees' paychecks. At the time the plan was implemented, National City Bank stock traded—and these low-level employees were charged—$200 to $220 per share. By the time of the hearing, National City Bank stock was trading at $40 a share, and most of the employees in the plan owed more on the stock payments than the stock was worth, with interest on the amount owed still being charged by the bank. "And the National City Bank has not done anything to sustain the morale of the employees with regard to those stock commitments of theirs under this plan, has it?" Pecora asked Rentschler. Rentschler responded that National City Bank employees "are, far and wide, entirely well-satisfied with the fact of their part in this plan," and that morale at the bank was "strong and fine." In fact, he testified, "there is no higher morale in any organization throughout the world."[19] Rentschler then admitted that the only way employees could be released of their obligations under the plan was to resign from the bank—a practicable impossibility for most of these employees when nationwide unemployment hovered at 25 percent.[20]

The strategic importance of shoring up the National City stock price in 1929 was heightened by the pending blockbuster merger Charles Mitchell had negotiated with the Corn Exchange Bank, which would have given National City Bank the most branches of any bank in New York. Under the terms of the merger agreement, Corn Exchange shareholders were provided a cash election option: They could elect to receive either 0.8 shares of National City Bank stock for each Corn Exchange share or $360 in cash. In other words, if the National City Bank stock price fell below $450 per share, shareholders would elect to receive cash. An all-cash deal would cost National City Bank $200,000,000 ($4,600,000,000 in today's dollars), an amount it could not afford to spend. In October 1929, in order to inflate the sinking share price (then around $300 per share), Mitchell borrowed heavily from J.P. Morgan & Co. to buy stock in the market ($250 million in today's dollars) and caused the securities affiliate to aggressively buy National City Bank stock as well. The effort, however, was futile. National City Bank stock continued to fall. Ultimately, Mitchell recommended to the National City Bank shareholders that they vote down the Corn Exchange merger, which, in November 1929, they did. Nonetheless, National City Company continued to own an enormous amount of National City Bank stock, which if sold in the market, would continue the downward pressure on the stock price. The employee stock purchase plan was a sinister effort to move this stock off the books of National City Company and into the portfolios of the mid- and low-level employees, who couldn't say no.[21]

The third day of the hearings brought more testimony regarding manipulation of the National City Bank stock by company management. This scheme involved deceiving new National City stockholders. Pecora called to the stand Hugh Baker, the president of National City Company, grilling him about the bank's decision to delist its stock in 1928. Baker explained that management was concerned about manipulation of the stock price if continued trading on the New York Stock Exchange was permitted. The genesis of his concern, he said, was a series of trades on a single day with what he deemed a suspicious fluctuation in share prices. When probed further by Pecora, Baker admitted the "suspicious" activity consisted of five trades of ten shares each, all trading within $5 of each other.[22] This at a time when there were 750,000 shares of City Bank stock outstanding and that day's closing price was $668.

The explanation convinced no one. Fluctuations of share prices of less than 1 percent were routine—and the idea that such a small volume of trading would prompt management to seek delisting was laughable. Furthermore, the New York Stock Exchange was then, as now, the most prestigious stock exchange in the world. Managements sought to have their company's stock listed on the New York Stock Exchange in order to *minimize* opportunities for others to manipulate their stock price, not the other way around.

New York Stock Exchange officials were initially unconvinced by National City Bank's rational for delisting:

> "While the Stock Exchange is most desirous of complying with the wishes of your board, it feels that it would not be justified in removing the stock of the National City Bank from its list upon the request of the board of directors alone and without the sanctions and approval of the stockholders of the bank.

> "It appears that the stock of the National City Bank has been listed on the Stock Exchange for many years and that, since the original listing of the stock, the bank has made applications from time to time for the listing of additional amounts of stock when the capital of the bank has been increased.

> "Under these circumstances, the removing of the stock of the National City Bank from the list of the Stock Exchange would affect the rights of the stockholders of the bank in that it would deprive them of a market for their stock which has existed for many years.

> "The Stock Exchange, therefore, cannot consider and act upon any request or application to remove the stock of the National City Bank from the list unless such request and application be authorized by the stockholders of the bank at a special meeting at which no substantial number of the stockholders vote against the proposed action."[23]

National City Bank sought and obtained shareholder approval, and the stock was delisted in January 1928. Why would the shareholders approve delisting? For precisely the opposite reason stated publically: Once unlisted, National City Company would have a much freer hand to promote (i.e., manipulate) the stock. A great deal of that stock was cross-sold by the National City Company to National City Bank depositors. After the delisting—and prior to the Crash the following year—the National City Bank share price quadrupled.

While Hugh Baker testified about the delisting, Indiana became the fourth state to declare a bank holiday.[24]

On Friday, February 24, the fourth day of hearings, Pecora continued questioning Hugh Baker on the activities of National City Bank's securities affiliate. In particular, Pecora questioned the very legality of National City Company. The company was born out of the original sin of the federal banking authorities and policymakers who chose to ignore their own laws. Despite repeated warnings over two decades about the dangerous conflicts of interest between banks and their unregulated securities affiliates, federal officials let the good times roll on Wall Street. Under the National Banking Act of 1863, federally chartered banks like National City Bank were prohibited from engaging in the securities business. To circumvent this prohibition, national banks implemented a number of schemes enabling themselves to do indirectly what they could not do directly. National City Bank's structure was typical of the legal maneuvering that attempted to comply with the letter, but not the spirit, of the law.

On June 1, 1911, National City Bank and three of its officers and directors (James Stillman, chairman of the board of directors; Frank A. Vanderlip, president; and Stephen S. Palmer, director) entered into an agreement, pursuant to which a company to be named "National City Company" was to be formed that enabled shareholders of the bank to take advantage of opportunities for investments "other than those which are possible in the ordinary course of the banking business." The agreement provided for the board of directors of National City Bank to declare a cash dividend of $10,000,000, payable only if the shareholder agreed to assign the right to a trust, which would in turn use that money to subscribe for the shares of National City Company. The shareholder would own a proportionate beneficial interest in the trust that owned all of the shares of National City Company. The trustees were the officers and directors of National City Bank.[25]

On November 6, 1911, Solicitor General of the United States Frederick W. Lehmann rendered a legal opinion to the attorney general concluding that both National City Bank and National City Company were in violation of law. Solicitor General Lehmann stated that National City Company was not independently organized but controlled by the bank in violation of the National Banking Act. In addition, Lehmann asserted that National City Company was in violation of the law because, through its intermingled relationship with National City Bank, it was engaging in the banking business in violation of both its charter, which prohibited it from acting as a bank, and federal law, because it had no federal banking license. The opinion not only attacked the creation of National City Company on legal grounds but prophetically pointed out the potential abuses and dangers that would arise from the interrelationship of banks and securities affiliates: "The temptation to speculate in funds of the banks at opportune times will prove to be irresistible. Examples are recent and significant of the peril to a bank incident to the dual and divisive interests of its officers and directors. If many enterprises and many banks are brought and bound together in the nexus of a great holding company, the failure of one may involve all in common disaster."[26]

And then nothing happened. Lehmann's opinion was buried in the files of the Department of Justice. President Taft had no desire to take on Wall Street over the issue, so National City Company and similar banking affiliates went unmolested by the federal government.

The legality of the securities affiliates was also called into question again during the Pujo Committee hearings the following year. The committee's report, issued in February 1913, recommended separating investment banking and securities operations from commercial banking:

"Your Committee is of the opinion that national banks should not be permitted to become inseparably tied together with security holding companies in an identity of ownership and management. These holding companies have unlimited powers to buy and sell and speculate in stocks. It is unsafe for banks to be united with them in interest in management. The temptation would be great at times to use the bank's funds to finance speculative operations of the holding company.

"The success and usefulness of a bank that holds the people's deposits are so dependent on public confidence that it cannot be safely linked by identity of stock interest and management with a private investment corporation of unlimited powers with no public duties or responsibilities and not dependent on public confidence. The mistakes or misfortunes of the latter are too likely to react upon the former. However profitable the participation of the bank, whether under the guise of a mere lender of money or underwriter or purchaser of securities in which the securities company is interested, the incentive to the bank to participate in these adventurous transactions is one that should be removed beyond the reach of its officers.

"The whole arrangement is a mere pretext—behind which the bank's officers are shielding themselves in making money for the bank's stockholders
through the prestige, resources, and organization of the bank and by means
that are forbidden to the bank."[27]

The committee recommended legislation expressly making illegal the "stapled" share and similar arrangements under which securities affiliates were
owned and operated by banks. The proposed bill required that the "stockholders of a national bank would be expressly prohibited from becoming associated as stockholders in any other corporation under agreements or arrangements
assuming that the stock of such other corporation shall always be owned
by the same persons or substantially the same persons who own the stock of
the bank or that their management be the same."[28]

Again, nothing happened. President Wilson, like his predecessor, decided
not to force the issue with Wall Street and the proposed legislation died in the
House. But this time Pecora got the nation's attention. By the weekend, the public was convinced that the game had been illegal all along, and even the banks
knew their breakup was now inevitable.

On Saturday, February 25, Maryland became the fifth state to declare a
bank holiday.[29]

On Sunday, February 26, Charles Mitchell and Hugh Baker announced
their resignations from National City Bank and National City Company, respectively. These first casualties of the Pecora Hearings blamed their demise
on "public misunderstanding" created by their testimony.[30] Pecora replied that
all newspaper reports of their testimony "were eminently consistent."

On Monday, February 27, the Pecora Hearings resumed. The day's topic
would be international banking. There is an old joke on Wall Street that an
international banker is a man who travels thousands of miles to make a loan
he would never dream of making at home. Pecora's witness that morning, Victor
Schoepperle, a vice president of the National City Company, might well have
been the genesis of that joke, except that he and National City had the last
laugh and bondholders ended up paying the price. Schoepperle testified
about National City Company's underwriting of three issues of Peruvian
government bonds in an aggregate principal amount of $90,000,000. The first
offering, involving the issuance of $15,000,000 of bonds, was consummated

on March 1, 1927. At the time of the offering, Schoepperle had written a memo for National City Company stating that the Peruvian government had "a bad debt record" and was "an adverse moral and political risk." Nowhere in the prospectus for the bond issue was there any mention of those risk factors. At the time of the hearing, the bonds were in default and were trading at 8 cents on the dollar. (The Securities Act of 1933, passed later that year, would require disclosure of all risks material to an issuance.)[31]

The second Peruvian bond issue involved a $50,000,000 offering on December 21, 1927. Between the two offerings, J.H. Durrell, a vice president and overseas manager of National City Bank, sent a report to Charles Mitchell regarding the then current situation in Peru:

"As I see it, there are two factors that will long retard the economic importance of Peru. First, its population of 5,500,000 is largely Indian, two-thirds of whom reside east of the Andes, and a majority consume almost no manufactured products. Second, its principal sources of wealth, the mines and oil wells, are nearly all foreign owned, and excepting for wages and taxes, no part of the value of their production remains in the country. Added to this, the sugar plantations are in the hands of a few families, a majority of whom reside and invest their profits abroad. Also, for political reasons, the present Government has deported some 400 prominent wealthy conservative families, but allows them to continue to receive and to make use of abroad the income from their Peruvian properties. As a whole, I have no great faith in any material betterment of Peru's economic condition in the near future."[32]

Again, no mention of those unfavorable factors was made in the bond-offering prospectus. At the time of the hearings, these bonds were also in default and trading at 8 cents on the dollar.

In October 1928, the third Peruvian bond offering was made in the amount of $25,000,000. Several months prior to the offering, on January 12, 1928, Schoepperle received a memo stating:

"The present low value of Peruvian money is due primarily to the fact that the balance of international payments is unfavorable to Peru, although the commercial sales show a favorable balance, this is apparent at a glance when one considers that metals and minerals, oils, bring into the country only a part of the real value as shown by the customhouse statistics, for the reason that the production of those articles is largely in the hands of foreign companies which sell exchange only sufficient to cover their operating costs, and many other articles leave a part of their value abroad."[33]

On August 25, 1928, the manager of the Lima, Peru, branch of National City Bank sent a report to the New York office:

"*Economic Conditions.*—Business continues to be extremely dull. Although there has been more activity in the cotton market during the past month, important growers estimate that the crop will be 25 percent below normal and probably a bit more. Our collection department reports that collections are becoming increasingly difficult. At every hand one hears complaints regarding slow sales and scarcity of money. Prices of securities and real estate are at extremely low levels, and new building operations have naturally been curtailed consistently.

"*Government Conditions.*—Financial condition of Government continues very tight. We understand that practically all of the Government dependencies are in arrears as regards salaries paid to employees. One of the members of the American Naval Mission informs us that for the first time in years they have been unable to secure their daily allowance of some Lp 4/500 from the Treasury. Although the Treasury has called upon a number of banks to effect the discount of some of its paper, we have received no such request of late."[34]

On October 8, 1928, a memorandum issued to J.H. Durrell pointed out that "economic conditions in [Peru] leave considerable amount to be desired. The last cotton crop was short on account of lack of water for proper irrigation."[35] No reference was made to the disturbing and deteriorating economic conditions in Peru in the prospectus. At the time of the hearings, the bonds were trading at 5 cents on the dollar.

Also not mentioned in any of the prospectuses was the fact that National City Company and another underwriter, J&W Seligman & Co., had made a $450,000 "loan" to Juan Leguia, the son of Peruvian president Agosto Leguia, contemporaneous with the selection of underwriters for the second bond offering.[36]

That Monday, after Pecora grilled Victor Schoepperle, Arkansas declared a bank holiday.[37]

On Tuesday, February 28, Pecora shifted his attention from Peru to Brazil and the underwriting by National City Company of two bond issuances, totaling $16,500,000, by the Brazilian state of Minas Gerais. A similar story was to be told with the same result: misleading disclosure and catastrophic bondholder losses. Ronald Byrnes, the former head of National City Company's foreign bond department, was called to testify before the subcommittee.[38]

On March 19, 1928, National City Company underwrote $8,500,000 of 6½ percent bonds of Minas Gerais. The prospectus stated that "the proceeds of this loan will be utilized for purposes designed to increase the economic productivity of the State." However, between $3,000,000 and $4,000,000 of the proceeds were used to repay short-term debt of Minas Gerais. This was not the first time the State of Minas Gerais failed to use the proceeds of a bond issuance as promised—and National City Company was aware of the prior misuse. French banks had underwritten bonds for Minas Gerais in 1911. The state defaulted and bondholders sued in French courts seeking repayment.[39]

On June 12, 1927, Ronald Byrnes received a letter from National City Company executive George F. Train concerning Minas Gerais's previous handling of the proceeds of French bond offerings:

"The 1911 contract was concluded in Brazil and apparently the same thing happened. I am unable to confirm this as I have as yet no photostats of the bonds, but the laxness of the State authorities borders on the fantastic. The 1916 bonds were admittedly signed by the then Secretary of Finance in Paris, who carelessly overlooked the wording not being in accordance with the contract. It would be hard to find anywhere a sadder combination of inefficiency and ineptitude than that displayed by the various State officials on the several occasions."

"The foregoing recital served to show the complete ignorance, carelessness and negligence of the former State officials in respect of external long-term borrowing."[40]

Notwithstanding the foregoing view by the executive, the prospectus for the Minas Gerais bonds contained the following assertion:

"Prudent and careful management of the State's finances has been characteristic of successive administrations in Minas Gerais."[41]

This disclosure remained in the prospectus despite the following comment from an executive in the National City Company foreign bond department:

"'Prudent and careful administration of the State's finances has been axiomatic with successive administrations in Minas Gerais.' I am not trying to criticize, and no doubt I am too much saturated with material dealing with the French issues of the State, but in view of the extensively loose way in which the external debt of the State was managed, do you think the statement quoted above would be subjected to criticism?"[42]

Citing the comment, Pecora asked Byrnes, "Why wasn't the investor told that the purpose of the issue was for the paying out of the short-term loans instead of for purposes of increasing the productivity of the state?" Byrnes responded: "Because in my opinion, no investor would be in the slightest interested or his investment in the least affected."[43] The State of Minas Gerais defaulted on both issues of bonds on March 1, 1932. At the time of the hearings, they were quoted at 22 cents on the dollar.[44]

Ohio declared a bank holiday while Pecora was questioning Byrnes.[45]

On Wednesday, March 1, Pecora called as a witness Horace Sylvester, the vice president of National City Company. Pecora was keenly interested in a $10,200 "syndicate expense" incurred in connection with a $66,000,000 bond offering for the Port Authority of New York in 1931. It turns out that payoffs for underwriting business worked as well domestically as they did overseas. Sylvester told the subcommittee that he had given the cash to a National City Bank employee named Edward Barrett who, in turn, "loaned" the money to John Ramsey, general manager of the Port Authority. When Barrett took the stand, he testified that Ramsey had executed a note to memorialize the loan, but he had lost it. Barrett provided no explanation as to why the loan was made in cash, rather than by check.[46]

As *The Nation* magazine described the episode, "Of course this was not a bribe, or a bid for future business from the Port Authority. Heaven forbid! It was just a generous kindly act to take care of a good man who happened to be in a jam. Why not give him $10,200 of the stockholders' money and overlook such matters as collateral and interest? That's the way to make friends for the bank!"[47]

By the end of Wednesday's hearing, Alabama, Kentucky, West Virginia, Idaho, and Minnesota had announced bank holidays.[48]

On the last day of hearings before the new Congress convened, Pecora addressed National City Company's handling of the initial public offering of airplane manufacturing company Boeing. It turned out National City was also cheating its investment-banking clients. The National City Company investment banker managing the deal recommended a public offering of Boeing stock to raise capital but was overruled by Charles Mitchell, who concluded it was too speculative for a public offering and should only be issued in a private placement. National City Company agreed to buy the entire offering, placing it with National City officers and directors, bankers at J.P. Morgan & Co., lawyers from Shearman & Sterling, and other friends of National City Bank.[49]

On October 21, 1928, just nine days after the closing of the private placement, National City Company requested that the Boeing stock be listed for trading on the New York Curb Exchange (predecessor of the American Stock Exchange). When trading commenced, the stock traded at a 50 percent premium over the private placement price. Insiders made a profit of over $1,600,000 ($21,500,000 in today's dollars).[50]

A few hours after the hearings adjourned, President-elect Roosevelt arrived at Washington's Union Station to a crowd of 1,500 supporters waiting in the icy rain.[51] That day, Arizona, California, Mississippi, Oklahoma, and Oregon closed their banks.[52] Roosevelt carried with him an inaugural address that would go through many drafts over the next two days as the banking crisis grew even worse.

The following day, Ferdinand Pecora boarded a train at Union Station bound for New York City. He was now a national figure, a celebrity. He became the face of justice for the average man served upon by the malefactors of Wall Street. Seventy-five years later, despite months of hearings by various congressional committees into all aspects of the Lehman Brothers collapse and the subsequent financial crisis, no comparable figure would emerge. Indeed, none could. With the complexity of twenty-first century financial markets and the cacophony that is the blogosphere and twenty-four-hour cable slug-fist, simple narratives of "good guys" versus "bad guys" are no longer possible. Pecora's success was due in large part to his lack of sophistication in matters of high finance. Unlike Untermyer, he had no pretentions of knowing how the financial system should be regulated and would make no proposals for reform. He was a meat-and-potatoes big-city prosecutor who saw his role as uncovering the wrongdoing and letting others decide what to do about it.

The New York Federal Reserve Bank was desperately trying to prevent the collapse of the national banking system, having created a program calling for a guarantee by the Federal Reserve Banks of 50 percent of all banking deposits nationwide. President-elect Roosevelt indicated he would not support the program, wisely concluding that the public needed to feel that *all* of their deposits were safe in the banks. New York City banks faced acute gold losses. Most troubling, the Federal Reserve Bank of New York could not convince the Federal Reserve Bank of Chicago to lend it money.[53] The unthinkable had happened: the Federal Reserve System had collapsed.

On March 3, Hoover's last day in office, Georgia, New Mexico, Utah, and Wisconsin declared bank holidays.[54] New York governor Herbert Lehman canceled his trip to Washington for the inauguration and set up a command center in his apartment with the State Superintendent of Banks, partners from J.P. Morgan, and George L. Harrison of the New York Federal Reserve Bank.[55]

At 2:30 a.m. on Saturday, March 4—Inauguration Day—Governor Lehman closed New York's banks. An hour later Illinois followed suit.[56]

THREE

BACK FROM THE ABYSS:
The Emergency Banking Act

While the Reverend Endicott Peabody, Roosevelt's headmaster at the Groton School and lifelong spiritual adviser, finalized the prayer he would give later that morning, notices were quietly slipped under Washington hotel-room doors informing guests attending the inauguration that checks written on banks outside the District of Columbia would not be accepted as payment. The District of Columbia and every state had some form of bank holiday. (Pittsburgh was the only big city where banks were open because the family of Hoover's Treasury Secretary, Andrew Mellon, controlled most of Pittsburgh's banks and refused to close them.)[1] On that cold and gray Saturday, in the parlance of twenty-first-century financial catastrophe, the ATMs stopped working.

Roosevelt had chosen St. John's Episcopal Church for that morning's service principally for ease of entry—it was close to the Mayflower Hotel, where he was staying, and it had a side entrance, with few steps. Months earlier, Bishop James E. Freeman had invited Roosevelt to attend Mass on the morning of his inauguration at the Washington Cathedral, but the problem of ascending the steps had forced him to decline. Amid members of Roosevelt's family, his cabinet members, and their families, Peabody prayed, "O God we most heartily beseech thee, with thy favor to behold and bless thy servant, Franklin, chosen to be President of the United States." Each year thereafter, Roosevelt took his cabinet to private services at St. John's on the anniversary of his first inauguration.[2] (Peabody, who had also officiated at Franklin and Eleanor's wedding, nonetheless had voted for Hoover, thinking him the abler man for the job.[3])

After the twenty-minute service, Roosevelt returned to his hotel room and continued refining his address. The draft of the speech he carried from New York had been substantially rewritten the night before to reflect the complete collapse of the banking system. At the president-elect's side at the Mayflower Hotel, tasked with helping redraft the speech, was secretary of the Treasury–designee William H. Woodin and Roosevelt's first choice for that job, Senator Carter Glass.[4]

Woodin hadn't gotten much sleep. He spent the night developing a plan of action for the new president with Hoover's secretary of the Treasury, Ogden Mills; his undersecretary of the Treasury, Arthur Ballantine; and the acting comptroller of the currency, F. Gloyd Awalt. They offered three recommendations: close all banks in the nation by proclamation; call a special session of Congress to validate the order and pass appropriate emergency legislation; and summon the nation's most important bankers to Washington on March 5 for consultation.[5]

Shortly after 1:00 p.m., Chief Justice Charles Evans Hughes administered the oath of office on the East Portico of the Capitol and President Roosevelt turned to address the nation. His speech—famous for the assertion in its opening paragraph "that the only thing we have to fear is fear itself"—combined a somber acknowledgement of the bleak economic realities with a strident assignment of blame and an extraordinary promise of executive action to address the national crisis.

"Only a foolish optimist can deny the dark realities of the moment," acknowledged Roosevelt. And with Pecora's bombshell disclosures fresh in the public mind, he left no doubt as to whom he held responsible: "Practices of the unscrupulous money changers stand indicted in the court of public opinion, rejected by the hearts and minds of men. True they have tried, but their efforts have been cast in the pattern of an outworn tradition. Faced by failure of credit they have proposed only the lending of more money. Stripped of the lure of profit by which to induce our people to follow their false leadership, they have resorted to exhortations, pleading tearfully for restored confidence. They know only the rules of a generation of self-seekers. They have no vision, and when there is no vision the people perish. The money changers have fled from their high seats in the temple of our civilization. We may now restore that temple to the ancient truths."[6]

At the crescendo of the address, Roosevelt warned Congress that if it failed to act, he would seek broad executive power—the equivalent of martial law: "I shall ask the Congress for the one remaining instrument to meet the crisis—to wage a war against the emergency, as great as the power that would be given to me if we were in fact invaded by a foreign foe."[7]

On his first day in office, Roosevelt issued a proclamation calling on Congress to meet in special session to consider emergency banking legislation.[8] That evening, it was decided that Congress would be called in session on Thursday, March 9, and Secretary Woodin promised Roosevelt he would have emergency legislation ready by then to permit reopening the banks. The White House released a presidential proclamation declaring a national bank holiday from March 6 through March 9, during which no banking institutions would be allowed to transact any business. The proclamation authorized the secretary of the Treasury to allow the issuance of "clearinghouse certificates" (or "scrip"), supplementing currency reserves and permitting banks to open new deposit accounts that could be withdrawn without restriction. This would, it was hoped, encourage those hoarding dollars to return them into the banking system.[9]

New York prepared for a long crisis. At the American Bank Note Company in the Bronx, New York, high-speed presses had been whirling twenty-four hours a day since the inauguration, printing certificates guaranteed by the New York Clearing House and bearing the facsimile signature of Mortimer N. Buckner, president of the Clearing House Association.[10] The total amount printed was kept secret but was roughly equal to the amount of unpledged liquid assets of the New York banks. Governor Herbert Lehman of New York tapped former governor and Democratic presidential nominee Al Smith to chair the newly formed Emergency Certificate Corporation. Ultimately, $250,000,000 in scrip was printed. None of it was used.[11]

President Roosevelt floated an alternative to scrip to address the currency hoarding issue. He proposed that all $21,000,000,000 of U.S. government bonds become immediately convertible into cash, no matter their maturity. Bankers and Treasury officials were aghast when told of the president's scheme. It would have the effect of reducing the value of the dollar by 80 percent. With no means of contracting the currency after conversion, the resulting unprecedented currency inflation would destroy the nation's credit. Embarrassed by his show of ignorance, Roosevelt quickly shelved the idea.[12] It would not be his last half-baked currency scheme.

Woodin also summoned to Washington many of the nation's leading bankers to assist in the drafting of the emergency legislation. (The migration of bankers to the White House and Treasury building gave rise to a joke that Roosevelt "cast the money changers out of the temple on Saturday, but let them in the back door on Sunday.") There was no consensus among the bankers on what the emergency legislation should provide.

As Raymond Moley remembered, "Some of the bankers insisted there must be a nationwide issue of scrip. Others urged that currency be issued against the sound assets of the banks. Others concentrated on the argument that the banks could not be made safe unless the state banking systems were forced into the Federal Reserve System. There was talk of the need for converting the Reserve Banks into government-owned deposit banks, talk of guaranteeing deposits, even talk of nationalizing the banking business—talk that went on and on in circles."[13]

The public response to the bank holiday proclamation was a remarkable calm. The feared hoarding of food and other essential supplies never materialized. In New York City, grocery stores reported heavy buying but nothing approaching panic. The New York Telephone Company and the Consolidated Gas Company announced they would continue to accept checks for payment and would also accept the new scrip, if issued. Small merchants continued to accept checks and even IOUs from customers in good standing. The most pressing problem was a shortage of nickels—needed in large quantities for bus and subway fares and automat payments.[14] There was standing room only in the reading room of the New York Public Library, as ordinary citizens showed unprecedented interest in banking and finance materials. In Reno, Nevada, quickie divorces came to a halt when clients couldn't pay filing fees. The governor of California granted two stays of execution because "a bank holiday was no time to hang a man."[15]

There were also those who believed that the fundamental problems of the banking system had been exaggerated and that the crisis was essentially "psychological." Alexander Noyes, finance editor of *The New York Times,* wrote of the banking moratorium: "It has its roots very loosely in the mental attitude which has always prevailed in the later stages of a severe depression—that the country has economically gone to the dogs and has no future. When the older men told Wall Street, in 1928 or 1929, of how that identical conception of the American situation had been proclaimed in the prolapsed reaction after 1893 and 1873, the listeners were utterly incredulous. The prevalent attitude of 1933 should make it easier to understand the Nineties and the Seventies. But the true time will come when description of the ideas entertained in 1933 regarding the country's economic future will be equally unbelievable."[16]

The news from Europe contributed to the mood of crisis. The results of Germany's parliamentary elections saw Adolf Hitler's National Socialist Party winning 44 percent of the vote, and Hitler would lead the next coalition government.

In St. Petersburg, Florida, another financial crisis was capturing the country's attention. The day the bank holiday was declared, a throng of reporters surrounded Babe Ruth on the links of the Pasadena Golf Club. In January, Yankees owner Colonel Jacob Ruppert offered Ruth a $50,000 contract for the 1933 season, a one-third pay cut from the $75,000 he was paid for the 1932 season. He refused to sign. Coming off a four-game sweep of the Chicago Cubs in the World Series, during which he batted .333 with two home runs and six RBIs, the Babe was prepared to take at most a 15 percent pay cut. When asked whether the banking crisis changed his mind about accepting the offer, Ruth was unbending. "Absolutely not," he said. "This money situation isn't a permanent thing. Colonel Ruppert will be able to sign checks after a few days and will be able to continue writing and signing them for a long time after this condition is forgotten. He knows what I am worth to the club and he knows what I think I am worth to him."[17] In today's dollars, Ruppert was offering Ruth slightly less than $900,000.

On March 7, James H. Perkins, the newly elected chairman of the board of directors of National City Bank, announced that National City would immediately separate its securities and investment-banking operations from its commercial banking operations. Only one week after "Sunshine Charlie"

Mitchell resigned, his "financial supermarket" was voluntarily broken up.[18] Sixty years later, a successor at Citi, Sandy Weill, would resurrect Mitchell's strategy.

From the moment the bank holiday proclamation was issued, Woodin, together with Senator Glass, Representative Henry B. Steagall, chairman of the House Committee on Banking and Currency, and the bankers, worked nearly around the clock to prepare legislation allowing the reopening of the banks in time for a special session of Congress on Thursday, March 9. By Tuesday morning, Woodin had developed the broad outline of what the emergency banking legislation would be. As Moley recalled:

"Early Tuesday morning, as I came in to breakfast with him, he yelled at me with wild enthusiasm, 'I've got it! I've got it!'

"Not being given to cheerfulness myself at breakfast time, I looked at him pretty glumly and said, 'Got what?'

"'Well,' said Will, 'after you left, I played my guitar a little while and then read a little while and then slept a little while and then awakened and then thought about this scrip thing and then played some more and read some more and slept some more and thought some more. And by gum, if I didn't hit on the answer that way! Why didn't I see it before? We don't have to issue scrip!'

"Here Will's tiny fist came crashing down on the table.

"'We don't need it. These bankers have hypnotized themselves and us. We can issue currency against the sound assets of the banks. The Reserve Act lets us print all we need. And it won't frighten people. It won't look like stage money. It'll be money that looks like money.'

"This, I can state positively, was the origin of the Emergency Banking legislation. The way in which Will made his decision was characteristic of him. Half businessman, half artist, he had succeeded in brushing away the confusing advice of the days previous and come cleanly to the simplest of all possible solutions.

"We jumped up from table and made straight for the White House. Roosevelt listened to the whole plan with mounting enthusiasm. In twenty minutes we had his O.K. Then we were off for forty-eight hours of wrangling over details in the meetings at the Treasury, of bill drafting, message drafting, and conferring with the congressional leaders."[19]

Significant concern over the legality of the bank-closing proclamation continued. President Roosevelt based his authority for issuing the proclamation on the 1917 Trading with the Enemy Act, which allowed the president to regulate "any transactions in foreign exchange and the export, hoarding, melting, or earmarking of gold or silver coin or bullion or currency . . ." Because the Senate voted against ratification of the Treaty of Versailles, the United States had not officially ended involvement in World War I. On March 2, 1933, President Hoover, himself considering the feasibility of declaring a bank holiday, was advised by then–attorney general William DeWitt Mitchell that the authority for such a presidential proclamation under the Trading with the Enemy Act was weak.[20] Senator Glass even admitted as much on the Senate floor, stating, "Some of us are disposed to think these proclamations have been invalid and unconstitutional."[21]

Work on the emergency banking bill continued until 1:00 a.m. on Thursday. Commenting to reporters about the bill in an off-the-record press conference, Roosevelt said, "The general thought at the present time is that it is absolutely impossible by tomorrow to draft any complete or permanent legislation either on banking or on budget balancing, or on anything else, because the situation, as you all know is changing very much from day to day, so much so that if I were to ask for any specific and detailed legislation it might be that the details will have to be changed a week from today. Therefore, it is necessary—I think you can make a pretty good guess—that I shall ask for fairly broad powers, in regard to banking, such powers as would make it possible to meet the changing situation from day to day in different parts of the country. We cannot write a permanent banking act for the nation in three days."[22]

The president's message in support of the bill was not communicated until 11:45 a.m., fifteen minutes before the special session of Congress was to open. In the message, President Roosevelt stated: "Our first task is to reopen all sound banks. This is an essential preliminary to subsequent legislation directed against speculation with the funds of depositors or other violations of positions of trust. In order that the final objective—the opening of banks—may be accomplished, I ask of the Congress the immediate creation of legislation giving to the executive branch of the government control over banks for the protection of depositors and authority forthwith to reorganize and reopen such banks as may be found to require reorganization to put them on a sound basis."[23]

He impressed upon Congress that prompt action on the bill was necessary. "I cannot too strongly urge the Congress the clear necessity for immediate action. A continuation of the strangulation of banking facilities is unthinkable. The passage of the proposed legislation will end this condition, and I trust within a short space of time will result in a resumption of business activities."[24]

Importantly, Roosevelt also implied that the federal government would be warranting the safety of all deposits of reopened banks (even though he decided against including an explicit deposit guarantee provision in the bill): "In addition, it is my belief that this legislation will not only lift immediately all unwarranted doubts and suspicions in regards to banks which are 100 percent sound, but will also mark the beginning of a new relationship between the banks and the people of this country."[25] Raymond Moley, who attended many of the drafting sessions for the emergency banking bill, later candidly described the legislative sleight of hand: "We knew how much banking depended upon make-believe or, stated more conservatively, the vital part that public confidence had in assuring solvency."[26]

Few members of Congress had even seen the bill. Even fewer had read it. It was rumored that Representative Steagall was the only member of the House who even had a copy. Waving it over his head, Steagall entered the House Chamber at 2:55 p.m., shouting, "Here's the bill. Let's pass it."[27] After only forty minutes of debate, it was passed by unanimous voice vote.[28] In the Senate, the bill was introduced at 1:40 p.m. and referred to the Banking and Currency Committee. Only one witness, F. Gloyd Awalt, acting comptroller of the currency, was called before Carter Glass's committee. He was asked how many national banks could open if the legislation passed and gave an emphatic answer: 5,000 if the bill became law; 2,600 if it didn't.[29] This was all the committee members needed to hear.

The bill was reported out of committee at 4:10 p.m.[30]

On the Senate floor, a small firestorm of opposition arose, organized by Huey Long, seeking more protection for smaller state banks, which he feared would be sacrificed to save the larger banks. Long offered an amendment authorizing the president to declare any state bank a member of the Federal Reserve System.

Rather than working behind the scenes with the Senate Democratic leadership to advance his populist agenda, Long decided early on that it would better serve his presidential ambitions to become an obstructionist in the Senate. Media attention is what he craved, a spotlight to promote himself. He arrived in the Senate on January 25, 1932, smoking a cigar (in violation of protocol), leaving it burning on a fellow senator's desk as he raised his hand to take the oath. The next day, he went back to New Orleans. He didn't return to the Senate until April, when he promptly made a motion to remove Joseph Robinson as Democratic majority leader, shocking his fellow legislators. After that failed, on May 12, he resigned from all committee appointments, this time producing scorn from his colleagues. On May 14, he began his first filibuster. Long's hysterically funny marathon floor speeches would soon gain a reputation as the best show in town. Committee work would stop so senators and staff could come to the floor to hear him carry on. A young congressional aide from Texas named Lyndon Baines Johnson paid a Senate doorkeeper to call him whenever Long took the floor.[31]

The filibusters made him a national figure—and he made the most of it. After the 1932 Democratic Convention in Chicago, Long met with Roosevelt campaign manager James Farley to offer his services to the campaign, insisting on a private train for himself along with a pair of sound trucks to trail him at every stop. Farley politely demurred, thinking it best to keep Long in remote rural areas—where either Roosevelt had no chance of winning or no chance of losing—to contain any possible public relations debacles.[32]

Word from the field soon trickled back to Farley. Long was surprisingly effective. Then reports cascaded back. Long was a huge hit. Wherever he went, crowds thronged and the press reports were glowing. Huey Long was a phenomenon. "We never again underestimated him," Farley later remembered.[33] Soon after the election, relations between the president-elect and Senator Long cooled. Long's patronage demands were increasingly outrageous, and his populist, socialist policies, for which he sought FDR's endorsement, were never seriously considered. Roosevelt would soon call Long one of the two most dangerous men in America (the other being General Douglas MacArthur).

Senator Glass, who felt similarly about Long, quickly acted to squelch any attempt to further burden the Federal Reserve System. Despite his Southern agrarian roots, Glass had little sympathy for small banking institutions, preferring a banking system dominated by large, solvent, big-city banks, particularly

New York banks. Glass stated that the bill expanded "in a degree that is almost shocking to me—the currency and credit facilities of the Federal Reserve Banking System, and further extends these facilities to state banks, which are not members of the Federal Reserve Banking System."[34] Long rose to defend the amendment, setting off a rare public display of senator-to-senator unpleasantries:

LONG: The Senator has misstated the facts. He wants to get his record straight.

GLASS: My record is quite straight and I do not relish hearing the Senator say I misrepresented anything. The Senator has to be more civil. . . .

LONG: The Senator is honestly in error. . . .

GLASS: The Senator has such ignorance of the whole problem, such a lack of appreciation, that he wants the President to cover 14,000 state banks into the Federal Reserve without knowing a thing in the world about them. . . .

LONG: What will the little banks do in the little county seats?

GLASS: "Little banks!" Little corner grocery men who got together $10,000 or $15,000 who then invite the deposits of their community and then at the very first gust of disaster topple over and ruin their depositors! What we need in this country is real banks with real bankers.[35]

Later, when they left the Senate floor, the seventy-five-year-old Senator Glass continued his confrontation with the thirty-nine-year-old Long, throwing a punch that nearly connected with the Kingfish's nose.

At 7:23 p.m., the bill passed by a vote of seventy-three to seven. At 8:36 p.m., seven hours and fifty-nine minutes after the special session opened, President Roosevelt signed it into law, obtaining for himself the largest peacetime grant of power over the U.S. financial system ever given.[36]

The Emergency Banking Act was divided into four operative titles. Title I approved and ratified the bank holiday proclamation and all regulations promulgated thereunder. It also granted to the president extraordinarily broad power to regulate all banking functions, including "any transaction in foreign exchange, transfers of credit between or payments by banking institutions, as defined by the President." It further empowered the secretary of the Treasury to require delivery to the Treasury of all gold and gold certificates held by anybody in the country. Violations of Title I were made punishable by fines of up to $10,000 and up to ten years' imprisonment.

Title II, known as the Bank Conservation Act, authorized the comptroller of the currency to appoint a conservator for any national bank if he deemed it necessary to conserve the bank's assets. It also authorized the reorganization of insolvent national banks upon the approval of the comptroller of the currency and depositors who held 75 percent of total deposits or holders of two-thirds of the outstanding capital stock of the bank. Prior to this law, consent of all creditors and stockholders was required to reorganize, allowing a small minority to block it.

Title III provided for the issuance of preferred stock by national banks and for the purchase of preferred stock of either national banks or state banks by the Reconstruction Finance Corporation (or loans to banks by the RFC secured by such preferred stock), if the president determined a bank required additional funds. This provision enabled banks to raise equity capital through preferred stock, as common stocks during this period often carried "double liability": if a bank failed, its receiver could assess shareholders for an amount up to the par value of their stock, meaning troubled banks had limited access to equity funding.

Title IV provided for the issuance by the Federal Reserve Banks of emergency currency called Federal Reserve Bank Notes. The notes were not required to be backed by gold, short-term commercial paper, or U.S. government obligations, but rather any notes, drafts, bills of exchange, or banks' acceptances valued at 90 percent of face value. This essentially allowed any loan or obligation, no matter how shaky the borrower was, to serve as collateral for new currency issued by the Treasury. The new Federal Reserve Bank Notes would be interchangeable with normal Federal Reserve Notes because the law provided that they "shall be receivable at par in all parts of the United States . . . and shall be redeemable in lawful money of the United States on presentation at the United States Treasury."[37]

Approximately $2,000,000,000 of the new notes would be issued to replace the hoarded currency taken out of circulation. As reported by *Time* magazine: "To manufacture the new money, the Bureau of Engraving & Printing went into 24-hour operation, its blue lights gleaming through the night across the Tidal Basin. Its 4,500 employees turned out crisp new bales of cash. Trucks, airplanes and trains rushed it cross-country to the twelve Federal Reserve Banks from which it was distributed like a financial blood transfusion to member banks."[38]

The expansion of the currency via Federal Reserve Bank Notes eliminated the need for scrip, except in small communities where banks were not agile enough to put the new currency into circulation. The scrip plan was abandoned primarily because of the lack of fungibility of various clearinghouses. For example, if bank assets underlying scrip issued in New York were of a higher quality than those underlying scrip in Chicago, the Chicago scrip would circulate at a discount to the New York scrip. In addition, both would circulate at a discount to Federal Reserve notes. "Where would we be if we had IOUs, scrip and certificates floating all around the country?"[39] asked Secretary Woodin. The millions of dollars of scrip paper printed at the American Bank Note Company in the Bronx would be trashed, costing taxpayers $100,000.

Secretary Woodin issued a statement after the passage of the Emergency Banking Act, stating, "It will be the policy of the Treasury to permit as rapidly as possible the opening of sound banks. There are, of course, many thousands of such banks which will promptly be restored to the performance of their normal function. The Treasury has already taken steps to secure information through the proper authorities as to the condition of the various banks of the country and immediately invites the banks' applications for reopening. While much information has already been assembled, the completion of the information and of the arrangements of the banks for resuming their functions takes some time. It has therefore been decided not to authorize any reopenings before Saturday, March 11. It is obvious that it will not be possible to act upon all of the applications even by Saturday. Resolutions governing reopenings and also other subjects governed by legislation will immediately be published."[40]

The New York Times headlined its story on the Emergency Banking Act, "Roosevelt Gets Power of Dictator." Arthur Krock wrote: "There are members of the House and Senate . . . who were aghast yesterday when they listened to Title One of the banking bill and stupefied today when they heard the clerk in the Chamber read the text of the economy bill. But these persons have been expressing themselves privately, if at all. The overshadowing presence of the national emergency has apparently silenced them."[41]

Shortly after the Emergency Banking bill was signed into law, President Roosevelt issued a proclamation under Title I of the act extending the bank holiday "until further proclamation by the president."[42] The following day, Roosevelt issued an executive order under Title I authorizing the secretary of the Treasury to reopen any member bank of the Federal Reserve System. The basic legal framework for the reopening of Federal Reserve member banks was simple: "All banks which are members of the Federal Reserve System, desiring to reopen for the performance of all usual and normal banking functions, except as otherwise prohibited shall apply for a license therefor to the Secretary of the Treasury. Licensing will be issued by the Federal Reserve Bank upon approval of the Secretary of the Treasury. The Federal Reserve Banks were designated as agents of the Secretary of the Treasury for the receiving of the applications and the issuance of licenses in his behalf and upon his instructions."[43]

The Federal Reserve Banks were concerned that issuing a license to reopen a bank would effectively constitute a guarantee of that bank's solvency, requiring they keep afloat reopened banks even at significant losses to themselves. If the Federal Reserve Banks rejected offered collateral and did not liberally issue the new Federal Reserve Bank Notes, as was their right, the hoped for anti-hoarding effect of Title IV would die on the vine. Recognizing that the cooperation of the Federal Reserve Banks was vital to the reopening plan, Roosevelt agreed to indemnify the Federal Reserve Banks against losses. "It is inevitable that some losses may be made by the Federal Reserve in loans to their member banks. The country appreciates, however, the twelve regional Federal Reserve Banks are operating entirely under Federal law and the recent Emergency Banking Act greatly enlarges their powers to adapt their facilities to a national emergency. Therefore, there is definitely an obligation on the federal government to reimburse the twelve regional Federal Reserve Banks for losses which they may make on loans made under those ensuing powers. I do not hesitate to assure you that I shall ask the Congress to indemnify any of the twelve Federal Reserve Banks for such losses. I am confident that Congress will recognize its obligation to the Federal Reserve Banks should the occasion arise, and grant such request."[44] The import of Roosevelt's promise was of historic significance: he had unilaterally pledged that the U.S. taxpayers would bear the cost of the bank bailout.

It was obvious to bankers and regulators that there was no effective way to examine the nation's 17,600 banks—in little more than a week—to determine which were solvent. It was equally obvious that this reality had to be hidden from the public. But if banks that were certified as solvent by the Treasury and the Federal Reserve Banks failed upon reopening, the banking system might fall into long-lasting chaos. In short, Roosevelt would have only one bite at the apple.

On March 11, Roosevelt announced a definitive program for the bank reopenings:

> "The Secretary of the Treasury will issue licenses to banks which are members of the Federal Reserve System, whether national bank or State, located in each of the twelve Federal Reserve Bank cities, to open Monday morning. So also the state authorities having supervision over State banks which are not members of the Federal Reserve System will be asked to permit any such state institutions located in any one of the twelve Federal Reserve Bank cities to open for business on Monday morning if in their judgment they deem it wise to do so. Under this progressive plan, banks located in any city having an active, recognized clearing house association, of which there are 250 cities, will receive licenses for reopening on Tuesday morning and banks located elsewhere will receive their licenses permitting reopening for Wednesday."[45]

Roosevelt emphasized that the chronology of bank reopenings was not related to the solvency condition of the banks. "The fact that banks will be opened under this plan does not mean that anyone should draw the inference that the banks opening Monday are in any different condition as to soundness from the banks licensed to open on Tuesday or Wednesday or any subsequent day."[46] Roosevelt also announced that he would address the nation that evening to explain the bank reopening plan.

In addition to arming banks with legal authority to limit large withdrawals that could fuel runs, the Treasury adopted an anti-hoarding rule: "No banking institution shall permit any withdrawal by any person when such institution, acting in good faith, shall deem that the withdrawal is intended for hoarding. Any banking institution, before permitting the withdrawal of large or unusual amounts of currency, may require from the person requesting such withdrawal a full statement under oath of the purpose for which the currency is requested."[47]

The most dramatic decision made by the administration in the lead-up to the bank reopenings involved A.P. Giannini's Bank of America National Trust and Savings Association in California. The first opinion of the responsible officials in California was that the bank should not be permitted to open. But Woodin believed that it would be unwise to accept this judgment. The failure of the Bank of America to reopen would mean much more than the failure of almost any other bank. The Bank of America had 410 branches. With its one million depositors it was in a very real sense the bank of the common people of California. To keep it closed would shock the state beyond description.

As Moley later recalled: "Woodin met the problem with such courage as I have rarely seen. He directed Awalt to go over the figures with him again. When everything was taken into consideration, the two men reached the conclusion that the bank was by no means insolvent. Then ensued a long telephone conversation with a high banking official in San Francisco—a conversation punctuated by some pretty strong language on Woodin's end. It wound up with Woodin's, 'Are you willing to take the responsibility for keeping this institution closed?' and the answer, from California, that the official refused to take that responsibility. 'Well, then,' said Will, 'the bank will open.'"[48]

President Roosevelt summoned a number of officials to the White House on Saturday to preview that evening's radio address. It was to be his first so-called fireside chat. Along with Secretary Woodin, the officials included acting comptroller of the currency Awalt, Federal Reserve Board Governor Adolph Miller, and Louis M. Howe, the president's chief of staff. As Awalt described it, "Mr. Roosevelt read the speech, turned to Woodin, and asked him what he thought of it. Woodin replied that he thought it was great. He then asked Miller his reaction, and [he] replied that it was an excellent speech and would accomplish its purpose. The president then asked what I thought of it and I, not knowing the president's disposition too well, rushed in as a fool where angels fear to tread, and said that it was a fine speech, but—. This was as far as I got when the president snapped 'But what?' I told him he had stated that we would open only sound banks and, in our hurry to complete the program, there might be some exceptions. He stated in no uncertain terms that that was what we were going to do, 'open only sound banks.' I had nothing more to say."[49]

It would be the most important peacetime address of his presidency. Roosevelt knew all too well that much of the reopening plan was "make believe"—he had to make the American people believe banks would be sound or his one bite at the apple would be wasted. It was his do-or-die moment.

Speaking from his study in the White House, the president addressed the nation:

"I want to talk for a few minutes with the people of the United States about banking. With the comparatively few who understand the mechanics of banking but more particularly with the overwhelming majority who use banks for the making of deposits and the drawing of checks. I want to tell you what has been done in the last few days, why it was done, and what the next steps are going to be. I recognize that the many proclamations from the state capitols and from Washington, the legislation, the Treasury regulations, etc., couched for the most part in banking and legal terms should be explained for the benefit of the average citizen. I owe this in particular because of the fortitude and good temper with which everybody has accepted the inconvenience and hardships of the banking holiday. I know that when you understand what we in Washington have been about, I shall continue to have your cooperation as fully as I have had your sympathy and help during the past week."[50]

He then tried to explain the origin of the banking crisis:

"First of all let me state the simple fact that when you deposit money in a bank the bank does not put the money into a safe deposit vault. It invests your money in many different forms of credit—bonds, commercial paper, mortgages, and many other kinds of loans. In other words, the bank puts your money to work to keep the wheels of industry and of agriculture turning around. A comparatively small part of the money you put into the bank is kept in currency—an amount which in normal times is wholly sufficient to cover the cash needs of the average citizen. In other words the total amount of all the currency in the country is only a small fraction of the total deposits in all the banks. What, then, happened during the last few days of February and the first few days of March? Because of undermined confidence on the part of the public, there was a general rush by a large portion of our population to turn bank deposits into currency or gold—a rush so great that the soundest banks could not get enough currency to meet the demand. The reason for this was that on the spur of the moment it was, of course, impossible to sell perfectly sound assets of a bank and convert them into cash except at panic prices far below their real value. By the afternoon of March 3 scarcely a bank in the country was open to do business. Proclamations temporarily closing them in whole or in part had been issued by the Governors in almost all the states."[51]

The president then laid out the actions his administration had recently undertaken:

"It was then that I issued the proclamation providing for the nation-wide bank holiday, and this was the first step in the Government's reconstruction of our financial and economic fabric. The second step was the legislation promptly and patriotically passed by the Congress confirming my proclamation and broadening my powers so that it became possible, in view of the requirement of time, to extend the holiday and lift the ban of that holiday gradually. This law also gave authority to develop a program of rehabilitation of our banking facilities. I want to tell our citizens in every part of the Nation that the national Congress—Republicans and Democrats alike—showed by this action a devotion to public welfare and a realization of the emergency and the necessity for speed that it is difficult to match in our history. The third stage has been the series of regulations permitting the banks to continue their functions to take care of the distribution of food and household necessities and the payment of payrolls. This bank holiday while resulting in many cases in great inconvenience is affording us the opportunity to supply the currency necessary to meet the situation. No sound bank is a dollar worse off than it was when it closed its doors last Monday. Neither is any bank which may turn out not to be in a position for immediate opening. The new law allows the twelve Federal Reserve banks to issue additional currency on good assets and thus the banks which reopen will

be able to meet every legitimate call. The new currency is being sent out by
the Bureau of Engraving and Printing in large volume to every part of the
country. It is sound currency because it is based by actual, good assets."[52]

Roosevelt then explained the schedule of bank reopenings to commence
the following day:

"As a result we start tomorrow, Monday, with the opening of banks in the
twelve Federal Reserve bank cities—those banks which on first examination
by the Treasury have already been found to be all right. This will be followed
on Tuesday by the resumption of all their functions by banks already found
to be sound in cities where there are recognized clearinghouses. That means
about 250 cities of the United States.

"On Wednesday and succeeding days banks in smaller places all through
the country will resume business, subject, of course, to the Government's
physical ability to complete its survey. It is necessary that the reopening of
banks be extended over a period in order to permit the banks to take applications for necessary loans, to obtain currency needed to meet their requirements, and to enable the Government to make common sense checkups.
Let me make it clear to you that if your bank does not open the first day you
are by no means justified in believing that it will not open. A bank that opens
on one of the subsequent days is in exactly the same status as the bank that
opens tomorrow. I know that many people are worrying about state banks
not members of the Federal Reserve System. These banks can and will receive assistance from member banks and from the Reconstruction Finance
Corporation. These state banks are following the same course as the national
banks except that they get their licenses to resume business from the state
authorities, and these authorities have been asked by the Secretary of the Treasury to permit their good banks to open up on the same schedule as the national banks. I am confident that the state banking departments will be as
careful as the National Government in the policy relating to the opening of
banks and will follow the same broad policy. It is possible that when the banks
resume a very few people who have not recovered from their fear may again
begin withdrawals. Let me make it clear that the banks will take care of all
needs—and it is my belief that hoarding during the past week has become

an exceedingly unfashionable pastime. I need no prophet to tell you that when the people find that they can get their money—that they can get it when they want it for all legitimate purposes—the phantom of fear will soon be laid. People will again be glad to have their money where it will be safely taken care of and where they can use it conveniently at any time. I can assure you that it is safer to keep your money in a reopened bank than under the mattress. The success of our whole great national program depends, of course, upon the cooperation of the public—on its intelligent support and use of a reliable system. Remember that the essential accomplishment of the new legislation is that it makes it possible for banks more readily to convert their assets into cash than was the case before. More liberal provision has been made for banks to borrow on these assets at the Reserve Banks and more liberal provision has also been made for issuing currency on the security of those good assets. This currency is not fiat currency. It is issued only on adequate security—and every good bank has an abundance of such security."[53]

But he was also careful to point out that many insolvent banks would never reopen:

"One more point before I close. There will be, of course, some banks unable to reopen without being reorganized. The new law allows the Government to assist in making these reorganizations quickly and effectively and even allows the Government to subscribe to at least a part of new capital which may be required. I hope you can see from this elemental recital of what your Government is doing that there is nothing complex, or radical in the process. We had a bad banking situation. Some of our bankers had shown themselves either incompetent or dishonest in their handling of the people's funds. They had used the money entrusted to them in speculations and unwise loans. This was, of course, not true in the vast majority of our banks but it was true in enough of them to shock the people for a time into a sense of insecurity and to put them into a frame of mind where they did not differentiate, but seemed to assume that the acts of a comparative few had tainted them all. It was the Government's job to straighten out this situation and do it as quickly as possible—and the job is being performed. I do not promise you that every bank will be reopened or that individual losses will not be suffered, but there will be no losses that possibly could be avoided;

and there would have been more and greater losses had we continued to drift. I can even promise you salvation for some at least of the sorely pressed banks. We shall be engaged not merely in reopening sound banks but in the creation of sound banks through reorganization. It has been wonderful to me to catch the note of confidence from all over the country. I can never be sufficiently grateful to the people for the loyal support they have given me in their acceptance of the judgment that has dictated our course, even though all of our processes may not have seemed clear to them."[54]

In closing, Roosevelt reiterated themes of confidence, courage, and faith:

"After all there is an element in the readjustment of our financial system more important than currency, more important than gold, and that is the confidence of the people. Confidence and courage are the essentials of success in carrying out our plan. You people must have faith; you must not be stampeded by rumors or guesses. Let us unite in banishing fear. We have provided the machinery to restore our financial system; it is up to you to support and make it work. It is your problem no less than it is mine. Together we cannot fail."[55]

Roosevelt and his advisers were happy with the address. But they couldn't know for sure if it had accomplished its purpose until Monday when the banks in the Federal Reserve cities were to open.

Shortly after the president's fifteen-minute talk concluded, Secretary Woodin released the list of Federal Reserve member banks licensed to reopen. Banks quickly advertised receiving the Fed's stamp of approval. Upon receiving notice of its license to resume unrestricted banking business, New York's Irving Trust Company immediately mailed notices of its reopening to 45,000 customers and sent more than 800 cables and 1,000 telegrams notifying clients all around the world.[56]

One area of significant concern was a feared disadvantage non-member state banks would have in accessing liquidity from Federal Reserve Banks, as compared with national banks and member state banks, since they didn't have direct access to currency from Federal Reserve Banks (particularly new Federal Reserve Bank Notes, with their liberal collateral requirements). Many governors, including Governor Lehman of New York, complained to the White

House that lack of access would severely handicap non-member banks. In response, Secretary Woodin indicated that Federal Reserve member banks would be encouraged to supply currency to the state non-member banks.[57] A consequence of this disparate treatment was a dramatic increase in the number of state banks seeking Federal Reserve membership. In the Chicago Federal Reserve district alone, thirty-nine state banks applied for membership and a hundred more asked for applications.[58]

Throughout the weekend, the new currency was delivered in quantity to the Federal Reserve Bank cities for the Monday reopenings. Approximately $200,000,000 was printed in the first run. In New York City, fifty-two out of sixty-one Federal Reserve member banks were allowed to open. In the eleven other Federal Reserve cities, 200 member and non-member state banks were to open.[59]

The tension in the White House built as dawn broke Monday morning. Local officials were on the lookout to report any telltale signs of a bank run. And when the tellers' windows opened that morning, something unexpected happened. There were long lines, but few customers sought withdrawals. Ordinary citizens showed up in huge numbers to deposit money. Roosevelt's fireside chat had succeeded far beyond expectations. The American people trusted the new president and wanted him to succeed. And with their votes of confidence—evidenced by their deposit slips—his political power grew.

Little of the new currency would actually be needed, as deposits by no-longer-panicked Americans far outnumbered withdrawals. Perhaps the strongest driver of withdrawals was curiosity—many people wanted to look at or collect the new bills. While older notes were inscribed with "National Currency—secured by United States bonds deposited with the Treasurer of the United States of America," the new bills bore an additional phrase—"or by like deposit of other securities."[60] They remain a collector's item.

New York on that first day saw a net deposit of currency of about $20,000,000, and gold receipts increased dramatically. In Chicago, over $7,000,000 of gold was deposited.[61] Attendants reported that safety deposit box renters were hauling out their gold and currency and taking it upstairs to the tellers' windows to be deposited.

The White House and the Treasury were delighted with the smooth functioning of the bank reopenings. "Reports from all sections of the country from which we have heard," Secretary Woodin observed, "indicate that the reopening of the banks in the twelve Federal Reserve cities has caused not excitement, but of course considerable gratification. The people have responded to the first step in the government's plan of financial reconstruction with common sense and sober realization of actual conditions. A great many inquiries have come to us about San Francisco, where banks opened to regular schedule as in the other Reserve cities. Deposits and withdrawals are proceeding normally. Word from New York is that all the reopened banks are functioning as if there had been no interruption in their activities. People are satisfied that their deposits are safe in these banks, a feeling doubtless to a large extent the result of President Roosevelt's radio speech last night."[62] When asked if opening the banks on the thirteenth made anyone superstitious, Woodin said it was now his lucky number.

Buoyed by the success of the big-city reopenings, Senate Majority Leader Joseph Robinson of Arkansas introduced an amendment to the Emergency Banking Act permitting state banks that were not members of the Federal Reserve System to obtain direct loans from Federal Reserve Banks, provided a state banking regulator deemed the bank in sound condition. Robinson's bill passed the Senate the next day.[63]

There was even progress in Babe Ruth's contract negotiations. He lowered his asking price to $60,000, but Colonel Ruppert continued to hold the line: "I think I have been liberal with all my players. I have the most expensive ball club in the business and I would gladly pay without quibbling any reasonable amount to any ball players. But I have reached the limit in offering $50,000 to Ruth."[64]

On Tuesday, March 14, approximately 1,500 banks opened in the 250 cities with recognized clearinghouse associations. The result was the same in the Federal Reserve Bank cities—deposits far exceeded withdrawals.[65]

In Newark, the Fidelity Union Trust Company received cash deposits that Tuesday estimated at $4,500,000—so much money that all bank employees, even the president, were put to work counting it. The inflow of deposits continued unabated in the twelve Federal Reserve Bank cities. In New York, net deposits on Tuesday were again estimated at $20,000,000.[66]

On Wednesday, the national banking holiday ended, with licensed banks in smaller communities opening. As with the large cities, deposits significantly outpaced withdrawals. During the three-day reopening period, net receipts of currency totaled $143,000,000.[67] Wednesday also saw the reopening of the stock exchanges. The trading results were even more spectacular than the deposit figures. The Dow Jones industrial average increased by 15.34 percent, the largest single-day price increase ever recorded. *The New York Times* observed: "The robust advance in stocks and bonds was interpreted—and correctly so— as Wall Street's mark of approval of the steps taken by the president and Congress in the interval to end the financial disorder."[68]

The success of the bank reopening plan depended almost entirely on public confidence in the ability of the federal government to ensure the solvency of the banks. There was no rational economic reason why banks the public believed insolvent on March 3 were thought to be solvent on March 15. This triumph of irrationality was, without question, a personal triumph of Franklin D. Roosevelt. Secretary Woodin performed surprisingly well under extraordinary pressure, and Senator Glass and Representative Steagall moved the Emergency Banking Act through Congress at breakneck speed.

Another key to the longer-term success of the bank reopening plan was the Title III preferred stock purchase authorization. Through the purchase of preferred stock, capital notes, and debentures, the RFC invested more than $1,171,000,000 in over 6,000 banking institutions in eighteen years, the equivalent of one-third of total bank capital in the United States in 1933. The RFC lost only $13,660,000, and just 206 of the 6,000 banks it helped were later compelled to close.[69]

The comparison of national leadership during the 2008 financial crisis with that of March 1933 is striking. President Bush did not make himself the personal spokesperson for the bailout as President Roosevelt had done. And the House of Representatives initially failed in passing TARP. When finally implemented, TARP's infusion of capital into banks was a virtual clone of the Emergency Banking Act Title III preferred stock purchase plan. Not surprisingly, the 2008 bailout never gained widespread public approval. Roosevelt's program did.

A final factor cannot be overlooked in explaining Roosevelt's success: good luck. During that critical two-week period after his inauguration, no major unsettling financial events challenged the shaky confidence-building efforts of the new administration. It is fortunate that the Pecora hearings were on recess during this period, for if a blockbuster disclosure of financial malfeasance had occurred, it is possible that confidence in the banks might not have been restored.

By the end of the week, more than 13,500 of the approximately 17,600 banks in the nation were open.[70] In New Wilmington, Pennsylvania, the First National Bank of New Wilmington, organized by George H. Getty in 1895 and taken over by his son Howard in 1907, was working with regulators toward a scheduled full opening on March 20. On the Friday before the bank was to reopen, Howard Getty's automobile was found unattended on Mercer Road in New Wilmington. A few feet away, his lifeless body was discovered alongside a gun. He had shot himself in the head. He left his hat, glasses, and a note in the car: "The $50,000 insurance policy which the bank holds on my life will pay the depreciation on the bond account to allow the bank to reopen."[71]

On March 22, Babe Ruth finally came to terms with Colonel Ruppert—for $52,000. It was a clear win for the Yankees ownership, and Ruth could barely muster a brave face in his perfunctory remarks to the press: "I'll take $52,000, I told him that was alright, and that ended the matter."[72]

FOUR

MORE LIVES THAN A CAT:

The Glass-Steagall Banking Act of 1933

The success of the bank reopenings earned Roosevelt an unexpected windfall of political capital for financial reform. But how best to deploy it—or how not to squander it—was not a simple matter. So much needed to be done and every option was fraught with risk. Roosevelt knew that Wall Street was flat on its back after the disastrous performance by the National City Bank officers at the Pecora Hearings and the humiliation of the nationwide bank shutdown and bailout. But he also knew that Wall Street would bounce back, and when it did, it would fight any permanent reform proposals tooth and nail. Time was not the president's ally.

Roosevelt's skeletal financial reform agenda had four essential elements: first, "truth in advertising" in the sale of new securities; second, elimination of stock manipulation and unfair dealing on the securities exchanges; third, stricter control over margin lending to limit stock speculation; and fourth, the separation of commercial banking and investment banking.

In broad strokes, Roosevelt outlined his seven-point reform program to implement this agenda during an August 20, 1932, campaign speech in Columbus, Ohio:

"Government cannot prevent some individuals from making errors of judgment. But Government can prevent to a very great degree the fooling of sensible people through misstatements and through the withholding of information on the part of private organizations, great and small, which seek to sell investments to the people of the Nation. First, toward that end and to inspire truth telling, I propose that every effort be made to prevent the issue of manufactured and unnecessary securities of all kinds which are brought out merely for the purpose of enriching those who handle their sale to the public; and I further propose that with respect to legitimate securities the sellers shall tell the uses to which the money is to be put. This truth telling requires that definite and accurate statements be made to the buyers in respect to the bonuses and commissions the sellers are to receive, and, furthermore, true information as to the investment of principal, as to the true earnings, true liabilities and true assets of the corporation itself. Second, we are well aware of the difficulty and often the impossibility under which State Governments have labored in the regulation of holding companies that sell securities in interstate commerce. It is logical, it is necessary and it is right that Federal power be applied to such regulation. Third, for the very simple reason that many exchanges in the business of buying and selling securities and commodities can by the practical expedient of moving elsewhere avoid regulation by any given state, I propose the use of Federal authority in the regulation of stock exchanges. Fourth, the events of the past three years prove that the supervision of national banks for the protection of the public has been ineffective. I propose vastly more rigid supervision. Fifth, we have witnessed not only the unrestrained use of bank deposits in speculation to the detriment of local credit, but we are also aware that this speculation was encouraged by the Government itself. I propose that such speculation be discouraged and prevented. Sixth, investment banking is a legitimate business. Commercial banking is another wholly separate and distinct business. Their consolidation and mingling are contrary to public policy. I propose their separation. Seventh, prior to the panic of 1929, the funds of the Federal

Reserve System were used practically without check for many speculative enterprises. I propose the restriction of Federal Reserve Banks in accordance with the original plans and earlier practices of the Federal Reserve System under Woodrow Wilson. Finally, my friends, I propose two new policies for which legislation is not required. They are policies of fair and open dealing on the part of the officials of the American Government[1] with the American investing public."

In truth, Roosevelt had no particular priority regarding which of his reforms he wanted to implement first, but he wanted a victory, because success would build his political power and make each successive reform bill easier to shepherd through Congress. He was, more than anything, a pragmatist, but he was also an economic and financial policy neophyte and dilettante and it showed, badly at times. His great strength—a willingness to try, and abandon if necessary, new and unorthodox approaches to economic problems—could also be a liability. He would whipsaw his economic team by his abrupt and fundamental course changes. During the first year of his presidency, he would go from a budget hawk to a deficit spender, a champion of sound money to removing America from the gold standard (only to later put the country back on it). He would create his alphabet soup of legislative programs and agencies during his first hundred days and beyond, keeping what seemed to work and casting aside what didn't. There is a degree of truth to David Stockman's characterization of Roosevelt's New Deal as "a political gong show, not a golden era of enlightened economic policy."

Regulation of new securities issuances and exchanges would require essentially de novo legislation in Congress—not so legislation limiting the activities of the banks. A banking bill sponsored by Carter Glass embodying many of the banking reforms proposed by Roosevelt in the Columbus, Ohio, speech had already traveled a long and bumpy legislative road.

Glass's legislation was less born of the 1933 banking crisis than it was interrupted by it. As the bank failure rate skyrocketed throughout the 1920s, concern about the strength of the Federal Reserve System had grown in Congress. In May 1929—months before the October Crash—Senator William H. King of Utah called for an investigation into the impact of the securities activities of banks on the Federal Reserve System. Huge profits were being made by banks' lending to stock market speculators; and many of the larger banks were borrowing cheaply from the Fed and lending at high rates to securities brokers and dealers.

Many policymakers, in particular Senator Glass, were concerned that the Federal Reserve Banks, established to essentially provide working capital to banks under times of stress, were becoming the house lenders in the Wall Street casino. After the Crash, support for Senator King's resolution grew and it was adopted on May 5, 1930. A subcommittee of the Senate Committee on Banking and Currency, chaired by Glass, conducted the investigation and focused on five areas of interest: use of banking facilities for trading in speculative securities; the extent of loans to brokers for securities transactions; the effect of the formation of investment trusts; the desirability of branch banking; and the development of branch banking within the national banking system.[2] Branch banking was a pet cause of Glass, and an anathema to populists like Huey Long. Glass wanted nationwide consolidation within the banking system. He believed fewer, larger banks with many branches promoted stability, and he was willing to allow rural areas to be "underbanked" if that was the price of stability. Banks like National City might behave badly, but they were smart and they were solvent. The best-intentioned mom-and-pop banking operations, which were unsophisticated and undercapitalized—and there were many hundreds of them—had gotten the country into the mess it was in, in large part, so Glass thought, even if many of their losses resulted from purchasing the worthless bonds aggressively sold to them by Charles Mitchell's salesmen. Glass believed that too many banks that were "too small to save" were a far greater risk than banks that were "too big to fail."

Over the course of thirteen days in January and February 1931, Glass's subcommittee heard testimony from top banking regulators, senior officials of banks (both large and small), and leading academics. The subcommittee prepared and distributed a series of questionnaires to banks, bank examiners, the twelve Federal Reserve Banks, and stock exchange members and officials. Upon conclusion of the investigation, the subcommittee produced a 1,100-page volume memorializing its conclusions.[3]

On January 21, 1932, Senator Glass introduced a banking reform bill implementing the subcommittee's recommendations. The bill provided for limitations on the operating policies of the Federal Reserve Banks, essentially bringing them more in line with his "lender of last resort" principle by preventing them from extending loans to a member bank for its ordinary course of business financing and specifically barring loans to finance speculation. No member bank would be permitted to increase its securities transaction lending if it had an outstanding loan owing to a Federal Reserve Bank. The bill also required Federal Reserve member banks to provide reports on the financial condition of their securities affiliates. It did not go so far as to require the disposing of securities affiliates. A provision Glass claimed was motivated by a desire to depoliticize and strengthen the Federal Reserve Board would have removed the secretary of the Treasury as a member of the board and would have required that at least two board members have substantial banking experience. Beginning during World War I, the Federal Reserve Banks started acquiring U.S. government bonds, first to fund the war, but continued to do so during the Depression to fund government deficits. Glass believed that it was totally contrary to the Federal Reserve's mission to finance U.S. government operations. This cozy relationship between the Treasury and the Fed was subverting the legislative purpose of the Federal Reserve System—ensuring the liquidity and solvency of the member banks, Glass believed; and removing the Treasury secretary from the Federal Reserve Board would help sever that too-close relationship. Senator Long argued this provision was intended by Glass to make the Federal Reserve even less accountable to the public and more dominated by Wall Street.

The bill also would have limited the amount banks could loan their affiliates to not more than 10 percent of capital and surplus for any one affiliate or 20 percent for all affiliates. The legislation would have also provided for regulation of bank holding companies, requiring regular examination and financial reporting, and disenfranchising holding companies from voting the stock of member banks if they failed to comply with these requirements. And it would give the Federal Reserve Board and the comptroller of the currency power to remove any officer or director of a member bank who continued to violate banking laws or engage in unsafe or unsound banking practices.[4]

The two most controversial features of the bill were provisions permitting branch banking by national banks and the creation of a federal "liquidating corporation" to wind up the operations of failed banks. The bill authorized national banks to establish branches anywhere in a state they operated (and, subject to Federal Reserve approval, in adjacent states but not beyond fifty miles from the seat of the parent bank). This embodied a compromise of Senator Glass's desire to strengthen the banking system by allowing the larger, healthier banks to expand and replace or absorb weaker, smaller banks—particularly in rural areas where banks were failing at an alarming rate and weakening the Federal Reserve System—with Senator Long's populist desire to preserve community banking.

The federal liquidating corporation was Glass's attempt to preempt the federal deposit insurance movement, which was gaining popularity as the Depression deepened and was strongly advocated in the House of Representatives by Glass's counterpart, Alabama representative Henry Steagall. Glass believed deposit insurance would reward poorly managed banks and those too small to survive economic stress. If guaranteed, he argued, deposits would remain in unstable banks, putting the financial burden on viable banks. The result would be a weaker banking system, with the dying dragging down the healthy. Roosevelt was in accord with Carter Glass on the deposit insurance question.

Glass proposed that the liquidating corporation be authorized to acquire and liquidate the assets of member banks closed by the comptroller of the currency (for national banks), state banking authorities (for state banks), or voluntarily by a bank's board of directors. Glass's liquidating corporation would be capitalized with a quarter of the Federal Reserve Banks' aggregate surplus (about $68,500,000), 0.25 of 1 percent of member banks aggregate deposits (about $75,000,000), and $125,000,000 from the U.S. Treasury.

The bill was received with intense opposition from small banks who, in March 1932, succeeded in forcing additional hearings before the full Senate Banking and Currency Committee. The bill's opponents focused on the branch banking provision, but surprisingly, there was little Wall Street opposition to the regulation of securities affiliates. Perhaps emboldened by this, Glass, who believed that banking activities should be limited to traditional commercial lending, drafted a revised bill requiring separation of commercial banks from their securities affiliates. The revised bill did not require "private banks" like J.P. Morgan & Co., Kuhn, Loeb & Company, or Dillon, Read & Co. that did not take deposits from the general public to dispose of their securities operations. After three years, member banks would have to eliminate all affiliations with entities principally engaged in the issuance, underwriting, or distribution of securities.[5]

Debate on the revised bill began in the Senate on May 9, 1932, but other pressing business resulted in it being tabled for the remainder of the session. The Senate adjourned for the 1932 election season without acting on the bill.[6]

As debate resumed during the lame-duck session of the 72nd Congress, Senator Huey Long emerged as the principal opponent of the bill, arguing that the expansion of branch banking would spell the end of the state banks and result in the consolidation of financial power on Wall Street, to the detriment of rural America. When it reached the floor on January 10, 1933, Long began a filibuster of the bill with a meandering four-hour speech that quoted heavily from scripture: "Go to now, ye rich men, weep and howl for your mischief that shall come upon you."[7] On January 21, 1933, Long ended his marathon of talk after an amendment was added by Senator Sam Bratton of New Mexico limiting branch banking by national banks in each state to what was permitted to state chartered banks under that state's law.[8]

On January 25, 1933, a final vote was taken on the bill, as amended, with fifty-four senators voting in favor and nine opposed.[9]

The bill died in the House Committee on Banking and Currency, where it was not taken up before the legislative session ended.

The House, too, had been actively pursuing a banking bill. Representative Steagall had been sponsoring legislation to create a federal deposit insurance plan since 1923. On March 7, 1932, he again introduced deposit insurance legislation. Steagall's bill contemplated insuring 100 percent of deposits, to be funded by a corporation capitalized with $150,000,000 from the U.S. Treasury, $150,000,000 from the Federal Reserve Banks, an initial $100,000,000 from Federal Reserve member banks (pro rata based on their respective deposits), and up to $100,000,000 per annum from member banks thereafter, if needed. State non-member banks with at least $25,000 in capital and surplus would be permitted to join the insurance program if certified financially sound by the board of the new corporation. Alternatively, state non-member banks would be permitted to participate for a period of not more than three years if they were certified to be financially sound by their state regulator and agreed to pay twice the assessments required of member banks with the same deposit base.[10]

Steagall's bill also required that national banks possess a minimum capital and surplus of $50,000. The bill would also have eliminated double liability for common shareholders, provided for immediate check clearing among Federal Reserve member banks, capped interest on deposits at 4 percent, and permitted the Federal Reserve Board to remove any officer or director of a national bank.[11]

Debate on the Steagall bill began on May 25, 1932. The two biggest sources of controversy were the taxpayer-funded aspects of the deposit insurance plan and the double contribution required for state non-member banks not submitting to federal supervision. Representative Wright Patman of Texas led the attack on taxpayer subsidies but was unsuccessful in modifying the provisions. However, the requirement that state non-member banks not subject to federal supervision pay twice the premium of federally supervised banks was eliminated, allowing them to enter the insurance program on the same financial terms. A second amendment to retain double liability for bank shareholders was also approved. The amended bill passed the House on May 27, 1932, but died in committee in the Senate.[12]

After the banks were reopened, Roosevelt used the Glass bill as the nucleus of permanent banking reform legislation. The White House was concerned about timing—did it make sense to push for an extensive overhaul of the banking system so soon after the collapse of the banking system? And Roosevelt, Secretary Woodin, and Senator Glass all remained opposed to deposit insurance but realized that they might have to allow it to obtain House approval of any banking bill. There was no doubt the separation of investment banking from commercial banking would be a feature of any administration-backed bill. In his book *Looking Forward*, which set forth his New Deal objectives, Roosevelt proclaimed: "Investment banking is a legitimate business. Commercial banking is another wholly distinct legitimate business. Their consolidation and mingling is contrary to public policy. I propose their separation."[13]

The administration's opposition to deposit insurance was not solely based on philosophical grounds; it was very much based on historical, practical experience. Everywhere it had been tried in America theretofore, deposit insurance had been an abject failure. New York first created a deposit insurance fund in 1829, but it was depleted by the Panic of 1837. Eight states reacted to the Panic of 1907 by establishing bank deposit guarantees: Oklahoma, Kansas, Nebraska, Texas, Mississippi, South Dakota, North Dakota, and Washington. By 1929, all these laws had either been repealed or were inactive. In every case, the insurance funds collapsed whenever any large number of banks failed, most during the agricultural depression of the 1920s.[14]

By April, Senator Glass had conceded to including a bona fide deposit insurance program in lieu of the "liquidating corporation" contained in his Senate bill. His consent was conditioned on a requirement that all participating banks in the deposit insurance program be subject to federal examination and supervision and be required to join the Federal Reserve System within a specified period of time. Glass, believing that no bank without deposit insurance would be able to compete against one with deposit insurance, was hopeful that deposit insurance would be a back door to a consolidated federal banking system. He hoped that capital requirements and financial soundness standards for participation in the insurance program would be set at a level rigorous enough to exclude, and thereby shutter, weak state banks that he believed posed the greatest risk to the banking system. Glass thought it possible that the failure of the state deposit insurance programs of the past could be avoided if supervision and participation standards were not compromised.[15]

On April 4, 1933, Glass announced that his subcommittee would be reporting his bill to the full Senate Banking and Currency Committee, with the deposit insurance provision added. He also indicated that it would contain a provision prohibiting the payment of interest on demand deposits (in order to avoid banks competing for insured deposits for risky lending by paying higher interest than competing banks) and a ban on interlocking directorates (where an official of a bank holds a position at a non-banking corporation).[16]

Representative Steagall prepared a similar but not identical bill for reintroduction in April. The principal differences involved eligibility requirements for the deposit insurance program and in branch banking. Steagall's version allowed state banks to participate in the deposit insurance program even if not subject to federal supervision, so long as state regulators certified the banks as solvent, and opposed Glass's provision allowing national banks to have local branches.

Throughout that April, tensions began to arise between Glass and Roosevelt over monetary policy. On April 5, Roosevelt took America off the "gold standard" when he issued Executive Order 6102 under power delegated to him by the Emergency Banking Act. This required all persons to deliver to a Federal Reserve member bank all gold coin and bullion and gold certificates owned by them with value in excess of $100 (other than gold for industrial uses or jewelry) by May 1, 1933, in exchange for currency at a rate of $20.67 per ounce.

The stated reason for the president's action was to prevent hoarding and the resulting restriction of the nation's currency supply and deflation. This action was not in and of itself inflationary, but would certainly pave the way for a future devaluation of the dollar by eliminating the market discipline of free conversion of dollars into gold at $20.67 per ounce—the rate in effect since 1879 (except for a temporary conversion suspension during World War I).[17]

It did not take long for Roosevelt and Congress to take longer steps down the path of dollar devaluation. The political expediency of inflation was obvious: the resulting price appreciation of agricultural commodities would revive the desperate farming sector, and the relative reduction in price of American manufactured goods would hopefully spur exports, production, and jobs. The risks of inflation were equally obvious, but longer term: losses to debt holders as old debts incurred under a gold standard dollar could be paid in less valuable inflated dollars and the risks that other nations will respond in kind with protectionist measures of their own, such as higher tariffs or devaluing their own currencies. More than any other risk, however, it was the volatility of a fiat currency system—the politicization of money—that motivated the hard-money advocates like Carter Glass to oppose these measures.

On April 18, Roosevelt, to the shock and fury of Glass and the others who insisted on the "strong dollar" plank in the 1932 Democratic platform, threw his lot in with the inflationists and broke his campaign promise of sound money when he approved an amendment to the Agricultural Adjustment Act offered by Oklahoma senator John William Elmer Thomas that empowered the president to substantially increase the money supply with a view toward increasing farm product prices. When the Thomas Amendment passed the Senate on April 28, becoming law on May 12, it permitted the president to authorize the Open Market Committee of the Federal Reserve Board to purchase up to $3,000,000,000 of outstanding federal government bonds, have the U.S. Treasury issue up to $3,000,000,000 of fiat currency (and nearly double the amount of currency then in circulation), to reduce the gold content of the dollar by up to 50 percent, to monetize silver by purchasing the nation's entire production of mined silver at $1.25 per ounce (three and a half times the then–market price) and coin that silver into circulating money, and to accept silver as payment for up to $200,000,000 of World War I war debts owed by European nations, at a rate not to exceed $0.50 per ounce.

Later, on June 5, the break from gold was extended when Congress passed a joint resolution declaring invalid and illegal every public and private contractual provision that required a repayment in gold. All such contracts were effectively rewritten to permit repayment in dollars.

Roosevelt had obtained the legal power he needed to effect inflation but did not yet exercise that power. He could have used the Treasury authority to print currency to support deficit spending, but he remained publicly in favor of a balanced budget. Currency and gold hoarding had been nearly completely eliminated with the bank reopenings, and the banking system was awash in excess reserves. It was simply not the case any longer that banks were afraid to lend; qualified borrowers were scarce. Glass feared—correctly, it would turn out—that Roosevelt would find some way to use this new power to appease rural voters and neutralize populists like Huey Long by inflationary policy actions.

In mid-April, the tension between Glass and the president intensified when the White House voiced concern over both banking bills. President Roosevelt continued to oppose deposit insurance. The administration also objected to the provision that would remove the secretary of the Treasury as a member of the Federal Reserve Board. In addition, the president was wary of the political fallout in rural states from the branch banking proposal. This could well become an issue that Huey Long could exploit in a national campaign, Roosevelt feared. And despite being publicly supportive of the separation of commercial and investment banking, concerns were raised by Treasury officials over the possible disruption separation might cause to government bond underwritings.[18] Steagall tried to downplay differences with the White House. On April 12, 1933, he told reporters: "Naturally, in a measure of this transcendent importance, there will be differences of views and these cannot be threshed out in a day. But a bill will be passed."[19]

On April 13, Glass's subcommittee unanimously agreed on the details of a modified bill, subject to obtaining sign-off on the bill from the Federal Reserve Board and the Treasury Department.[20] A week later, Secretary Woodin appeared before Glass's subcommittee, objecting to both the deposit insurance provisions and to his removal as a member of the Federal Reserve Board.[21] On April 25, Glass met for an hour with the president in a productive meeting that repaired their strained relationship. The two proposed a compromise: a limited guarantee of bank deposits—100 percent for the first $10,000 of deposits, 75 percent of deposits between $10,000 and $50,000, and 50 percent of deposits in excess of $50,000. "The president is going along nicely with us on the bank bill," Senator Glass said. "He listed some modifications of the insurance of deposit features of the bill which the subcommittee thinks were valuable. These modifications, I think, will be made. We may meet in a day or two."[22]

On May 1, Glass reported that the subcommittee had reached agreement on President Roosevelt's proposal: "We expect an interview with the Secretary of the Treasury and the President before reporting the bill."[23]

On May 4, Senator Glass led a contingent of senators from the subcommittee to a conference at the White House with the president, Treasury Secretary Woodin, and Undersecretary of the Treasury Dean Acheson. The group met for approximately ninety minutes.[24] Two of Woodin's objections would be accommodated: the secretary of the Treasury would remain a member of the Federal Reserve Board, and the effectiveness of the deposit insurance provisions would be delayed for a year after the bill's approval.[25]

Despite the compromise, Roosevelt remained lukewarm on forcing the bill through Congress.

As the *Wall Street Journal* reported on May 6, 1933, "The Administration view on the banking bill seems to be that the permanent bank reform legislation is not essential at present, and may be unsettling to the banking structure of the country which is beginning to show definite signs of stability.... There is still lacking complete Administration support of the Glass measure for various reasons, most important of which is the belief that the measure is not essential at this time, and may create disorder in a banking situation which is beginning to right itself."[26]

On May 10, Glass reintroduced his bill in the Senate. The new bill provided immediate insurance on 100 percent of deposits up to $5,000, increasing to $10,000 after six months. The old bill provided for 100 percent insurance of deposits up to the $10,000 level, but was not to take effect for one year. A last-minute rider to the bill, inserted at the urging of Winthrop W. Aldrich, chairman of Chase National Bank, prohibited private banks from underwriting and dealing in securities while concurrently receiving the deposits, effective two years after enactment. Aldrich was greatly concerned that if "retail" commercial banks (those that took deposits from the public) like

Chase and National City could not engage in securities activities, but private banks (which only took deposits from large institutions and very wealthy individuals) could, Chase would lose its institutional and wealthy customer base to private banks like J.P. Morgan & Co., Kuhn, Loeb & Company, and Dillon, Read & Co. It was reported that the "private bank" rider was supported by President Roosevelt, over the objection of Secretary Woodin.[27]

Senator Glass held a two-hour meeting of the Senate Banking and Currency Committee to explain the provisions of the new bill. On May 13, the committee favorably reported the bill to the full Senate by a vote of eleven to one.[28] Three days later, the House Banking and Currency Committee favorably reported the Steagall bill to the full House of Representatives.[29] The bills differed in two meaningful respects: first, the House bill did not permit branch banking by federally chartered banks; and second, state banks (not members of the Federal Reserve System) would be permitted to join the deposit insurance plan on the same terms as Federal Reserve member banks if they were certified to be financially sound by state banking authorities.

As debate on the banking bills was set to begin, the banking industry objections centered on deposit insurance—not on separation of investment banking from commercial banking. On May 19, Francis H. Sisson, vice president of the Guaranty Trust Co. and president of the American Banking Association, told the Pennsylvania Bankers' Association convention that banks "cannot give their endorsement to the deposit insurance proposal. . . . The fundamental needs of banking reform are so obvious that they should not be obscured with palliatives of this character. . . . Fewer banks, more adequately capitalized, better supervised and better managed by standardization of laws and methods, greater and more intelligent cooperation between government and banking, better understanding by the public of its joint responsibility in maintaining banking solvency and efficiency—these are the primary needs of banking reform which should be given first consideration and be the foundation of our banking system of the future. For such a system, no guaranty of deposits would be necessary and the depositors' interests would be fully protected. No considerations of political expediency can warrant Congress in avoiding these essential steps in reform by shifting the burden of an inadequate system upon the sound banks and taxing the shareholders and depositors of good banks to cover the errors and losses of the unsound."[30]

That day, the House took up debate on the Steagall bill. After four days of debate, it passed by a vote of 262 to nineteen.[31]

Also on May 19, Carter Glass took to the floor of the Senate to speak in favor of his bill. He had grown tired of Secretary Woodin's opposition to separation of commercial banking and investment banking and his insistence on maintaining a seat on the Federal Reserve Board. He spent a good deal of time criticizing the Treasury Department, which he argued made the Federal Reserve Board its "floor mat" to finance government debt:

"The Federal Reserve banking system was devised for the purpose of responding to the business of industrial and agricultural requirements of this country. It is owned exclusively by the member banks. It was never intended that the Federal Reserve banking system should be used as an adjunct of the Treasury Department and particularly it was never contemplated that it should be so used to such an extent as recently has been done as to very materially curtail the capabilities of the Federal Reserve Banks to serve the business interests of the country.

"There has not been a bond issue floated by the government since the beginning of the World War up to within two weeks ago that was not floated through the agencies of the Federal Reserve Banking system.

"In later years, the Federal Reserve Banks notably and the member banks of the system substantively have been compelled to subscribe to the issues of the United States bonds. I say compelled in the sense that it was regarded as dangerous for a member bank or a Federal Reserve Bank to decline to take its allotment of securities, whether long-time bonds or Treasury notes as apportioned by the Secretary of the Treasury.

"The major part of those issues have been taken by the Federal Reserve Banks and the member banks. That largely means in time of stress that these banks, just in that measure, are disqualified from responding generously and liberally to the requirements of commerce, industry and agriculture.

"That has largely been done, your committee thinks, through the dominating influence of the Secretary of the Treasury as a member of the Federal Reserve Board."[32]

Glass specifically called Woodin out on the Federal Reserve Board membership issue:

> "That provision is not included only by reason of the fact that the Secretary of the Treasury seemed to regard it as a personal affront to him and as a curtailment of this power which he ought to have at this particular time."[33]

When discussing the separation of banks from their securities affiliates, Glass said, "These affiliates were the most unscrupulous contributors, next after the debauch of the New York Stock Exchange, to the financial catastrophe which visited this country, and were mainly responsible for the depression under which we have been suffering since, and they ought to be speedily separated from the parent banks, and in this bill we have done that."[34]

An amendment was offered by Senator Arthur Vandenberg of Michigan providing for an interim deposit insurance plan covering the period between enactment and July 1, 1934, when the permanent plan was to take effect. Vandenberg's interim plan provided for 100 percent insurance up to $2,500 and allowed membership to state non-member banks on the favorable terms, as provided in the Steagall bill.[35]

The Vandenberg Amendment was strongly opposed by the administration because of the non-member bank provision, leading to rumors that Roosevelt might veto the bill.[36]

As the Glass bill was being debated in the Senate, the Pecora Hearings resumed. With strong public support, Roosevelt and the Democratic Senate leaders in the new Congress encouraged Pecora to continue his investigation of Wall Street. Pecora next trained his sights on the premier private banks, J.P. Morgan & Co., Kuhn, Loeb & Company, and Dillon, Read & Co. The private banks were market leaders in merger and acquisition advice and securities underwriting—the predecessors of what would later be called an investment bank. Unlike National City Bank, they did not deal in their own securities nor engage in high-pressure sales tactics. In short, they had fewer conflicts.

Pecora's first target was J.P. Morgan & Co., and J.P. Morgan Jr. would be his first witness: a showdown between the king of Wall Street and the now-feared inquisitor of financial titans. As financial historian John Brooks observed, the two men couldn't have been more different:

"Morgan seemed to be thought of variously or in combination as a king and as a master thief. He presented himself as neither, but as a gentleman and a businessman with the gentleman coming first in a pinch. Pecora, an immigrant in childhood from Sicily, was the other face of American life, short and squarish where Morgan was tall and commanding, swarthy where Morgan was fair-skinned, energetic and ambitious where Morgan was languid, all conscience and earnest intellect where Morgan was all style. Neither was afraid of the other. It was a confrontation out of Kipling."[37]

But the standoff would not live up to the advance billing. Few punches were landed by Pecora, and the two developed a cautious respect—if not admiration—for each other.

In Pecora's own words:

"Mr. Morgan as a witness proved to be courteous to a degree and cooperative in his attitude. He made no attempt to fence with his examiners. He was accompanied by his brilliant counsel, John W. Davis, sometime Democratic candidate for President and ex-ambassador to Great Britain. His was the attitude of a man who, far from having any guilty secrets to hide, manifested a pride in his firm and its works which was obvious and deeply genuine. And, in truth, the investigation of the Morgan firm elicited no such disclosures or glowing abuses as we shall meet later on in connection with various other great banking institutions and personalities. Mr. Morgan was undoubtedly wholly candid when he declared at the outset of his testimony: 'I state without hesitation that I consider the private banker a national asset and not a national danger.'"[38]

The main attack on J.P. Morgan & Co. involved its practice of allocating stock offerings to clients and friends on "preferred lists." These individuals were offered stock by J.P. Morgan at cost, even though the market or trading price for the stock was, or very shortly would be, substantially higher. (The maneuvering by National City in the Boeing IPO process was an egregious version of this practice.)

In the case of a stock offering for Allegheny Corporation in February 1929, 575,000 shares of common stock were offered to individuals on the preferred list at a price of $20 per share while the stock was trading on the New York Stock Exchange on a "when issued" basis at $35 to $37 per share. It was, in short, a sure thing—to the tune of over $8,000,000 ($109,000,000 in today's dollars).[39]

The Allegheny preferred list read like a who's who of the American business and political elite: J.P. Morgan Jr. was personally allocated 40,000 shares; his partner Thomas Lamont was allocated 8,000 shares; Richard Whitney was allocated 1,000; John W. Davis, J.P. Morgan's chief counsel, received 400 shares; John J. Raskob, chairman of the Democratic National Committee, was allocated 2,000 shares, while Joseph R. Nutter, treasurer of the Republican National Committee, received 3,000 shares; former Secretary of the Treasury Williams Gibbs McAdoo received 500 shares; and future Secretary of the Treasury William Woodin was allocated 1,000 shares.[40]

The other shocking public disclosure was the sheer reach and influence of J.P. Morgan & Co., whose partners, held directorships in fifteen large banks with total assets of $3,811,400,000. They also held twelve directorships in ten large railroads with assets of $3,430,000,000, nineteen directorships in thirteen public utilities with total assets of $6,222,000,000, and fifty-five directorships in thirty-eight industrial corporations with total assets in excess of $6,000,000,000. In total, 126 directorships in eighty-nine corporations, with total assets in excess of $20,000,000,000. Pecora called it "incomparably the greatest reach of power in private hands in our entire history."[41]

The most memorable moment of J.P. Morgan Jr.'s testimony did not involve his mammoth wealth and power but rather his interaction with a tiny woman named Lya Graf. A press agent for Ringling Bros. and Barnum & Bailey Circus managed to evade security in the Senate Hearing Room and place Graf, a two foot, three inch–tall circus lady, on the knee of Morgan while news photographers snapped away. He remained good-natured throughout the stunt, smiling and striking up conversation with Graf. The pictures, which appeared in papers all over the world, had a humanizing effect on the public's perception of Morgan. Lya Graf's story, though, did not end happily. The photographs made her famous, but she disliked the media attention and left the United States for her native Germany in 1935. A Jew, Graf was arrested by the Nazis in 1937, designated a "useless person," and later shipped to the Auschwitz concentration camp where she was killed.[42]

On May 25, the Senate passed the Glass bill—including the Vandenberg Amendment—on a voice vote.[43]

On June 1, the first day the House and Senate conferees met on the bill, President Roosevelt summoned Senator Glass and Representative Steagall to the White House, along with Secretary Woodin, Governor Black of the Federal Reserve Board, J.F.T. O'Connor, controller of the currency, and Dean Acheson, undersecretary of the Treasury. The administration voiced its opposition to the Vandenberg Amendment, expressing fear that the banking system was not yet stabilized, that many weak banks had not yet been reorganized, and that granting those banks access to the deposit insurance fund might render the fund insolvent. The White House was also concerned that the insurance premium banks would be required to pay might further weaken marginal banks. Given prior experiences with state deposit insurance schemes, Roosevelt feared this one might fail too, or be believed by the public to be at risk of failing, resulting in more panic. And state bank examiners could not be relied on to accurately portray the solvency of their banks—they had every incentive to get them in the insurance program, offloading them on the federal government. Roosevelt and Woodin wanted time to determine which banks should be allowed to fail.[44]

On June 5, on the floor of the Senate, Vandenberg rose to defend his amendment:

> "I understand that the Treasury Department and perhaps even higher authority recommended the rejection of my amendment. This is utterly inconsistent with the Treasury's own attitude on the same subject within the past two weeks. I want to lay down a plain warning that we must have an explanation of the proposition which came from the Secretary of the Treasury, two weeks ago if it now develops that the thoroughly limited proposition upon which the Senate has agreed is to be rejected upon the Treasury's recommendation."[45]

The following day, Senator Long weighed in with support for Vandenberg: "Let's demand that Congress do its duty. There are enough men in Congress to override a veto if necessary."[46]

On June 7, the Senate conferees reached a compromise with Roosevelt: Vandenberg's temporary issuance fund would come into being on June 1, 1934, with the permanent insurance fund becoming effective on January 1, 1935.

Steagall was not yet on board: "Because of this situation," he said, "it might be better to delay a conference report until the next session. I understand that Senator Vandenberg is ready to filibuster if we don't adopt his amendment making the insurance effective immediately. We can't do that."[47]

As the few remaining days in the congressional session elapsed and more threats of filibuster in the Senate were expressed, Glass was expecting the bill to be held over until the January 1934 session. However, on June 12, a compromise on deposit insurance was reached. There would be no immediate deposit insurance, as hoped for by Vandenberg. Instead, the plan would begin on January 1, 1934, in a preliminary form, insuring 100 percent of deposits up to $2,500, and taking full effect on July 1, 1934. But the president could elect to fix a date earlier than January 1, 1934, to implement the preliminary insurance plan. State non-member banks would be given membership in the deposit plan on the favorable terms contained in the Steagall bill but would be required to become members of the Federal Reserve System by July 1936 or be required to withdraw.[48]

On June 13, the House of Representatives approved the Glass-Steagall bill by a vote of 191 to six, and the Senate approved it the same day without a recorded vote. The American Bankers Association, fighting deposit insurance to the bitter end, wired its member banks, urging them to contact the president and request that he veto the legislation.[49] On June 16, President Roosevelt signed the bill into law.[50]

The act created the Federal Deposit Insurance Corporation (FDIC), to be governed by a three-person board of directors comprised of the comptroller of the currency and two members appointed by the president, with the advice and consent of the Senate. Not more than two members of the board were to be from the same political party. The appointed members were to serve for six-year terms.[51]

The FDIC was capitalized with an appropriation of $150,000,000 from the U.S. Treasury, a subscription by each Federal Reserve Bank of half of its surplus as of January 1, 1933, and a subscription by each FDIC member bank equal to 0.5 of 1 percent of its total deposits. The FDIC was also authorized to issue tax-exempt debentures in an amount not to exceed three times the amount of its equity capital. All moneys of the FDIC not deployed were required to be invested in U.S. government securities or deposited in a Federal Reserve Bank or with the U.S. Treasury.[52]

Any national bank certified as solvent by the comptroller of the currency was eligible to become an FDIC member. Any state bank so certified by the Federal Reserve Board was also eligible to become a member. Any national bank that did not become a member by July 1, 1934, was to be placed into receivership, with any Federal Reserve member state bank that hadn't to be expelled from the Federal Reserve System. State banks that were not members of the Federal Reserve System were permitted to become FDIC members until July 1, 1936, at which time they were required to either become Federal Reserve System members or be expelled from FDIC membership.[53]

The FDIC's permanent deposit insurance was to commence on July 1, 1934, unless the president fixed an earlier date, and would insure 100 percent of deposits up to $10,000, 75 percent in excess of $10,000 up to $50,000, and 50 percent in excess of $50,000. The permanent deposit plan, however, never became operational. The temporary plan was extended from July 1, 1934, to August 23, 1935, when the provisions of the Banking Act of 1935 became effective.[54] Under the Banking Act of 1935, deposits up to $5,000 were covered in full (but none in excess of that amount), and all non–Federal Reserve member banks were required to become members by July 1, 1942.[55]

The separation of commercial banking from investment banking would occur one year following the law's enactment, at which time no Federal Reserve member bank would be permitted to affiliate with a securities dealer. In addition, dealings in investment securities by member banks would generally be limited to transactions for customer accounts. No member bank would be permitted to underwrite securities issuances. Member banks would be limited in their own investment in securities to not more than 10 percent of any particular issue of securities, and the amount of such investment in any one obligor was not to exceed 15 percent of the bank's paid-up unimpaired capital and 25 percent of its unimpaired surplus. After one year from enactment, no entity engaged in underwriting or selling of securities would be permitted to receive deposits.[56]

In addition, the act provided that after January 1, 1934, no officer or director of a bank which was a member of the Federal Reserve System would be permitted to be an officer, director, or manager of an organization that engaged primarily in the securities business. And no officer, director, or employer of a national bank would be permitted to be an officer, director, or employee of an entity that made margin loans. The act forbade Federal Reserve member banks from acting as agents of a non-banking entity in making loans secured by securities to brokers or dealers. The act also prohibited "stapled shares" with respect to stock of member banks. After one year from enactment, no certificate of stock of a member bank would be permitted to represent the stock of any other corporation (other than another bank that was a member of the Federal Reserve System).[57]

The act authorized statewide branch banking by national banks to the extent that state banks in the particular state were permitted to engage in branch banking. Double liability for shareholders of national banks was eliminated.[58]

Each bank holding company affiliate was required to submit to examinations by the applicable regulators. The act also prohibited bank holding companies from acquiring interest in or managing any company in the securities business and required bank holding companies to divest of their securities affiliates within five years.[59]

The act prohibited Federal Reserve member banks from paying interest on demand deposits and authorized the Federal Reserve Board to regulate the amount of interest that may be paid on time deposits.[60]

The act also implemented a number of reforms to the Federal Reserve System. Federal Reserve Banks were required to act impartially in their treatment of member banks. Member banks under the same holding company were given only one vote in the nomination or election of Federal Reserve Bank directors. The act provided that the principal offices of the Federal Reserve Board would be in Washington, D.C., and that the secretary of the Treasury would serve as chairman of the Federal Reserve Board. It created the Federal Reserve Open Market Committee, consisting of twelve members, one being appointed by each Federal Reserve Bank, with authority to set regulations for all open-market activities in which it engaged. It contained a provision for the removal of a director or officer of a Federal Reserve member bank who continued to violate the law or continued unsafe or unsound practices in conducting the business of the bank after being warned by the comptroller of the currency (as to a national bank) or the Federal Reserve Bank of his district (as to a state member bank) to discontinue such violations or practices.[61]

The board of directors for the FDIC met for the first time on September 11, 1933. The two members appointed by the president were Walter J. Cummings, an assistant to Treasury Secretary Woodin, and E. G. Bennett, a Republican banker from Utah selected as chairman. The third member of the board was J.F.T. O'Connor, comptroller of the currency, as required by the act. Most of its activities in the months leading up to the establishment of the temporary deposit insurance fund involved the examination of the nearly 8,000 state non-member banks seeking admission to the FDIC.[62]

On January 1, 1934, the temporary federal deposit insurance fund opened with 13,201 banks approved for insurance, approximately 90 percent of all commercial banks (and 36 percent of all mutual savings banks) in the country. In January 1934, E.G. Bennett stepped down from the FDIC to become chairman of Continental Illinois National Bank & Trust Company in Chicago. He was replaced by Leo T. Crowley, who would serve as chairman for the next twelve years. By the end of 1934, insured banks held 98 percent of the assets of all commercial banks. During 1934, only nine insured banks failed, while fifty-two uninsured banks failed. Given the immediate success of deposit insurance, public support of the plan was overwhelming. Even opposition from the banking industry faded. In April 1934, the executive council of the American Bankers Association publicly endorsed deposit insurance.[63]

With the exception of some muted, ineffectual protests against deposit insurance, the financial industry was essentially absent from the debate over the Glass-Steagall Banking Act. Wall Street was, for all practical purposes, completely silent, having run for cover even as its businesses were being split up. On the heels of Pecora's revelations regarding National City Bank, the nationwide banking shutdown, and the subsequent bank bailout, the momentum for reform was overwhelming. And with J.P. Morgan Jr. in the dock while the act was being finalized, no one on Wall Street dared to raise their head above the parapet—they might be Pecora's next target. Even Huey Long fell into line, pointing to the liberalization of state banks' entry into the FDIC as grounds for his about-face.

Just after New Year's Day 1934, one of the oldest firms on Wall Street issued a press release announcing that after 137 years in business, it was breaking up. Roosevelt & Son was started as a hardware store at 97 Maiden Lane in Manhattan in 1797 by Jacobus Roosevelt. Despite the yellow fever epidemic that plagued the city that year, his business flourished. By the end of the Civil War, Roosevelt & Son had exited the hardware business, having become a full-fledged banking house (it would finance the first trans-Atlantic cable and many of the country's railroads). Jacobus Roosevelt's great-grandson Theodore became the 26th president of the United States. His second cousin, thrice removed, became the 32nd president.

When President Roosevelt signed the Glass-Steagall Banking Act of 1933, Roosevelt & Son was forced to split into three firms. George Emlen Roosevelt and Philip James Roosevelt continued the firm's money management business and retained the firm's name. Their second cousin, Archibald Cox, with partner Charles E. Weigold, took the municipal bond business under the name Roosevelt & Weigold, Inc. The general securities business would be conducted by partners Fairman Rogers Dick, Van S. Merle Smith, Charles B. Robinson, and John K. Roosevelt under the name Dick & Merle Smith.[64]

Many on Wall Street—including some of his own family members, it was whispered—now called Franklin Roosevelt a "traitor to his class." Many of the reformers—some even in his brain trust—thought Roosevelt had gone too far in bailing out the banks and not far enough in punishing them. Seventy-five years later, the balance achieved by Glass-Steagall would be pointed to as an almost-sacred mandate and the erosion of its wall of separation blamed for the worst financial crisis since winter 1933. "Your bill had more lives than a cat," Roosevelt quipped to Carter Glass as he signed it into law. Glass-Steagall would have even more lives many decades later.

FIVE

FRANKFURTER'S HOT DOGS:
The Securities Act of 1933

While the Glass-Steagall Banking Act of 1933 was working its way toward enactment, the administration was proceeding rapidly with a bill regulating the
securities offering process. The administration would endure two false starts,
with flawed proposals from prominent reformers from an earlier era, before a
team of three young lawyers handpicked by Harvard law professor Felix
Frankfurter would draft a bill that would be relentlessly driven through Congress by a Texas representative with his sights set on the Speaker's chair. That
bill ultimately passed both houses without a single vote recorded in opposition.

Securities offering regulation was one of the four prominent planks in the
1932 Democratic Party financial reform platform.[1] Unlike banking reform,
there was no bill pending in Congress to serve as a template for Roosevelt. In
fact, federal securities legislation had been a dead letter for more than a decade,
though great activity toward federal regulation of securities had taken place
earlier, in the dozen or so years following the Panic of 1907. By necessity,
those who Roosevelt looked to were old Wilsonian reformers, though many
youthful New Dealers thought them simply old and woefully out of touch

with modern markets. In preparation for making good on his campaign promise, Roosevelt authorized top aide Raymond Moley to reach out to Samuel Untermyer, the seventy-four-year-old crusading (and some said self-promoting) lawyer who'd been chief counsel to the Pujo Committee twenty years earlier.[2] By 1932, Untermyer had become a "wise man" of the Wall Street reform movement and had been a key player in many of the numerous, failed prior attempts at regulating the securities industry. In December 1932, at Moley's urging, Untermyer began drafting a proposal for Roosevelt, starting with the same securities bill he recommended to the House of Representatives from the Pujo Committee in 1913.[3] Unfortunately, he would end with a bill not terribly different from the one he started with, one more suitable to prewar markets than those of 1933.

Untermyer's Pujo Committee bill provided that no written information concerning transactions in securities listed or quoted on any stock exchange could be carried in the mail unless the exchange was either incorporated under the laws of the state where it operated, thereby subjecting itself to state corporation law regulation, or its governing documents contained protections satisfactory to the U.S. postmaster general.[4] These protections included requiring a sworn disclosure statement describing the issuer and the offering. The bill also outlawed a number of manipulative trading practices on exchanges and limited margin to 80 percent.[5] The postmaster general was authorized to prevent the delivery of any mail relating to securities traded on exchanges that didn't adhere to these requirements. Telegraph and telephone companies were also prohibited from transmitting any information that could not be legally transported in the mail under a similar criminal penalty.[6] Untermyer's bill faced vigorous and organized opposition from the securities exchanges in 1913, which argued that the proposed law was unconstitutional and the exchanges should not be required to act as de facto agents of the federal government, enacting and enforcing regulations that the federal government could not—or would not—enact and enforce itself. Opponents also believed that states were already effectively regulating the securities industry and that federal legislation was not required and conflicted with states' rights.[7]

In fact, with New York in the lead, the states had been very active in enacting securities laws during the previous decade, and the argument that these relatively new state laws should be given time to work prior to creating a new federal regulatory overlay was compelling to many. Even before the Panic of 1907, the New York state legislature created the Tompkins Law, requiring that a prospectus containing basic specified information about the issuer and offering be used whenever a public offering was to be made.[8] In 1908, New York outlawed "bucket shops"—places where a ticker tape machine allowed purchasers to bet on the movement in prices of stocks, but where no actual stock was bought or sold.[9] In the wake of the Panic of 1907, New York governor Charles Evans Hughes appointed a committee to determine what legal changes were advisable to control speculation in securities.[10] On June 7, 1909, the Hughes Commission released a report containing twelve recommendations for reform of the New York Stock Exchange and proposed legislation providing for "truth in advertising" in securities issuances.[11] On May 9, 1913, New York enacted a truth-in-advertising securities law, making violations a felony (punishable by a fine of not more than $5,000, or by imprisonment for not more than three years, or by both).[12] Also in 1913, New York passed laws regulating brokers and exchange members with respect to a number of manipulative and unfair practices.[13]

While New York was not surprisingly the leader in securities legislation, given that it was home to the major exchanges and most large banking houses, all across the country during the 1910s, states experimented with substantive securities legislation. The explosive post–Civil War industrial growth in America had resulted in history's largest investment of capital. By the 1910s, that investment was reaping enormous gains, and not only for the very rich. A burgeoning middle class with investment capital had emerged. And as night follows day, an industry of hucksters and cheats had arisen to rob them. The failure of existing state corporation statutes to prevent securities fraud gave rise to enactment of what became known as "blue sky" laws—named after stock swindlers who, it was said, "would sell building lots in the blue sky." The first such law was passed in Kansas in 1911 at the behest of state banking commissioner J.N. Dolley. "History and statistics show that losses through banks are but a drop in the bucket compared with the money which is lost through investment in worthless stocks and bonds," Dolley said.[14] The Kansas law, which was the model for nearly all the subsequently adopted blue sky laws, required issuers to receive a permit to sell the securities, which could be denied if the offering was found to be "unfair, unjust, inequitable, or oppressive," or if the company "does not intend to do a fair and honest business" or "does not promise a fair return" on the securities offered. By 1933, every state except Nevada had adopted a blue sky law.[15] But the blue sky laws suffered from a basic jurisdictional flaw: They could only be applied to persons present in the state. Sales made by advertisements or sales calls originating outside a particular state were beyond the reach of the law. And most states' securities divisions lacked the resources to effectively investigate suspected fraud and prosecute violators.

The opposition to Untermyer's Pujo Committee bill in 1913 was coordinated by John G. Milburn, a partner in the Wall Street law firm of Carter Ledyard & Milburn, who served as counsel to the New York Stock Exchange. Milburn argued that the New York Stock Exchange was organized as a private club, not as a corporation, and could govern itself and discipline its members without the involvement of judicial review. Requiring exchanges to face federal regulation would, he argued, impair their ability to enforce their rules, since disciplined members could tie up proceedings in the courts. Milburn also warned that the Pujo Committee bill would drive securities off the New York Stock Exchange and into the less regulated "over the counter" market, where fraud would be easier to perpetrate.[16] The New York Stock Exchange–led counteroffensive succeeded. The Pujo Committee bill died in the Senate, having failed to garner the backing of President Wilson, who was unwilling to antagonize Wall Street, with war clouds gathering in Europe.

The first federal securities law passed was the War Finance Corporation Act, which became law on April 5, 1918.[17] The act created the Capital Issues Committee, which determined whether a proposed securities offering was compatible with the wartime national interest.[18] As a result of the November 11, 1918, armistice, the committee announced it would wind up its affairs. For a brief period of time after the end of World War I, however, it looked like federal regulation of securities offerings might well become a permanent peacetime reform. Charles S. Hamlin, chairman of the Capital Issues Committee, issued a statement warning the public of the dangers of fraudulent securities sales and urging Congress to take action to permanently regulate security issuances in peacetime: "While legislative business may safely be left to work out its own problems, the Capital Issues Committee feels that it would be unfaithful to its responsibility if it failed to warn the public respecting the enormous losses sustained by the nation through the sale of worthless and fraudulent securities. In the opinion of the committee the sale of such securities should be restrained in times of peace as well as in war, and strongly urges that Congress establish adequate machinery to put a stop to this traffic. It is the intention of the committee to make a supplementary report to Congress recommending a law to prevent these existing abuses and such impositions upon the investing public."[19]

Carter Glass, then President Wilson's secretary of the Treasury, issued a companion statement also calling for federal securities legislation: "I intend to ask Congress immediately for legislation that will check the traffic in worthless securities while imposing no undue restrictions upon the financing of legitimate business, and shall urge that it be made effective before the close of the present session."[20]

In its final report to Congress, delivered on February 19, 1919, the Capital Issues Committee renewed its call for Congress to pass securities oversight legislation: "Having in view the inability of the several States to control financial operations beyond their boundaries, it follows that there is but one agency which can check the major part of the traffic in fraudulent and worthless securities and that agency is the National Government. As long as its powers are not invoked to suppress this traffic, the organization of irresponsible companies, the sale of their securities and the deception of the public will proceed."[21] In response to the Capital Issues Committee report, a bill co-drafted by Huston Thompson was introduced into the House by Colorado Democrat Edward T. Taylor requiring the registration of all new issues of securities with a new bureau within the Treasury Department. But the Taylor bill was never reported out of the House Judiciary Committee.[22]

Nonetheless, the final year of the Wilson presidency saw serious congressional attention to securities reform legislation. On June 28, 1920, the Transportation Act of 1920 went into effect, rendering it unlawful for any interstate railroad company to issue securities unless the Interstate Commerce Commission found that such issue was compatible with the public interest.[23] This legislation, however, was driven less by investor protection and more by a desire to rationalize an unwieldy and often duplicative railroad system that had produced spectacular failures. Illinois Republican Edward Dennison also introduced a bill that year that would have made it a violation of federal law to sell securities into any state without complying with that state's blue sky laws. The bill passed the House but was never reported out of the Senate Judiciary Committee.[24]

By 1921, with Calvin Coolidge now in the White House, there would be no extension of federal intervention in the markets; and until Franklin Roosevelt's administration no significant securities legislation would pass either house of Congress. It had lost interest in even the most mild of securities reform measures. In 1922, a bill by Minnesota Republican Andrew Volstead would have empowered the attorney general to investigate fraudulent practices in interstate sales of securities and to seek injunctions to prohibit such sales. It wasn't even given a hearing in the House Interstate and Foreign Commerce Committee.[25]

With this frustrating history that included no small measure of personal disappointment very much on his mind, Untermyer spent the waning days of 1932 refining his 1913 bill for presentation to the president-elect. In January 1933, he delivered his draft bill to Raymond Moley. It was hoped that the legislation would be ready for introduction by Inauguration Day to spearhead the administration's response to the growing financial crisis. That hope was quickly dashed. Moley and Roosevelt were deeply disappointed by Untermyer's work product. Like his 1913 bill, Untermyer's updated bill would have empowered the post office to function as the federal securities regulator and rulemaker. "The Post Office Department was essentially a service organization," Moley later wrote. "The idea of sticking an immense regulatory machine into it horrified my sense of administrative and legal proprieties."[26] Roosevelt and Moley were equally shocked that Untermyer would seriously propose having Postmaster General Farley, the patronage czar of the Roosevelt administration who'd never graduated college, deciding complex rules for the securities markets. Untermyer's approach also betrayed his outdated view of federal constitutional power. In the earlier reforms, serious constitutional questions had arisen regarding the ability of the federal government to regulate economic activity. Use of the mail was the hook to justify federal regulation, since the operation of the postal system was unquestionably a federal power. By the 1930s, the New Dealers were ready to assert federal power more broadly, willing to declare that any activity bearing upon interstate commerce could be directly regulated by the federal government, even through the creation of new agencies explicitly for that purpose. Both Roosevelt and Moley concluded that

Untermyer was hopelessly out of touch with modern markets and theories of their regulation.

Another problem was the behavior of Untermyer himself. A relentless self-promoter and press hound, his self-serving leaking of his meetings with Roosevelt were annoying the president-elect. In a January 2, 1933, article in *The New York Times*, Untermyer denied that a visit to Albany was for the purpose of conferring with Roosevelt on stock regulation but said he would call on Mr. Roosevelt if he—Untermyer—"was not too busy."[27] A week later, Untermyer issued a press release from his winter home in Palm Springs, California, predicting enactment of securities legislation at a special session of Congress that Roosevelt would call soon after his inauguration. The article noted that "Mr. Untermyer, it is understood, has discussed with Mr. Roosevelt on several occasions the activities of the New York Stock Exchange and the problem of governmental regulation."[28] By Inauguration Day, Roosevelt had shelved the Untermyer proposal and was deciding how best to freeze him out without provoking a messy public break.

Roosevelt next turned to another experienced Wilsonian hand in securities matters, Huston Thompson, a former chairman of the Federal Trade Commission and a disciple of Supreme Court Justice Louis Brandeis. Thompson, who had been tapped to assist in drafting the Taylor bill in 1919, was profoundly influenced by Brandeis's criticism of big business—and big banking in particular. He had written Brandeis on May 20, 1919: "I have completed the reading of your book entitled *Other People's Money* and enjoyed every part of it. In my study of the blue sky laws of the different states and in the prosecution of the investigation of unfair competition produced by the sale of 'wild-cat' stocks, it has occurred to me that some legislation is necessary and I am drafting a bill which on its completion, I would like to show you, if you care to see it."[29] It is not known whether Justice Brandeis ever commented on Thompson's draft of the Taylor bill, but it appears that Thompson was rather more impressed with Brandeis than Brandeis with Thompson. Brandeis later said of Thompson he had "every quality that matters for a great lawyer, except one—brains."[30]

Thompson had also authored the securities regulation plank of the 1932 Democratic Party platform. It stated: "We advocate the protection of the investing public by requiring to be filed with the government and carried in advertisements of all offerings of foreign and domestic stocks and bonds true information as to bonuses, commissions, principal invested and interests of sellers. Regulation to the full extent of federal power of: (a) holding companies which sell securities in interstate commerce; (b) rates of utilities companies operating across state lines; and (c) exchanges in securities and commodities."[31]

Leaving nothing to chance, Roosevelt assigned a team to work with Thompson on a new securities bill, which included Attorney General Homer Cummings, Secretary of Commerce David Roper, and two of Roper's staff attorneys, Walter Miller, chief of the Commerce Department's Foreign Service Division, and Ollie Butler, counsel to the Foreign Services Division. The drafting of the bill was undertaken principally by Thompson though, with the assistance of Miller and Butler.[32]

On March 19, 1933, on the weekend following the bank reopenings, Thompson presented his draft bill to Roosevelt, Moley, and Roper. On March 23, the press was informed that a securities bill prepared under the supervision of Roper and Cummings would soon be introduced. Roosevelt had not yet told Untermyer that his draft bill had been scrapped, and word of Untermyer's displeasure quickly reached Moley. Roosevelt had earlier decided to let Thompson take the initial fall with Untermyer, and only after the bad news was brought to him would the president discuss the matter with him. Roosevelt suggested that Thompson meet with Untermyer to convince him that his bill was essentially a stock exchange regulation bill, which would be submitted later, while Thompson's was a securities sales bill. Untermyer wasn't buying it. As Thompson wrote in his diary:

"In the morning I was required . . . to call upon Mr. Samuel Untermyer at the Shoreham Hotel at ten o'clock. I found Mr. Untermyer in bed. He was in an irritable mood and suggested that I would be hostile to his bill. I laughed and said I knew nothing about his bill and felt sure there was no conflict between our bills and soon demonstrated this fact, leaving a copy of my bill with him.

"In the afternoon at four o'clock, at the request of the President, I met in a room on the second floor of the White House with the President and Messrs. Moley, Untermyer, Cummings, Roper and Taussig, an economist, and several others . . .

"The President directed most of the conversation to Mr. Untermyer and myself. He had a draft of Thompson's and Roper's proposed bill before him and discussed it. He criticized its length and detail, suggesting that we cut down both. . . . He distinguished clearly between our bill and Untermyer's and said there was no conflict, the latter covering sales on exchanges.

"After an hour's discussion we retired to tea in an adjoining room where [the President's] daughter, her children and some British lords were present. I had a separate discussion with Messrs. Roper and Cummings and we all agreed to keep our bill entirely apart from Untermyer's bill. I had a talk with the President and he also agreed to this.

"The President asked me to make the changes in the bill and bring it back in two days. He seemed in [a] very good mood and handled Mr. Untermyer cheerfully and successfully." [33]

By March 28, Thompson's bill was revised and shortened in accordance with the president's suggestions (principally by eliminating a provision empowering the Federal Trade Commission to refuse to register foreign securities).[34] The following day, Roosevelt had Thompson's bill submitted simultaneously to both the Senate and the House of Representatives with the following accompanying message:

To the Congress:

I recommend to the Congress legislation for Federal supervision of traffic in investment securities in interstate commerce.

In spite of many State statutes the public in the past has sustained severe losses through practices neither ethical nor honest on the part of many persons and corporations selling securities.

Of course, the Federal Government cannot and should not take any action which might be construed as approving or guaranteeing that newly issued securities are sound in the sense that their value will be maintained or that the properties they represent will earn profit.

There is, however, an obligation upon us to insist that every issue of new securities to be sold in interstate commerce shall be accompanied by full publicity and information, and that no essentially important element attending the issue shall be concealed from the buying public.

This proposal adds to the ancient rule of caveat emptor the further doctrine, "Let the seller also beware." It puts the burden of telling the whole truth on the seller. It should give impetus to honest dealing in securities and thereby bring back public confidence.

The purpose of the legislation I suggest is to protect the public with the least possible interference to honest business.

This is but one step in our broad purpose of protecting investors and depositors. It should be followed by legislation relating to the better supervision of all property dealt in on exchanges, and by legislation to correct unethical and unsafe practices on the part of officers and directors of banks and other corporations.

What we seek is a return to a clearer understanding of the ancient truth that those who manage banks, corporations and other agencies handling or using other people's money are trustees acting for others.

FRANKLIN D. ROOSEVELT
The White House March 29, 1933[35]

At a press conference announcing submission of the bill, Roosevelt explained that the proposed law would only require disclosure of risks, not prevent investors from taking foolish ones:

"Well, the simplest example is this: If a company is organized to develop a gold mine and they have got what they and the engineers honestly believe to be a perfectly good speculation and it is not overcapitalized, there is no reason why they should not get a license to operate provided it is said to the public that it is, like most gold mining operations, a speculative venture. Of course, it must be stated in good faith. In other words, what we are trying to do is get the kind of information as to each issue before the investing public so that, if they then invest, they will know at least the representations that have been made to them are true."[36]

The Thompson bill established the Federal Trade Commission as the national securities regulator. It made it unlawful to publicly offer securities unless the issuer filed with the FTC a registration statement signed by the issuer, its principal executive officer, principal financial officer, and all of the issuer's directors, trustees, or managers. In addition, if the securities to be registered were issued by a foreign government or foreign corporation, the underwriters of the securities in the United States were also all required to sign the registration statement.[37] The registration statements were required to contain basic information about the issuer, including a business description, detailed description of the capitalization of the issuer, list of all 1 percent or greater stockholders, a balance sheet not more than ninety days old, three years of income statements, detailed information regarding the plan of distribution and underwriting compensation and the security offered and any collateral therefor, and a description of the use of proceeds of the offering.[38] Registration statements were "effective" upon filing, but the Federal Trade Commission was to be given the power to revoke or suspend the effectiveness of a registration statement if it found that the issuer violated the act or an order of the FTC thereunder, had been engaged in—or was about to engage in—fraudulent transactions, had affairs in an unsound condition or was insolvent, or was offering securities not based on sound principles. It was this delegation of power to the FTC—to prohibit offerings based on its view of what is "sound"—that would alarm even the president's closest allies in Congress. In its examination of a registration statement, the FTC was given access to all files and records of the issuer and underwriters, was given the power to question under oath officers of the issuer and the underwriters, and could require the issuer and underwriters to produce an audited balance sheet and income statement. The issuer was entitled to a public hearing if suspension of a registration statement was ordered by the FTC. The issuer could appeal registration suspension to the U.S. Court of Appeals for the District of Columbia.[39] The Thompson bill required that any advertisement in connection with a public offering of securities contain certain specified information, including the name of the issuer, its principal place of business and incorporation, the names of the officers and directors of the issuer, the names of the underwriters, the price to the public and the underwriting compensation to be paid, a statement of the issuer's assets and liabilities with the profit and loss during its most recent fiscal year, and a statement that additional information may be obtained from the FTC. Copies of all such advertisements and the transcripts of all radio advertising were required to be filed with the FTC within five days of their dissemination.[40]

The Thompson bill further provided that if any information in a registration statement was false in any material respect, a buyer had the right to rescind its purchase and have its money returned from any vendor knowing of the falsity of the statement or from persons signing the registration statement. The aggrieved purchaser also had the right to obtain damages for any losses sustained as a result of false statements.[41] The Thompson bill included a provision federalizing state blue sky laws, making it unlawful to sell securities in a state without complying with the laws of that state as if present therein. Willful violation of the law would be punishable by a fine up to $5,000 and five years' imprisonment.[42]

In the House, Thompson's bill was introduced by the chairman of the Committee on Interstate and Foreign Commerce, a staunch ally of the president and a rising star, Representative Sam Rayburn of Texas. He was by background predisposed to believe the worst about Wall Street and was committed to passing the president's securities reform legislation no matter what the hue and cry might be from the bankers.

Samuel Taliaferro Rayburn was born in Kingston, Tennessee, on January 6, 1882, the eighth of eleven children of William and Martha Rayburn. When Sam was five, the family moved to Fannin County, Texas, northeast of Dallas. At the age of twenty-four, Rayburn won a seat in the Texas legislature. At thirty, he was elected to the House of Representatives, representing Texas's fourth district, a seat he would hold for more than forty-eight years.[43] Over the twelve-year period between his election and elevation to chairman of the Committee on Interstate and Foreign Commerce, Rayburn worked tirelessly to learn the ways of the House, the details of legislation, and his fellow legislators and their districts. He was knowledgeable, loyal, trustworthy, and tough. And he was perhaps the loneliest man in the House.

What Rayburn said he wanted more than anything else was a family—a wife and a house full of children. Despite Rayburn's enormous talent as a legislator, persuader, and negotiator, he was socially awkward and painfully shy, particularly with women. But at thirty-six, he declared his love for Metze Jones, the eighteen-year-old sister of another Texas congressman. It took nine years for Rayburn to propose marriage in 1927 (some friends joked that it took him that long to steel his nerves). The engagement was short and they married almost immediately, "before she changed her mind," Rayburn joked to friends. But three months after the wedding, the marriage was over. Months, years, and decades passed, but he never seemed to be able to recover from the break-up. He rarely mentioned the marriage even to his closest friends, and close associates who met Rayburn after the divorce never knew he'd been married.[44] It was assumed that the heartbreak was too painful for him to discuss. He threw himself into the work of the House. And now, six years after the divorce, with the country in economic turmoil—but with a Democratic president and a solid Democratic majority in the Senate— Sam Rayburn knew it was his time. He would work at a killing pace, and the next two years would seal his fate for greatness.

In the Senate, Thompson's bill was introduced by Democratic Majority Leader Joseph Robinson and was referred initially to the Judiciary Committee. The chairman of the Judiciary Committee, Arizona senator Henry F. Ashurst, called a meeting the following day to take up consideration of the bill. On March 30, members of the Senate Banking and Currency Committee objected to the referral of the bill to the Judiciary Committee, believing that their committee should consider the bill. Florida senator Duncan Fletcher, chairman of the Banking and Currency Committee, prevailed and the bill was reassigned.[45]

With demagoguery always at the ready, Huey Long accused J.P. Morgan & Co. of orchestrating the change in committee and Majority Leader Robinson and Chairman Fletcher of being J.P. Morgan & Co.'s lackeys: "I was thinking that the Banking and Currency Committee which is at this time having the help of the Treasury Department—which means the help of Mr. S. Parker Gilbert, one of J.P. Morgan's firm, and other members of the Morgan house— in the preparation of legislation, might be a little inconvenienced or embarrassed in examining the helpers and the progenitors of our present day potential legislation. I thought, therefore, that it would probably relieve the committee of some embarrassment if the bill went to the Judiciary Committee. In other words, I thought the committee probably would hate to be sitting one day with S. Parker Gilbert drawing the laws that they are proposing to the Senate for enactment and the same day be turning around to investigate the gentleman who is very kindly, as a matter of help to the Government, volunteering his time here. I do not want embarrassment to come between the committees."[46]

Senator Fletcher quickly responded. "The senator is mistaken. Neither Mr. S. Parker Gilbert nor any member of J.P. Morgan & Co. has appeared before the Banking and Currency Committee. Moreover, the committee has not had anything to do with any person connected with that company."[47]

Long didn't know it, but after poring over the Thompson bill, Wall Street was breathing a bit easier. It had been expecting worse. With the exception of foreign securities offerings—which were a dead market after the disastrous Latin America offerings of the prior decade—the bill created no substantive new liabilities for underwriters, only for issuers and their directors and officers. Although the registration requirements would be time-consuming and costly, those costs would be borne by issuers, not by the Wall Street banks. The initial reaction of Wall Street to the Thompson bill was, as *The New York Times* reported, "mixed and for the most part, apathetic." Most of the Wall Street criticism centered on the federalization of blue sky laws, arguing that it was an onerous condition because it required state-by-state licensing of offerings by the underwriters.[48]

Nevertheless, Wall Street organized a cautious opposition to the bill but not directly from the banks themselves: Fearful of Pecora's subpoenas, they relied on their cadre of lawyers. The opposition was coordinated by Sullivan & Cromwell, the Wall Street firm that represented many of the large investment banks in the securities offering business. This initial adversarial engagement between Sullivan & Cromwell and the Roosevelt administration over the Securities Act of 1933 gave rise to a complex relationship between the firm and the federal government that would evolve over a generation. The firm would often be battling the U.S. government on behalf of its Wall Street clients, while at the same time sending its partners into government service in positions at the highest level in administrations of both parties and assisting congressional committees in the drafting of legislation and agencies in drafting regulations. It was no exaggeration when observers noting these intricate Wall Street–Washington connections would refer to Sullivan & Cromwell as the "general counsel for the American Establishment."

The first Sullivan & Cromwell partner to publicly and prominently criticize the bill was Eustace Seligman. In an April 1, 1933, editorial in *The New York Times*, Seligman attacked the broad power granted to the FTC to suspend registration statements: "The Commission is given the power to forbid the issuance of securities of any corporation if, in its opinion, the business of that corporation is in an 'unsound condition' or is 'not based upon sound principles.' The definition of these terms is obviously so much a matter of judgment that the effect of this proposal if enacted into law would be to give the Federal Trade Commission the power of a dictator over American business." Not surprisingly, Seligman harshly attacked the provisions subjecting underwriters to liability for foreign securities sales: "The effect of this provision is thus to single out from all securities the bonds of foreign governments and in that case alone make the underwriting bankers guarantors. It is difficult to see any justification for this proposal unless it is to prevent the sale of bonds of foreign governments in the United States."[49] On the strict liability of directors, Seligman wrote: "If such a proposal was to become law, the incurable effect would be that every director of any responsibility would resign his directorship and that boards of directors would be entirely made up of dummies, for it is not conceivable that any director would expose himself to a risk of unlimited financial responsibility which might result from acts entirely beyond his control. This proposal is indeed a revolutionary one and without precedent in Anglo Saxon law or practice."[50] Seligman also criticized the requirements for advertisements as overly burdensome and impractical: "For example, the financial pages of *The New York Times* contain numerous advertisements with respect to the sale of securities; none of the advertisements will be permitted in the future unless they are elaborated and extended so as to include, among other things, the balance sheet and earnings statement of the company in question. The impracticability of this must be obvious."[51]

Seligman's editorial was likely the first time many in the administration and in Congress became aware of the details of how the bill would operate in practice. The bill had been drafted in relative secrecy and had not been vetted in a careful fashion as a result of the administration's preoccupation with the banking crisis. Seligman raised legitimate concerns about the bill, and it was apparent that modifications to the bill would be needed at the committee hearing stage.

On March 31, Rayburn's committee commenced hearings on the bill, with Huston Thompson taking the committee members through a section-by-section explanation of its provisions, referring numerous times to Brandeis's book *Other People's Money* as his inspiration for the legislation.[52] Thompson's testimony was thorough and well prepared, but it did not alleviate Rayburn's concerns that the bill had not been completely thought through and all of its implications understood.

Rayburn's committee next heard testimony from Wall Street. Frank M. Gordon, president of the Investment Bankers Association of America, and George W. Bovenizer of the investment bank Kuhn, Loeb & Company, both testified in support of the bill. They were ready to cut Wall Street's losses and accept the bill "as is," letting any rough edges in the bill be softened by revisions later on. Gordon testified that he knew of "no responsible securities dealer who is not eager to see effective laws to prevent and punish fraud and misrepresentations in the sale of securities. Such laws are not only in the interest of the public, but also of those who deal in legitimate securities and we are, therefore, thoroughly in accord with the intent of the bill now under consideration." Bovenizer stated that Kuhn, Loeb & Company was "wholeheartedly" in favor of the bill. "We have sat back for twelve years and watched the dressing down of the name of what has been called an investment banker because of some who should have never been in the business."[53]

The Senate Banking and Currency Committee also held hearings that day, with Arthur H. Carter, president of the New York State Society of Certified Public Accountants. Mr. Carter advocated that the three years of financial statements included in registration statements be required to be audited by independent accountants.[54] Carter correctly anticipated that federal regulation of securities offerings would be a boon to the accounting firms.

Despite the tepid opposition to the bill from Wall Street, Rayburn was troubled by the concentration of power over the economy the bill granted to the Federal Trade Commission, particularly by giving the FTC power to veto any securities offering it viewed not "sound." During the hearings, Rayburn's concern over the bill's delegation of authority grew as he questioned co-draftsman Ollie Butler about the powers granted to the FTC under the revocation provisions of the bill. Rayburn stated: "Now we have passed a lot of laws since we met here on the 5th of March, but I do not think we have given anybody that much power yet. . . . Do you believe that an administrative officer of the Government ought to be given that much power, as a general principle—to pass upon whether or not a man's business is based on sound principles? It is mighty easy when you go to write a statute, if you want to delegate absolute authority you can write that in a very short statute; but the question that this committee has got to determine is whether or not you want to give anybody that kind of authority."[55] Privately, Rayburn was already skeptical about the wisdom of proceeding with the bill in its current form. But fiercely loyal to the president, he would scrupulously avoid grandstanding his reservations. He wasn't sure what course of action in relation to the bill he should take.

The House hearings resumed on April 4 with securities industry representatives opposed to the bill providing testimony. In the Senate hearing that day, another lawyer from Sullivan & Cromwell, Arthur H. Dean, gave testimony critical of the bill. Dean called the bill "a hopeless confusion of ill-assorted provisions."[56] Against his natural instincts, Rayburn found himself agreeing with Dean.

Rayburn knew a bad bill would hurt the president's credibility and could cause further damage to an already greatly weakened economy. But he was under extraordinary pressure from the administration to get a securities bill to the House floor. Exhibiting great bravery and leadership, Rayburn decided to end consideration of the bill there and then and tell the president that the bill "was a hopeless mess" that needed substantial rewriting. Rayburn reached out to Raymond Moley. "It will have to be thrown out," Rayburn told him. "I want you to get me a draftsman who knows this stuff to write a new bill under my direction. And you've got to persuade the chief that this Thompson bill won't do."[57] Moley made no attempt to get Rayburn to reconsider. He knew the Texan had only the best interests of the president in mind.

After informing Roosevelt that Rayburn had lost faith in the Thompson bill, Moley received authorization to seek out yet a third drafting team for the legislation. This time the president broke with the past. He would not turn to a Wilsonian, Brandeis disciple, or a veteran of the battles of the previous generation. Instead he turned to the man who was in many ways Brandeis's successor—and rival. Within hours, he reached out to the brain behind the brain trust, Harvard Law School professor Felix Frankfurter. Frankfurter gave a prompt response: "Three of us will arrive at the Carlton Friday morning."[58]

The outsize influence of Felix Frankfurter at the beginning of the Roosevelt administration was the result of a unique confluence of events. At its simplest, the administrative law theory of Brandeis was centered on the need to protect society in its smallest units (the individual, small communities, small business) from the tyranny of "bigness" (big business, big government). Brandeis naturally appealed to reformers of the trust-busting generation.

Frankfurter's vision of administrative law, again at its simplest, embraced "bigness," particularly the use of the enormous power of the federal government to regulate—and, in truth, centrally plan—the nation's economy in order to eliminate vicious business cycles and financial panics. Frankfurter's legal theories provided intellectual underpinning for the New Deal legislative program and more important, perhaps, his energy and charisma attracted a small army of loyalists among his former students and colleagues. Requiring a large number of ideologically like-minded bright lawyers to staff his rapidly growing new regulatory agencies, Roosevelt needed Frankfurter more than any president would need any other academic.

Frankfurter's theories influenced much of the cornerstone early New Deal "central planning" legislation: the National Industrial Recovery Act, enacted on June 16, 1933, which created the National Recovery Administration, to establish "industrial codes" to centrally plan production and wages and working conditions, and the Public Works Administration, to oversee a $6,000,000,000 economic stimulus program to build roads and bridges and other public works; the Agricultural Adjustment Act, enacted on May 12, 1933, which created the Agricultural Adjustment Administration, to reduce crop surpluses and raise crop prices by paying farmers not to grow crops in exchange for subsidies paid for by a tax on food-processing companies and also authorized the president to effect currency inflation to raise crop prices; and the Tennessee Valley Authority Act, enacted on May 19, 1933, which created the Tennessee Valley Authority, to provide economic development in Tennessee, Alabama, Mississippi, Kentucky, Georgia, North Carolina, and Virginia. (The effectiveness of these programs was mixed, and the Agricultural Adjustment Act and the industrial code provisions of the National Industrial Recovery Act were struck down by the Supreme Court as unconstitutional.)

With Rayburn having already doomed the Thompson bill, the last day of scheduled hearings of the House Interstate and Foreign Commerce Committee was taken up principally by Huston Thompson desperately proposing revisions to address the myriad concerns raised.[59] At day's end, Rayburn told the press that a sweeping revision of the bill was required.[60] A subcommittee consisting of Rayburn and representatives George Huddleston of Alabama, Clarence Lea of California, James Parker of New York, and Carl Mapes of Michigan was appointed to oversee the redrafting process.[61]

Shortly after Moley's call for help, Felix Frankfurter considered who among his vast network of former students and protégés to assemble to quickly salvage the flailing legislative process. There was never any question that Tommy Corcoran, Frankfurter's man in Washington, would lead the team, given not only his knowledge and experience in the ways of the Capitol but also his practical experience in practicing corporate law on Wall Street with Cotton & Franklin.[62]

The second man Frankfurter chose was thirty-three-year-old James M. Landis, a colleague of Frankfurter's from Harvard Law School and its first professor of litigation. Landis grew up in Japan the son of a Presbyterian missionary. He had graduated from Princeton with honors and was first in his class at Harvard Law School. Like his law-school friend Corcoran, Landis had been selected by Frankfurter for a teaching fellowship at Harvard. Following the teaching fellowship, he had clerked for a year with Justice Brandeis. And at age twenty-seven, he joined the regular faculty of Harvard Law School. Unlike the gregarious Corcoran, Landis was intense and analytical—and at times testy and tactless.[63]

On April 6, Frankfurter asked Landis to join him in Washington. As Landis remembered it: "It was a Thursday in early April and my next classes were scheduled for the following Monday. Frankfurter, however, thought the job could be done over that weekend. We consequently left on the night train to Washington."[64] Landis would not return to Cambridge for nearly eight weeks. Also like Corcoran, Landis was not an early supporter of Franklin Roosevelt, having endorsed Al Smith for president in 1932.

The last man Frankfurter selected was thirty-nine-year-old Benjamin Cohen. Cohen, the son of a wealthy scrap-metal dealer from Muncie, Indiana, had received a degree in both economics and law from the University of Chicago. He was doing post-graduate work at Harvard Law School when he caught the eye of Frankfurter. Like he had done for Landis, Frankfurter had arranged a clerkship with Brandeis for Cohen.[65]

On April 7, Frankfurter, Landis, and Cohen arrived at Washington's Union Station aboard the *Federal Express*. Corcoran met them on the train platform, and they retired to a suite at the Carlton Hotel, where Frankfurter laid out the outlines of the bill he expected them to draft.[66] As Landis later described it: "After a brief session with Frankfurter, where we determined to take as the base of our work the English Companies Act, with which Cohen was very familiar, Cohen, Corcoran and I set to work. Frankfurter had other duties to attend to."[67]

Frankfurter's "other duties" involved meeting with Roosevelt that day to convince the president of his vision for the securities bill. While the two men had attended Harvard at the same time, they only became friends later, as young lawyers in New York, when Frankfurter was an assistant U.S. attorney and Roosevelt a junior associate of Carter Ledyard & Milburn.[68] They became closer friends during World War I, when both were officials in Washington for the war effort, Roosevelt as assistant secretary of the Navy and Frankfurter as chief of the War Labor Policies Board.[69] Despite this relationship, Frankfurter, too, initially backed Al Smith for the Democratic nomination in 1932. Even as the convention approached, he expressed reservations about his old friend: "I am wondering what will come out of Chicago. . . . If F.D.R. is nominated, it will certainly prove there is no limit to the amount of fumbling one can do and still win the game. Were I God, of course, I should want more of a fellow to guide our destiny during the next four years than is Roosevelt. . . ."[70]

During the campaign, Roosevelt used Frankfurter principally as an emissary to rally former Smith supporters. Only on one of the last days of the campaign—on November 5, 1932—did Frankfurter publicly support Roosevelt, giving a speech critical of Hoover's response to the Great Depression. It was between election and inauguration that Roosevelt saw Frankfurter's unique value—an ability to fill the rank and file of the New Deal bureaucracies with brilliant and motivated young lawyers.[71] Shortly after the inauguration, a grateful Roosevelt offered him the position of solicitor general—often a stepping-stone to a Supreme Court nomination. Frankfurter turned him down.[72] But he remained a trusted adviser.

After meeting with Frankfurter that Friday morning, Roosevelt curtly informed Huston Thompson that his bill was about to be rewritten without him. Inviting Thompson to the White House, the two met alone in the president's second-floor study, where he informed Thompson that he required him for a new assignment: checking into illegal use of power generated by the Army Corps of Engineers at Muscle Shoals, Alabama. Thompson did not want to believe what he was being told. Like Untermyer before him, Thompson was now most definitely out. He would blame Moley, Frankfurter, and Frankfurter's "boys," Corcoran, Landis, and Cohen, but in truth it was Rayburn who had killed his bill.

Throughout that weekend, Corcoran, Landis, and Cohen, along with Corcoran's secretary, Peggy Dowd (a cousin of *New York Times* columnist Maureen Dowd, and the future Mrs. Thomas Corcoran), worked virtually without sleep in their suite at the Carlton Hotel rewriting the securities bill. As Landis remembered it, "By late Saturday night we had a draft of the bill in reasonable shape. We had to work under certain limitations imposed upon us by the fact of the Thompson bill. Tactically it seemed wise to shape our proposal as 'perfecting,' amendments to that bill, with the result that our original bill embodied a number of proposals contained in the Thompson bill that were subsequently hopefully discarded."[73]

The bill they prepared provided for a thirty-day waiting period between the filing of the registration statement and its effectiveness to allow the FTC to review the disclosure. It scaled back the power of the FTC to deny or revoke effectiveness of a registration statement to only situations where disclosure was faulty or the rules of registration were not followed. The concept of "soundness" review of securities was abandoned. The bill also significantly modified liability provisions. Officers and directors of issuers were immunized from liability if they had a reasonable ground to believe statements in the registration statement were true. Most ominously for Wall Street, however, securities underwriters were now expressly added to the list of those subject to liability under the act, though they too could avoid liability if they performed a reasonable investigation of the issuing company and believed the statements in the registration statement to be true and complete.[74]

On Sunday night, Frankfurter returned to the Carlton Hotel to read the draft bill before he presented it to Chairman Rayburn the next morning. He then informed his team they now had the unhappy task of explaining to Thompson what they had done to his bill.[75]

On Monday morning, Corcoran, Landis, and Cohen met with Thompson and walked him through their bill. It would be the first of many occasions where the three young lawyers would confront an experienced Washington hand and deliver the always disheartening news that times had changed. A new generation of power players had arrived. The meeting concluded without incident, but Thompson would continue to lobby the Senate to pass his version of the bill and later try to persuade Roosevelt and Rayburn to reconcile the two pieces of legislation in his favor. Thompson told FDR secretary Marvin McIntyre "the brain trust crowd . . . ruined my bill."[76]

After breakfast, Corcoran, Landis, and Cohen joined Frankfurter in the House Interstate and Foreign Commerce Committee hearing room to present the new draft bill. Frankfurter spoke for the group. As Landis recalled: "Questions of detail were referred by him to Cohen and me, but he handled the main structure of the bill magnificently as well as the relationship of this bill in the nature of a 'perfecting' amendment to the Thompson bill. The session, punctuated by questions from members of the Committee, continued throughout the morning. We adjourned for lunch and returned in the afternoon. It was difficult for me to assess the effect of our draft upon the Committee, particularly Rayburn, whom I had never seen before. About five o'clock the meeting ended and the Committee held a brief executive session from which every non-member was excluded except Frankfurter. At its close, Rayburn and Frankfurter came out to talk to Cohen and myself, and Rayburn asked us to continue to work with the Committee and with Middleton Beaman's office as consultants to perfect our draft. Upon Frankfurter's assurance that my classes at Cambridge could be covered, I agreed to do so. Cohen and I stayed on, for what I believed would be only another few days. It became almost two months."[77]

Despite Frankfurter's prominence and his complete faith in his three young protégés, Rayburn had too much on the line personally to delegate the fate of the securities bill to Corcoran, Landis, and Cohen. He wanted an old hand, a man of the House, in the room and preferably controlling the process. Rayburn wanted Middleton Beaman in control of the drafting. Beaman was the first legislative counsel for the House of Representatives, a post he would hold for thirty years until his retirement in 1949. A fellow lawyer working with him on the Social Security Act described Beaman: "A tense, caustic, redheaded Yankee, [he] reminded me of a Vermont schoolmarm. It was this role that he played when he and I appeared, day after day, at the executive sessions of the Ways and Means Committee. The committee's procedure was to read the bill, paragraph by paragraph. No sooner was a sentence read, however, than Mr. Beaman was on his feet asking questions: Where the bill said that employees should recover old age benefits, did it mean to include American employees stationed abroad? If the committee member said no, then Mr. Beaman, terrier like, would ask: What about a contractor in Detroit who sent his regular crew on to a job for a few days in Windsor, Ontario? What about seamen on the Great Lakes? A cook on a ship that went from Seattle to Alaska, through Canadian waters? He insisted on answers, and the committee members generally complied."[78]

Despite his less than charming disposition, Beaman was perhaps the most important unelected official in Congress during the Roosevelt years. He was religiously non-partisan and exacting and was trusted by both parties to be a fair practitioner in the drafting of legislation.

Middleton Beaman's path to power in Washington ran through Columbia University Law School in New York. In 1911, Columbia accepted a gift by Joseph P. Chamberlain to establish a "bureau for the promotion of scientific study and investigation of legislative drafting and for the collection of materials relating thereto." Named the Legislative Drafting Research Fund and staffed by Columbia Law School professors, one of its earliest initiatives was to persuade Congress to set up a professional drafting service. In 1916, the fund dispatched Middleton Beaman to Washington to provide drafting aid to the House Ways and Means Committee and the House Committee on Merchant Marines and Fisheries. Beaman proved to be so successful on the job that in 1918, Congress passed a revenue act, creating and funding the legislative drafting office. He would be the office's first employee, remaining there until 1949.[79]

Over the course of ten days following submission of their draft bill, Corcoran, Landis, and Cohen, working with Beaman in the bowels of the House Office Building, painstakingly carved out the language of the next draft of the bill. Landis described the experience: "For days, Beaman would not allow us to draft a line. He insisted instead on exploring the implications of the bill to find exactly what we had or did not have in mind. He probed always for the extent and nature of those hiatuses that any proposed important legislation necessarily possesses."[80]

Beaman distilled from the team of young lawyers the core principles of securities regulation that are well understood by Wall Street lawyers to the present day. The famous words creating liability under the Securities Act of 1933 were Beaman's handiwork: "If the registration statement contains any untrue statement of a material fact or omits to state any material fact required to be stated therein or necessary to make the statements therein not misleading."[81]

A heated dispute arose between Landis and Cohen over how best to draft the information requirements included in registration statements. Landis believed the requirements should be referred to generally in the text of the statute (the FTC would fill in the details later); Cohen believed they should be set forth with specific detail. It was, of course, a distinction without much practical legal difference, reflecting more a personality clash between Landis and Cohen. Indeed, Cohen become so angry with Landis that on April 14 he threatened to quit the project unless Landis relented. Frankfurter reached out to Roosevelt to warn him of the dissension. On April 17, Frankfurter telegraphed Cohen, telling him that he was "indispensable and . . . must not leave till the ship is in port." Beaman was instructed to resolve the dispute among "Frankfurter's hot dogs," as the press would come to refer to his three young acolytes, and Corcoran was tasked with smoothing out feelings between the two men.[82]

Beaman sided with Cohen but said that disclosure requirements should be moved to schedules at the end of the bill, facilitating approval by the House Interstate and Foreign Commerce Committee who, exhausted from reading the main text of the legislation, would hardly have the energy to nitpick these provisions. Beaman proved to be right, as disproportionately more of the committee's attention was paid to the main body of the bill, even though the core of the registration disclosure requirements was included in those schedules.[83]

All three Frankfurter protégés had held their own with Beaman during the ten-day ordeal, and with Beaman's stamp of approval, Rayburn decided to keep them on for the duration of the battle in Congress. On April 19, a revised draft of the bill was circulated to the five-member subcommittee. Four additional drafts were circulated before Corcoran, Landis, Cohen, and Beaman were ready to meet with the subcommittee. Most notable in the revised drafts was an expanding list of securities to be exempted from coverage under the law. Among those added were municipal bonds, building and loan and savings and loan securities, and railroad securities.[84]

Two in-person meetings with the subcommittee were held, with the only significant revision being a reduction of the statute of limitations from six years to two years.[85]

Corcoran, Landis, and Cohen were nearly paranoid about the risk of leaks tipping off Wall Street that underwriters would have statutory liability for prospectus disclosure. Their fear of leaks was heightened by the coincidence that J.P. Morgan Jr., in town for the Pecora Hearings, was also staying at the Carlton Hotel. (Treasury Secretary Woodin, himself a bit too sympathetic to Wall Street, many New Dealers believed, also lived in the Carlton.) More than once they rode the elevator with Morgan, barely able to conceal their mix of fear and amusement that they were currently rewriting the rules of his industry.[86]

No members of the public or press were allowed at the meetings of the subcommittee, and there were remarkably few press leaks regarding its deliberations. Somehow, though, word leaked out to interested persons on Wall Street that a substantial rewrite of the liability provisions was being undertaken and that underwriters would be subject to liability: there was, perhaps, a chance to influence the final product.

Having been lobbied by his Wall Street friends, Raymond Moley convinced Rayburn to allow representatives of Wall Street to present their concerns to the drafting subcommittee. Representing Wall Street was, once again, Sullivan & Cromwell, led by the senior partner John Foster Dulles. Dulles had broad experience in government: he had served as legal counsel to the American delegation in Paris negotiating the Treaty of Versailles and later served on the War Reparations Committee, and he was instrumental in developing the Dawes Plan for the restructuring of Germany's war debts. He would later serve as President Eisenhower's secretary of state.[87]

Dulles's performance before Rayburn's subcommittee wasn't his finest hour. Assisted by Arthur Dean, as well as Alexander Henderson of Cravath, DeGersdorf, Swaine and Wood (predecessor of today's Cravath, Swaine & Moore LLP), Dulles aggressively criticized provisions that weren't even included in the bill and referenced provisions of the Thompson Senate bill not included in the House bill.[88] While Arthur Dean and Alexander Henderson were knowledgeable about the bill and well prepared for the hearing, they were unable to recover from Dulles's miscues. "Technically, I had him way out in left field," Landis remembered, "and he never got back to home base."[89] Dean and Henderson's low-key attempts to water down the liability provisions of the bill and eliminate the thirty-day waiting period likewise gained no traction with the subcommittee.

The subcommittee adjourned with instructions that Dean and Henderson would meet with Landis and Cohen to consider the technical drafting points raised by the Wall Street lawyers. Certain of the lawyers' proposals proved helpful and were included, particularly those relating to the bill's disclosure schedules. Later that day, Landis would hear what Rayburn thought of Dulles and his team: "I went back to my little cubbyhole office in the sub-basement. . . . About twenty minutes later, I got a call from Sam Rayburn to come up to his office. Well, naturally, I was worried. I thought maybe all our work was down the drain." Instead, Rayburn asked Landis, half-rhetorically, "What those people were doing there." With a snarl, Rayburn cussed the Wall Street lawyers "in very obscene language."[90]

By Monday, the Corcoran, Landis, and Cohen draft bill was ready for formal introduction to the House of Representatives by Rayburn. The bill, labeled H.R. 5480, was immediately referred to Rayburn's committee.[91]

On May 4, the committee on Interstate and Foreign Commerce took up the bill in a public hearing and recommended the bill for approval by the full House of Representatives.[92] Two committee members, California Democrat Clarence Lea and Connecticut Republican Schuyler Merritt, issued a minority report objecting to the provision federalizing state blue sky laws.[93]

Rayburn arranged to have the bill voted on by the full House the next day and invoked a special rule limiting debate to five hours and prohibiting the offering of amendments to the bill unless directed by the Committee on Interstate and Foreign Commerce (i.e., Rayburn himself). Rayburn justified the "no amendments" rule by arguing that the bill was so complex that an unstudied amendment might impact other portions of the bill, upsetting the careful balance of the bill's various sections.[94] The Republican minority wasn't buying this explanation. Though in favor of the bill for the most part, Representative Carl Mapes of Michigan objected, calling it a "gag rule," which is precisely what it was and what Rayburn intended it to be.[95]

The House debate on the merits of the bill provided little excitement. In his remarks on the floor, Rayburn stated: "Since the World War, some $50,000,000,000 in new securities have been floated and fully $25,000,000 have proved to be worthless. These figures spell tragedy in the lives of thousands of men and women who invested their life savings in these worthless securities." Rayburn laid this financial carnage squarely at the feet of Wall Street. "The flotation of such a mass of essentially fraudulent securities was made possible because of the complete abandonment by many underwriters and dealers in securities of those standards of fair, honest and prudent dealing that should be basic to the encouragement of investment in any enterprise."[96] Shortly before 5:00 p.m., the House passed the bill by an unrecorded voice vote, with no dissenting voices raised. Rayburn, turning to Benjamin Cohen when the vote was taken, quipped that he did not know whether the bill passed so readily because it was "so damned good or so damned incomprehensible."[97]

The reaction of Wall Street to passage of the bill was a predictable combination of anger and resignation. The Thompson bill's raising of hopes that underwriters might avoid liability was illusory. (Many astute observers doubted all along that any final bill would exempt them—they expected underwriters to be explicitly added during committee mock-ups.) Frank M. Gordon, president of the Investment Bankers Association of America, who had testified before the Senate Committee in favor of the Thompson bill, now issued a statement on May 7 strongly critical of the Corcoran, Landis, and Cohen bill, arguing that the "interests of the country's industries and of the investing public are as detrimentally affected by the federal securities bill passed by the House of Representatives on Friday, as are the interests of the investment banking business."[98] Gordon thought the liability provisions of the bill imposed on underwriters and experts "an extreme degree of diligence, accuracy and financial liability that is not only impracticable but dangerous."[99] He maintained that the bill, if it became law, would automatically prevent needed financing of many essential industries.

During the first week of May, with both the Securities Act and the Glass-Steagall Banking Act pending in Congress, rumors were circulating regarding a rift among Roosevelt's economic team. Specifically, it was alleged that Treasury Secretary Woodin was about to resign, having broken from Roosevelt over the president's inflation policy. In truth, Woodin was bedridden at his apartment in the Carlton Hotel with a bad sore throat he couldn't seem to shake. He called a press conference from his sickbed to dispel the rumors: "Reports that I am about to resign have been industriously promoted during my illness. I wish you would deny them as emphatically as you can. . . . I feel that my work in Treasury is just beginning. I am supremely happy. . . . It seems to me most unsportsmanlike that anyone should take advantage of my illness to circulate such falsehoods. . . . All these rumors including the comment that my seat in the Treasury would be so hot I would need a pair of asbestos pants can be relegated to the realm of dreams. I am with the Chief until the end and he is going to lead us out of this situation."[100]

In the Senate, the Committee on Banking and Currency was still working with the Thompson bill—and with far less bandwidth available to it than Rayburn's committee was devoting to securities legislation. The Senate Banking and Currency Committee was fully occupied with the Pecora Hearings and the Glass banking bill and had no figure with the gravitas of Middleton

Beaman to shepherd through a major bill-rewriting outside of a traditional committee structure. Most of the Senate work on the bill was done by the full committee itself, not a subcommittee, in a more public—and untidy—manner.

On April 8, the Senate committee circulated a new draft of the Thompson bill, addressing many concerns and criticisms raised during the committee hearings. The new draft eliminated "soundness" review, allowing the FTC to revoke registrations only in cases where the disclosure in a registration statement had failed to comply with the act or where the issuer or other signatory of the registration statement had otherwise violated the act. This draft of the bill also eliminated the provision federalizing state blue sky laws. The draft exempted commercial paper, mutual building and loan securities, and homestead association securities. It required that at least three-quarters of an issuer's directors sign a registration statement and made clear that the act only applied to new issues of securities.[101]

On April 19, Senator Fletcher announced that a third draft of the Thompson bill had been prepared. The new draft added a provision that any suspension or revocation of a registration statement would not apply to securities sold to bona fide purchasers prior to the date the FTC revoked a registration statement. In addition, it allowed for appeals of FTC orders to both the D.C. Circuit Court of Appeals and the circuit court of appeals where the person subject to the order resides.[102]

In late April, Frankfurter persuaded Senator James Byrnes, a member of the Banking and Currency Committee, to lobby Chairman Fletcher to withdraw the Thompson bill in favor of the House bill. But on April 27, the Senate Banking and Currency Committee voted to report out the revised Thompson bill. After the bill was reported, Frankfurter and Corcoran continued to lobby Majority Leader Joseph Robinson against the Thompson bill. At Robinson's request, Frankfurter prepared a memorandum outlining the bill's deficiencies, but Robinson was unwilling to challenge Senator Fletcher on the bill's floor vote.[103]

On May 8, with little debate, the Senate approved the revised Thompson bill by unanimous consent. The only unplanned development during the floor proceeding was an amendment offered by Senator Hiram Johnson to create a committee to negotiate with defaulting foreign borrowers on debt repayment. Called the Corporation of Foreign Bondholders, this body would be composed of twelve individuals chosen by the FTC, funded by the RFC, and authorized to represent American holders of defaulted foreign bonds in negotiations with foreign governments and corporations.[104]

Johnson's bill was strongly opposed by Cordell Hull, Roosevelt's secretary of state, who did not want a U.S. government–sponsored entity—at least one not controlled by the State Department—engaging in negotiations with foreign governments to protect the private economic interests of U.S. citizens. The concept behind the bill, though, was popular, given the significant losses incurred by those who owned foreign bonds that subsequently proved to be worthless or nearly worthless, as highlighted during Pecora's National City Bank hearings. President Roosevelt was noncommittal on Johnson's proposal, which was approved by the Senate as Title II to the securities bill.[105]

On May 9, Sam Rayburn selected a conference committee to negotiate a bill with the Senate, selecting himself and representatives George Huddleston of Alabama, Clarence Lea of California, James S. Parker of New York, and Carl Mapes of Michigan. On the Senate side, Chairman Fletcher chose himself, Carter Glass, Senator Robert Warner of New York, Senator Peter Norbeck of South Dakota, and Senator Phillips Lee Goldsborough of Maryland. When Senator Norbeck was required to leave Washington, D.C., for personal business, Senator John G. Townsend Jr. of Delaware replaced him. Later, senators James J. Couzens of Michigan and Hiram Johnson of California would substitute as well.[106]

On May 18, the conference committee held its first meeting. In addition to the conferees, James Landis, Benjamin Cohen, Middleton Beaman, Ganson Purcell (a member of the Senate Drafting Service and a former student of Landis's, who would become chairman of the Securities and Exchange Commission in 1942), and two other Senate staffers were in attendance. From the beginning, the conference committee was dominated by Rayburn, who skillfully outmaneuvered Fletcher. Rayburn asked Fletcher whether he preferred the Senate or House version of the bill as the base document that the conference committee would work off. Fletcher, of course, said the Senate bill. Rayburn then requested that Fletcher make a motion to that effect. The vote on the motion, predictably, ended in a five-to-five tie (Senate versus House members). Rayburn then declared that since the motion had failed, the House bill would be the starting point. "Except for an occasional reference to its provisions," Landis recalled, "that was the last we heard of the . . . Senate bill."[107]

The only senator who could have potentially challenged Rayburn was Carter Glass. But Glass, an early advocate of federal securities regulation from his days as Woodrow Wilson's secretary of the Treasury, was now preoccupied with his banking bill. Once Glass had satisfied himself that the securities bill did not encroach on his turf, especially with respect to banking regulation, he lost interest in the conference committee proceedings. As remembered by Landis, "He growled, thumbed the bill for any further reference to banks, found none, and shortly thereafter left the committee never to reappear."[108]

A number of constituencies made suggestions to the conference committee for revisions to the bill. Wall Street interests funneled their proposed revisions through Republican senator John G. Townsend of Delaware. The FTC prepared a memorandum, authored by Baldwin Bane, who would become the FTC's first chief of its Securities Division, favoring the House bill. Robert E. Healey, the chief counsel of the FTC, later to become an original member of the Securities and Exchange Commission, favored the Senate bill.[109]

The conference committee prepared four drafts of the bill before the final version was agreed upon. There were a number of relatively minor changes to the House bill included in the final version. The waiting period before registration statements could become effective was reduced from thirty to twenty days. The period of time during which a prospectus could be used was increased from twelve months to thirteen months. Bank securities, as well as securities of federal, state, and municipal entities, were exempted from the anti-fraud provisions of the act. Appeals of FTC orders were allowed in any circuit court of appeals rather than just the D.C. Circuit Court of Appeals. Securities of farmers' cooperatives and annuities issued by regulated insurance companies were added to the list of exempted securities. The FTC was given the power to grant confidential treatment to certain documents and information filed with registration statements. Consents were required to be obtained from any person named as an expert in the registration statement. And the provision federalizing the state blue sky laws was eliminated.[110]

The most heated disputes in the conference committee revolved around the civil liability provisions applicable to officers and directors of registrants. The Senate bill retained the essentially "strict liability" standard, while the House bill didn't impose liability on directors and officers exercising due care when determining the accuracy and completeness of registration statements and prospectuses. Again, the House version prevailed.[111]

The last order of business for the conference committee was Title II of the Senate bill: Hiram Johnson's Corporation of Foreign Bondholders Act. Rayburn wanted no part of the simmering controversy between Senator Johnson and the State Department and indicated that he would take his lead from President Roosevelt. By May 20, Rayburn still hadn't received specific guidance from the White House. On that morning, Senator Johnson requested Rayburn call the president directly and ask for his instructions. Rayburn broke out from the conference and, with Landis listening in, called Roosevelt, who was unhelpful in providing cover to Rayburn. Always mindful to preserve all of his options, Roosevelt told Rayburn to do what he thought best. Landis put the ball back in the president's court, though, proposing the approval of Title II but having it become effective only upon a presidential declaration. Middleton Beaman questioned the constitutionality of delegating to the president the authority to determine when a law becomes operative, but quietly dropped his objections. To everyone's amazement, Senator Johnson signed off on the approach as well.[112]

Later that day, the conference committee delivered its report, with all Democratic representatives from both the Senate and the House having signed. All Republican House members signed, but none from the Senate. The holdout Republican senators, however, failed to issue a minority disagreement in the report.[113]

On May 22, shortly after the opening of the House session, Sam Rayburn called up the conference report for consideration. Speaker of the House Henry Thomas Rainey approved Rayburn's request that the conference report be accepted by way of a voice vote; it was approved with no objections raised.[114]

On May 23, the Senate likewise approved the bill by a voice vote without objection.[115]

On May 27, President Roosevelt held a signing ceremony at the White House, attended by Representative Rayburn and Senator Fletcher, as well as Senate Majority Leader Robinson and a number of FTC officials. After signing the bill into law, Roosevelt presented the pen to Rayburn.[116] In his statement, Roosevelt said:

"It gives me much satisfaction to sign the Rayburn-Fletcher Securities Bill, and I know I express national feeling in congratulating Congress on its passage. For this measure at last translates some elementary standards of right and wrong into law.

"Events have made it abundantly clear that the merchandising of securities is really traffic in the economic and social welfare of our people. Such traffic demands the utmost good faith and fair dealing on the part of those engaged in it.

"If the country is to flourish, capital must be invested in enterprise. But those who seek to draw upon other people's money must be wholly candid regarding the facts on which the investor's judgment is asked.

"To that end, this bill requires the publicity necessary for sound investment. It is, of course, no insurance against errors of judgment. That is the function of no government. It does give assurance, however, that within the limits of its powers, the Federal Government will insist upon knowledge of the facts on which above judgment can be based.

"The new law will also safeguard against the abuse of high-powered salesmanship in securities flotations. It will require full disclosure of all the private interests on the part of those who seek to sell securities to the public.

"The Act is thus intended to correct some of the evils which have been so glaringly revealed in the private exploitation of the public's money. This law and its effective administration are steps in a program to restore some old-fashioned standards of rectitude. Without such an ethical foundation, economic well-being cannot be achieved."[117]

The FTC issued a statement saying it would be prepared to handle the registration statements in ten days' time, when the law became effective. In its statement to the press, the FTC also stated that "statistics indicate that the sale of worthless securities through misrepresentations and fraud has amounted to the colossal sum of $25,000,000,000 during the last ten years. This means $250 for every man, woman and child in the United States."[118]

On June 7, Benjamin Cohen sent a congratulatory but reflective letter to James Landis: "I am afraid it is a little unfortunate for us that the act passed so nearly as we drafted it. That gives us too much of a powerful interest in the darned thing. The rules and regulations and the decisions of the courts have as much chance of satisfying us as the clothes that strangers might choose for our babies."[119]

Frankfurter's "hot dogs" would serve as a useful lightning rod for both the proponents and the adversaries of the law. Rayburn, who in truth was more a father to the bill than Frankfurter, Corcoran, or anyone else, was happy to keep a comfortable distance from it until he saw how—and whether—it worked in practice. Nonetheless, his legislative brilliance was displayed and recognized by those who really mattered to him—Speaker Rainey and his fellow House Democrats.

On May 27, 1933, the day Roosevelt signed the Securities Act of 1933 into law, the Chicago World's Fair, formally named "A Century of Progress Exposition," opened. Arch Ward, the sports editor of the *Chicago Tribune,* came up with the idea for an exhibition baseball game to be played by the stars of the National League against their counterparts from the American League— a showcase of America's pastime for the world. Ward billed it as a onetime "Game of the Century," with fans choosing the lineups of each league's team. Ward's editor, the right-wing isolationist Colonel Robert R. McCormick, convinced that the game would not make money, balked at financing what he saw as a gimmick.

Since 1929, attendance at major league baseball games had plummeted 40 percent. Those who could afford tickets had migrated from $2 box seats to 50-cent bleacher seats. To win back fans, owners experimented with all manner of promotions, including ladies' nights (where women were given free admission), grocery giveaways, and the introduction of night games. Colonel McCormick thought Ward's brainchild was a similar gimmick. But when Ward offered to have any losses from the sponsorship taken out of his salary, the colonel approved his reaching out to team owners. Baseball commissioner Kenesaw Mountain Landis was eventually persuaded, and the game was set for July 6, 1933.

Ballots were printed in fifty-five newspapers, and several hundred thousand fans responded. The top vote getter, with more than 100,000 votes, was Babe Ruth.

On game day, 47,595 fans packed into Chicago's Comiskey Park. John McGraw was manager of the National League team, and Connie Mack helmed the American League squad. In the bottom of the third inning, with Charlie Gehringer on second base, Babe Ruth sent a pitch from St. Louis Cardinals left-hander Willie Hallahan into the right-field pavilion, propelling the American League into a four-to-two win. It was the first home run in All-Star Game history.[120]

The political chatter heard around the ball park that night was monopolized by talk of President Roosevelt's bombshell letter delivered earlier that week to the London Economic Conference, a gathering of representatives of more than sixty nations, who were meeting at the Geological Museum in London to reach an international accord for the elimination or reduction of trade tariffs and on currency exchange rates. A revival of international trade was critical to ending the worldwide economic depression, and protectionist currency devaluation—which Roosevelt had taken steps toward with his executive order confiscating all gold and with the inflationary Thomas Amendment—was hampering free trade.

While the administration publicly expressed hope that the conference might lead to an accord the United States would support, Roosevelt's choice of members for the American delegation preordained deadlock and possibly chaos. Secretary of State Cordell Hull, who chaired the delegation, was a free-trade, hard-money man, as was James M. Cox, the former governor of Ohio and Democratic presidential nominee in 1920. Two members, Ralph W. Morrison, a Texas businessman, and Samuel D. McReynolds, a Tennessee congressman, had expressed no particular views on the currency issue. The last two members, Michigan senator James Couzens and Nevada senator Key Pittman, were pro-inflation and protectionist leaning.

From June 12, when the conference began, until month's end, nothing was agreed. The conduct of the U.S. delegation was noteworthy only for its dysfunction. The members quarreled among themselves and the behavior of Senator Pittman—chairman of the Senate Foreign Relations Committee and president pro tempore of the Senate—was the scandal of the conference. He got drunk the day he arrived and drew hardly a sober breath thereafter. He refused to abide by the dress code in the dining room at Claridge's, where the American delegation was headquartered, showing up so slovenly looking that the hotel's first-class staff, not wanting to turn him away and create an international incident, but also not wanting to offend its refined clientele, allowed him to be served only behind a partitioning screen.[121] Displeased by Claridge's unaccommodating management, the chairman of the Foreign Relations Committee went on a hotel rampage that might have had Keith Moon taking notes. On one night where his drinking was curtailed while he could still remain upright, he returned to Claridge's with a prostitute on each arm.[122] The ladies were ejected by hotel security, further souring Pittman's mood. Pittman later had the idea that he needed a bath, but insisted on taking it in the large sink in the hotel's kitchen.[123] On yet another night of epic drinking, Pittman thought it would be great fun to shake up the stuffy residents of London's exclusive Mayfair neighborhood, so he raced down Brook Street and shot out the street lamps with his pistol. Later, when about to be presented to King George V and Mary, Queen Consort, he flaunted protocol by refusing to remove his raincoat. "I ain't going to get soaked for no King and Queen," he slurred. (It was reported that the king and queen were quite amused by Pittman's antics.)[124]

By early July, there were rumors that a currency stabilization scheme had been tentatively agreed to by the major powers. Those currencies not convertible into gold at a set rate would be tied to those currencies that were at agreed exchange rates or ranges. Roosevelt wanted nothing to do with it. He wasn't going to surrender the inflation option and incur the populist wrath of Huey Long and the farmers. From aboard the Navy cruiser *Indianapolis* off the Atlantic coast while on vacation, Roosevelt drafted a letter seethingly critical of the proposed stabilization plan, calling it the product of "old fetishes of so-called international bankers," and declared that the United States would not enter into any currency stabilization agreement. The conference was effectively over, dashing hopes of any quick end to the trade-crippling protectionist policies. This King George did not find amusing. "I will not have those people worrying my Prime Minister this way," he said to a crestfallen Ramsey MacDonald in reference to Roosevelt and the American delegation.[125]

Throughout that summer, the securities markets were moribund. A rally in the market sparked by the end of Prohibition faltered, and sober reality set in by June, as Wall Street sorted out the practical effect of the changes in its business mandated by the Glass-Steagall Banking Act and the Securities Act. Bankers had plenty of free time to arrange for the separation of their commercial and investment-banking businesses: There were no deals. Banks that had available reserves were afraid to lend them out, and stricken investors had no appetite for new securities purchases. As fall approached, talk of something else explaining the dearth of activity could be heard. On Wall Street, the talk was of a strangling of deal activity by punitive liability risks and exorbitant compliance costs brought about by the new laws. Among the reformers in Washington, the talk was of a "capital strike"—a vindictive Wall Street refusing to lend or underwrite securities needed to finance growth and jobs in order to blackmail Roosevelt into rolling back reform.

Before the ink was dry on the Securities Act of 1933, efforts began on Wall Street to repeal or weaken it. But with the exception of relatively minor tweaks, the act's provisions would survive intact. The Securities Act was a decisive victory for the New Deal reformers. The most vicious battle, though, lay ahead. In the fall of 1933, regulation of the securities exchanges was in the works. This would not be a proxy war fought by Wall Street lawyers and lobbyists. It would pit a hero of American capitalism willing to battle publicly against the brain trusters, Pecora, and even the president himself.

SIX

A PERFECT INSTITUTION:

The Securities Exchange Act of 1934

The New York Stock Exchange was the symbolic center of Wall Street power and historically led the resistance against regulation. Repeated efforts had been made to regulate the exchanges at both the state and federal level, most notably by Samuel Untermyer's Pujo Committee, but all of those efforts had failed, due in no small part to the power and superb lobbying of the New York Stock Exchange. In the spring of 1933, powerless to stop the Glass-Steagall Banking Act and the Securities Act, Wall Street was at its lowest and most impotent. With gallows humor demoralized members of the Union League Club, heavily populated by bankers and brokers, papered the walls of a room in the club with securities once worth millions. (When the market rallied in 1934, members asked club management to steam some of the certificates off the walls, as they regained value.)[1] Yet, despite the public anger over the Crash and despite the Pecora Hearings revelations, one man refused to be cowed and was preparing for a fight in Washington over exchange legislation. Richard Whitney remained unconvinced that federal oversight was inevitable.

There were a number of reasons why Richard Whitney was hopeful about his chances. Unlike the banks, first shuttered then bailed out by the federal government, the brokerage and trading firms that made up the New York Stock Exchange had weathered the Crash and Great Depression surprisingly well. The exchange membership was relatively easy to organize—there were only 1,375 members,[2] a great majority of whom were headquartered in the New York City area. Historically, their interests diverged on few regulatory issues. There was nothing similar to the big bank–small bank conflict ever present in the Glass-Steagall Banking Act debate, and Whitney had learned valuable lessons from the Securities Act hearings. His opposition narrative couldn't be limited to, or even principally focused on, the effects regulation would have on Wall Street. Main Street would need to figure prominently in his counterattack.

At first, Whitney attempted to convince President Roosevelt that self-regulation by the New York Stock Exchange would be sufficient to reform the market. On April 5, 1933 (coincidently, the day Roosevelt took America off the "gold standard"), Whitney and his general counsel, Roland L. Redmond, met with Roosevelt in the White House and outlined a slew of proposed rules changes that, he assured the president, would preclude the need for legislation.[3] He followed up with a letter to Roosevelt on April 14, 1933, stating that the New York Stock Exchange stood ready "to accomplish the purposes you have in mind." Whitney argued that federal legislation would subvert reform, with disciplined exchange members likely to be given judicial remedy if laws were enacted. "Any method of statutory regulation," he wrote, "must mean that persons affected by any action of the Governing Committee of the Exchange would have the right to appeal to the courts or some administrative tribunal."[4] It wasn't due process for disciplined members that Roosevelt was afraid of, it was the unwillingness of the exchanges to discipline their members.

After a two-week break following the J.P. Morgan & Co. hearings, Ferdinand Pecora resumed his investigation on June 27, 1933, questioning Otto H. Kahn, the senior partner of Kuhn, Loeb & Company, the second-most prestigious private investment-banking firm after J.P. Morgan & Co.[5] Kuhn, Loeb was then the leading "Jewish firm" on Wall Street, at a time when religion and ethnicity were as important as education and talent in determining what firm one might aspire to. Kuhn, Loeb was formed in 1867 by Abraham Kuhn and Solomon Loeb, but grew to prominence under the leadership of Jacob Schiff, Loeb's son-in-law, who focused the bank's attention on the rapidly growing and capital-intensive railroad industry. Allied with E.H. Harriman, Kuhn, Loeb had fought a bitter and successful struggle against J.P. Morgan & Co. for control of the Northern Pacific Railroad at the turn of the century, earning the begrudging respect of the House of Morgan. While nowhere near its equal in social prominence, Kuhn, Loeb was nearly J.P. Morgan & Co.'s equal in financial clout. Schiff died in 1920, leaving Otto Kahn to dominate the firm during the 1920s and 1930s.

After the Northern Pacific fight, a truce of sorts was established on Wall Street whereby Jews (particularly German Jews) would be admitted to the top tiers of the business establishment, while remaining strictly excluded from the social one. "You can do business with anyone," J.P. Morgan Sr. said. "But you only go sailing with a gentleman."[6] Unlike the Irish, the third predominant ethnic group on Wall Street then, the Jews generally preferred to keep to themselves socially and organized their own clubs and social institutions rather than try to gain entry into the WASP world. There would be no pictures or profiles in the society pages; the Schiffs, Kuhns, and Loebs kept a low profile.

But when it came to business, the Jews held more sway than the Irish, who at the time were principally traders and brokers, running no powerful Wall Street institutions. A few might get into the better clubs, but the Irish didn't have the capital or relationships to play in the investment-banking game with the likes of Jacob Schiff, Otto Kahn, and the Morgans.

The WASP–Jewish relationship on Wall Street was strained by World War I. On May 7, 1915, a German submarine sank the liner *Lusitania* off the Irish coast, killing many prominent Americans, including Alfred Vanderbilt. Many accused Kuhn, Loeb of having sympathies with the Germans (the firm did have strong business ties there). Morgan was unabashedly pro-English. When news of the sinking broke, Jacob Schiff walked to the Morgan office to tell J.P. Morgan Jr. that he fully supported the Allied cause and was horrified by the German outrage. Morgan offered a curt reply and turned his back on Schiff. Morgan's partners looked on tensely, wondering if the European hostilities would spill over and inflame the ethnic tensions on Wall Street into open conflict. "I suppose I went a little far. I suppose I ought to apologize?" Morgan later commented, as his partners stared at the floor silently. Partner Dwight Morrow scratched a note and handed it to Morgan, offering a biblical quote: "Not for thy sake, but for thy name's sake." Morgan grabbed his hat and hurriedly walked over to the offices of Kuhn, Loeb & Company and apologized to Jacob Schiff.[7] Peace was restored.

Like at the J.P. Morgan hearings, Pecora's questioning of the Kuhn, Loeb partners revealed "preferred lists" of investors cut into hot offerings, weak prospectus disclosure in foreign bond offerings, and wildly profitable deals that the bank took advantage of (and arguably, in the process, took advantage of its clients). But there was nothing that could be compared to the egregious conduct unveiled during the National City Bank hearings. When the subcommittee adjourned the hearings for the summer, there was a growing sense of apathy about them; it had been four months since any blockbuster disclosures. Maybe National City was an aberration.

In July, the Repeal bubble burst and stock exchange practices were once again under intense scrutiny. Rumors of pool operators manipulating Repeal stocks were all over the Street, notwithstanding the intense scrutiny of Pecora and the press.

In August, Whitney pushed a modest reform program through the governing committee of the New York Stock Exchange in another effort to preempt federal regulation. First, a margin requirement of 50 percent of debit balance would be required on all investor accounts less than $5,000 and a 30 percent debit balance margin requirement on all accounts of $5,000 or more. Second, members were required to report to the Exchange all pools, syndicates, and joint trading accounts. Third, brokers were prohibited from soliciting business from clients at home.[8] Although dismissed as window dressing by his critics, Whitney could point to the rule changes as evidence of Wall Street cleaning up its act.

The summer of 1933 saw a dramatic decrease in the number and volume of new securities offerings. Wall Street lawyers led by Sullivan & Cromwell's Arthur Dean blamed this on the Securities Act. In the August 1933 issue of *Fortune* magazine, Dean wrote a lengthy, detailed, and stark criticism of the legislation.[9] "The Act is drastically deflationary in nature," Dean argued, "and may seriously retard economic recovery. Many short-term loans now in the commercial banks, the liquidation of which depends on improvement in the bond market, may be frozen. Corporations with impending maturities, or those who face the problem of raising capital funds or of voluntary reorganizations are fearful that the Act will be a serious drag for the Act does far more than require that the sale of securities be accomplished by full publicity and information. It contains many provisions not apparent on the first reading which will have a profound effect on the entire economic system of the country. This is particularly true when it is read in connection with the Glass-Steagall Banking Act."[10]

Dean set forth a list of sixteen negative effects he believed the Securities Act would precipitate, which included the inability to refinance short-term bank debt with corporate bonds; an increase in unemployment because of difficulties in raising capital; the breakup of companies because of the difficulties in complying with the disclosure requirements of registration for large, complex business enterprises; the potential that new and speculative businesses would be shut out of capital markets; and the potential that the cost of capital would increase for all borrowers as a result of the costs of complying with the act and exposure to liability thereunder.[11]

At the annual convention of the Financial Advertisers Association on September 12, 1933, held at New York's Waldorf Hotel, Arthur Dean and Allan M. Pope, president of First Boston Corporation, were among the presenters addressing the effects of the new federal financial legislation.[12] "Since the passage of the Securities Act of 1933, no long-term borrower, without exception, is willing to apply for registration with the Federal Trade Commission for authority to issue any loan which is proper for an investment broker to underwrite," Pope asserted. "No necessary refunding of maturing obligations can be accomplished. If this keeps up, great numbers of defaults and bankruptcies are bound to occur."[13] Pope also claimed that the separation of commercial and investment banking, as mandated by the Glass-Steagall Banking Act, further damaged the functioning of the capital markets. Dissolution of the banking affiliates, he said, "will eliminate a very large part of the distributing power of securities of the United States Government. It will eliminate a larger part of the underwriting of municipal securities in the country. The bank affiliate, properly organized and properly regulated, is far from being a danger to its parent institution, and has so definitely a place in the investment-banking field in this country that its forced elimination is fraught with serious consequences."

Arthur Dean presented a detailed description of sixteen amendments that he believed would greatly improve the Securities Act. "Amendments to the Act will undoubtedly have to be made," said Dean, and "industry and the investment bankers can do a most constructive thing by suggesting amendments which will really carry out the president's message, [while giving] the public the maximum measure of protection without at the same time hampering industry."

The continuous criticism of the new laws began to attract adherents to the deregulation movement beyond Wall Street and its allies. The flat-lining securities and lending markets were now a two-edged sword: a painful object lesson either for further legislation to prevent future collapses or for a moratorium on additional constraints on Wall Street until the financial markets recovered. The liability provisions of the Securities Act applicable to officers and directors of issuers were very unpopular throughout corporate America, which began to feel that it was being punished for Wall Street's sins. Richard Whitney had engaged some of the best public relations people money could buy to help him tailor a message that would tap into this anti-Washington sentiment that was slowly growing in chambers of commerce and other business associations in the country's heartland. The fall of 1933 was a time of preparation for Whitney—the promised bill for exchange regulation was already in the works, with Pecora doing the spadework.

That fall, the New York Yankees were giving traders and brokers on the Exchange little to cheer about. On October 1, the Yankees hosted the Boston Red Sox for the last game of the 1933 season. The game meant nothing in the standings: both teams had been eliminated from pennant contention, with the Yankees in second place—seven games back—and the Red Sox languishing in seventh place. The Washington Senators won the American League pennant but would go on to lose the World Series to the New York Giants in five games.

Babe Ruth's declining performance was a large contributing factor to the Yankees' failure to repeat as American League champions. His average slid to a still respectable .301, but from .341 the prior year. He hit seven fewer home runs (thirty-four) and drove in sixteen fewer runners (114).

Attendance for the Yankees in 1933, like for most teams, was disappointing, down to 728,014 from 962,148 the previous year. To increase attendance for the last game of the season, the Yankees announced that Ruth would be their starting pitcher. He hadn't pitched in more than three years and had pitched exactly one game in the past dozen years. Over 25,000 came out to watch the Babe on the mound. He shut out the Red Sox for five innings and belted his thirty-fourth home run of the season, eking out a six-to-five win. It was the last game Ruth would ever pitch.[14]

Two days after Ruth's last pitching outing, the Pecora Hearings resumed, with Clarence Dillon, the chairman of Dillon, Read & Co., taking the stand. Dillon, Read, the third most powerful investment bank in the country, had risen to prominence in the 1920s by serving the automobile industry and promoting investment trusts, an early version of the mutual fund. Dillon, Read had nearly as many of its partners serving in high government positions as J.P. Morgan & Co. Dillon, Read partner James Forrestal was secretary of the Navy and later secretary of defense under presidents Roosevelt and Truman. Dillon's son, G. Douglas Dillon, would serve as secretary of the Treasury under presidents Kennedy and Johnson, and Dillon himself served as assistant chairman of the War Industries Board during World War I under President Wilson. Despite his bank's white-shoe status, Clarence Dillon himself was a Polish Jew, born Clarence Lapowski to immigrant parents, Samuel and Bertha Lapowski, from Lomza, Poland. The family settled in Texas and legally changed the family name to Dillon in 1901. They sent their son north to be educated, first to Worcester Academy and then Harvard, where Clarence graduated in 1905.[15]

Pecora's interrogation of Dillon was very much a replay of his questioning of J.P. Morgan Jr. and Otto Kahn. There were certainly embarrassing revelations but nothing on an order of magnitude approaching the Mitchell testimony. Pecora tried, without much success, to imply something inherently untoward about investment trusts, principally by highlighting the separation of voting and investment control from economic interests inherent in investment trusts. As manager of two of the largest investment trusts, United States and Foreign Securities Corporation and United States and International Securities Corporation, Dillon, Read controlled more than $90,000,000 of capital, principally in the form of preferred stock, by means of a $5,100,000 investment in common stock, giving it 75 percent voting control. The rest of the common stock was sold as a "kicker" to facilitate sales of the preferred stock to the public. But as *Time* magazine reported, "[the] pyramidal set-up was no secret; the public which bought the preferred had had a chance to cash in on their bonus of common at prices that they probably never dreamed they would get. U.S. & Foreign had paid $11,000,000 in dividends on the publicly owned preferred and were still paying. U.S. & International paid preferred dividends until this year but there was no reason to believe that eventually they would not be resumed."[16]

Pecora was more effective in criticizing Dillon, Read's lax underwriting practices in South American bond offerings. Pecora revealed that $131,000,000 of Brazilian and Bolivian bonds underwritten by Dillon, Read were in default, noting that the firm had made $9,000,000 in underwriting fees on the offerings. One bond offering for the Republic of Brazil was intended to fund the electrification of a national railroad (which was never electrified), and another for the city of Rio de Janeiro was to fund an urban renewal project in a notorious Rio slum (which was never completed). Dillon, Read's underwriting mistakes, however, failed to provoke outrage.[17]

On October 13, the final day of his testimony, Clarence Dillon read a prepared statement into the record: "We have calculated that if one may have bought the entire amount of securities sponsored by Dillon, Read & Co. from January 1, 1929, to June 30, 1933, and had sold on the latter date all issues then in default at their then market prices, he would have received on his investment cash income averaging more than 4-⅛ percent per annum over the entire period and, in addition, would have had sufficient cash income to make up the entire capital loss on the sale of his defaulted securities."[18] Pecora was silenced by the incontrovertible truth of Dillon's numbers.

It had been seven months since the National City hearings, and the officials of the premier private investment banks investigated by Pecora had weathered his questioning—perhaps the worse for wear but still employed and none disgraced. Carter Glass had even complained about Pecora's rough handling of these witnesses.

The strong performance of Dillon and his partners before Pecora further emboldened Whitney. He was ready to risk taking an overtly combative position with Pecora and the Senate committee. By the end of September, an opportunity presented itself, and Whitney seized it.

On September 30, Pecora sent Whitney a questionnaire he wanted the New York Stock Exchange to distribute to its members regarding pool accounts of which Exchange members had knowledge and margin accounts of members and their customers—information, he suspected, that might prove embarrassing. Whitney balked. Pecora sought a meeting. Whitney delayed. Finally, two of Pecora's staff members met with Whitney and his attorney Roland Redmond. One of the investigators Pecora sent was journalist John T. Flynn, whom Whitney loathed. Whitney entered the meeting room and announced: "You gentlemen are making a great mistake. The Exchange is a perfect institution."[19] Whitney refused to distribute the questionnaire, despite it being requested by a congressional committee with subpoena power.

Whitney's increasingly aggressive stance could only be maintained if his core constituency, the Exchange membership, remained solidly behind him. It had to that point, and nearly all cheered his willingness to stand up to Washington. Morale was bolstered by his hitting back at Pecora. But a schism in the New York Stock Exchange membership—usually minor and well concealed from public observation—made Whitney's position more fragile than it appeared. By culture and practice, the specialists and dealers who traded for their own accounts had power and status on the Exchange outsized relative to their numbers as compared with the brokers, or "customers' men," who executed trades on behalf of others. The pool operators and the other stock manipulators were usually specialists and dealers. Their victims were principally the customers of the brokers. Accordingly, the brokers, a majority of the Exchange members in number, could be convinced to restrain Whitney if he went too far in resisting reforms that protected their customers.

One New York Stock Exchange member not happy with Whitney's new defiance was E.A. Pierce, a commission broker and founder of the firm that would become Merrill Lynch, Pierce, Fenner & Smith. Pierce thought Whitney's unwillingness to distribute the questionnaire was unreasonable and bad for the Exchange's public image. It convinced Pierce to become a back-channel conduit between the congressional committees and more moderate elements of the Exchange membership.[20]

In a letter dated October 15, Whitney informed Pecora that the Exchange would not require its members to respond to the questionnaire because of cost and confidentiality concerns: "Certain of the questions, particularly those referring to income of members of the Exchange and to the number of, and the debit balances in, margin accounts carried by them in 1929 and in 1933, would have required the members of the Exchange to furnish to you information which they have already given or are currently furnishing to the Department of Internal Revenue. I was advised by your associate that the records of the Treasury Department are available to you and it therefore seemed grossly unfair to compel the members of the Exchange to furnish the same information, almost duplicate in certain aspects, to two departments of the government. . . . We have always been willing to cooperate to the fullest possible degree in securing information for the Senate Committee. We have at very great expense furnished it with a vast amount of information. We have, however, always taken the position that information in regard to the particular and personal affairs of members of the Exchange should be sought directly from them and not indirectly through the Exchange."[21]

Whitney's decision to stonewall the questionnaire process left Pecora's overworked subcommittee staff with the task of subpoenaing and gathering the hundreds of questionnaires from members of the New York Stock Exchange and the other exchanges. It was Pecora, and not Whitney, who would incur the ire of the profit-challenged brokerage firms incurring the expense and inconvenience of compiling the data, estimated to be from $1,500 for smaller firms up to $30,000 for larger institutions.[22]

Pecora knew that any softening of sentiment for reform was very likely temporary given what would soon be disclosed in hearings into the activities of the next and last Wall Street bank in his sights, Chase National Bank, the world's second-largest bank. A "retail" bank like National City Bank, its biggest competitor, Chase accepted deposits from the general public, had publicly traded stock, had securities affiliates, and had a myriad of conflicts of interest. Also, like National City, its management had behaved appallingly and perhaps criminally in the pursuit of personal profit at the expense of the bank's public shareholders.

On October 17, Albert H. Wiggin, former chairman of the board of directors of Chase, appeared before the stock market practices subcommittee.[23] Wiggin had joined Chase in 1904 as its youngest vice president, becoming president in 1911 and chairman in 1915. He had presided over tremendous growth, with Chase becoming the second-largest bank in the world after its merger with the Rockefeller-controlled Equitable Trust Company in 1930. Following the merger, Wiggin was no longer the bank's largest shareholder, as the combined bank was controlled by the Rockefeller family, but he remained chairman of its governing board.

On the first day of testimony, Wiggin revealed that after his resignation in December 1932 he had been generously awarded a pension of $100,000 per year for life, despite the bank incurring $212,000,000 in losses the previous three years.[24] The following day, Pecora began questioning Wiggin on trading activities in Chase stock undertaken by the bank and its affiliates. Pecora revealed that Chase had traded almost $900,000,000 of its stock in recent years. Wiggin explained that the bank was trying to stabilize the market for its stock—unsuccessfully, it turned out—as the price rose from $575 per share in 1927 to $1,415 in 1929, only to collapse to $89 in 1933.[25] By the third day of questioning, it was disclosed by Wiggin that he and his family-controlled corporations had engaged in trading in Chase stock while the bank's securities affiliates were also trading the stock.[26] But while the bank had made a mere $159,000 profit on more than $860,000,000 of transactions during the period from 1928 to 1932, Wiggin and his family corporations had made a $10,425,000 profit (over $135,000,000 in today's dollars), more than sixty-five times as much as the bank made.[27] When asked by Pecora whether the huge volume of trades by the bank was a scheme to churn the market for Chase stock in order to enable Wiggin to personally profit from his trading activities, Wiggin replied arrogantly, "I think the market was a God-given market," which drew sneers from the senators, staff, and press.[28]

When Wiggin returned to the witness chair on October 31, he had become a publicly reviled symbol of duplicitous greed. But by day's end, he had convicted himself of corporate treachery on a colossal scale. Under questioning by Pecora, Wiggin admitted that between September 19, 1929, and December 11, 1929, in the midst of the Crash, he had engaged in massive short selling of his bank's stock, netting himself and his family corporations a profit in excess of $4,000,000 ($52,000,000 in today's dollars). This was at precisely the same time that Wiggin was a leading member of the "bankers' consortium," which was publicly proclaiming from The Corner at 23 Wall Street that the market had overreacted and that bank stocks were cheap. Chase National Bank itself was actively in the market buying back its stock to demonstrate confidence. All the while, Wiggin was selling Chase stock short—with some sales directly to Chase itself. Worse still, rather than using his own stock to cover these short sales, Wiggin borrowed money from the bank to purchase stock from the bank's securities affiliates to cover the short sales.[29]

Certainly many of the officers and directors of Chase were aware of Wiggin's self-dealing, but they too were compromised. Nine senior Chase officials were also directors of one or more of the Wiggin family corporations. And these officers and directors, at the time of Wiggin's retirement, had more than $1,000,000 in outstanding loans from the Wiggin family entities. When Pecora asked what prompted him to sell the bank stock, Wiggin replied, "I must have had some trend of thought at that time. I thought all bank stocks were too high and that Chase was in line with the other stocks." "If you thought Chase bank stock was too high," Pecora responded, "why did you permit the Chase Securities Corporation and its wholly owned subsidiary, the Metpotan Corporation, to go into these various pools to stabilize the market?" Wiggin said that it was Chase that handled those transactions, not him. By the end of his testimony, the storm of public outcry was so great that Wiggin renounced his $100,000-a-year pension, hoping to preempt legal action against him.[30]

During the Chase hearings, Pecora also exposed the curious details of a stock distribution of Sinclair Consolidated Oil Corporation by a pool organized by Harry F. Sinclair, the chairman of the board of Sinclair Consolidated Oil, and operated by Arthur W. Cutten, a prominent commodities speculator.

Harry Sinclair had earlier gained notoriety in 1922 in connection with the Teapot Dome Scandal. Warren Harding's secretary of the interior, Albert Fall, had leased the huge Teapot Dome Oil Field in Wyoming to Sinclair Consolidated Oil without competitive bidding and on terms very favorable to Sinclair. It was later revealed that Fall had received gifts from Sinclair and others benefiting from the transaction worth more than $5,000,000 in today's dollars. Sinclair received a six-month prison sentence in connection with the scandal and cover-up.[31] Despite his criminal misdeeds at the expense of the taxpayers, Sinclair, the ex-con, was welcomed back to Wall Street with open arms by Albert Wiggin.

Sinclair Consolidated Oil Corporation sold 1,130,000 new shares of stock at $30 per share to a group that included Cutten, Sinclair; Blair and Company; Chase Securities Corporation; and Sherman Corporation, one of the Wiggin family companies. During the next six months, Cutten, on behalf of the group, distributed the stock at prices between $35 and $45 per share, yielding a profit of more than $12,000,000. Harry Sinclair and Arthur Cutten each made a profit of over $2,600,000. Albert Wiggin, through Sherman Corporation, received $877,000. Chase Securities Corporation netted $1,755,000, and Blair and Company $2,932,000. Why would the Sinclair Consolidated Oil Corporation board of directors allow the selling group to profit by more than $12,000,000 on a $33,900,000 stock issuance? Possibly because Henry Sinclair, Elisha Walker (then the president of Blair and Company), and a representative of Chase Securities Corporation were all members of the board of directors of Sinclair Consolidated Oil.[32]

More curious, however, was a 2½ percent subparticipation profit interest in the pool (worth $300,000) granted by Blair and Company to a Mr. William S. Fitzpatrick, president of Prairie Oil and Gas Company. Mr. Fitzpatrick claimed that the grant of this subparticipation had been arranged by the Rockefellers, the controlling shareholders of Prairie Oil, as a bonus for his years of loyal service. The Rockefellers, however, denied this, claiming they knew nothing of the pool interest grant to Fitzpatrick. Elisha Walker offered another explanation. As Blair and Company was leading the syndicate to purchase Prairie, they made the payment to Fitzpatrick to secure his loyalty. And there was perhaps a further possible explanation. Sinclair Oil, it was later learned, had held negotiations for a merger with Prairie in early 1928, and the two companies had finally agreed to a merger that would be consummated in 1932. Perhaps Harry Sinclair thought a $300,000 payment to the president of an acquisition target might facilitate negotiations on more favorable terms.[33]

The merger of Prairie Oil and Gas Company with Sinclair Consolidated Oil Corporation in 1932 was effectuated on the basis of one share of Sinclair Consolidated Oil for one share of Prairie Oil. It was never disclosed to Prairie Oil stockholders that Fitzpatrick had received the $300,000 payment. Nor was it disclosed to stockholders that in February 1929 Fitzpatrick and other officers of Prairie Oil were secretly offered the right to exchange their shares of Prairie Oil for shares of Sinclair Consolidated Oil on the basis of five shares of Sinclair for each share of Prairie Oil. Fitzpatrick and the other insiders at Prairie Oil exchanged 20,000 shares in this secret, sweetheart deal.[34]

The Chase disclosures once again turned public opinion strongly against Wall Street. Whatever seeds of doubt Arthur Dean, Richard Whitney, and the other critics of federal legislation might have succeeded in planting were killed by Pecora's dissection of Wiggin and the other Chase witnesses. There was now no realistic hope that Roosevelt could be persuaded to settle for a mild exchange regulation bill.

In addition to his duties as chief counsel for the Senate subcommittee that fall, Pecora was sent on a purely political mission by President Roosevelt. Attempting to wrest control of New York City politics away from Tammany Hall, Roosevelt and Bronx political leader Edward Flynn formed the Recovery Party, running a slate of candidates in the 1933 citywide elections. Earlier that year Pecora had been courted by Tammany, but he rebuffed their request. He could not say no to the president, however. Pecora would campaign for Manhattan district attorney on weekends after his Senate business was completed. But the anti-Tammany vote was split between Pecora and the Republican candidate, resulting in a victory in November for Tammany. Pecora, however, with his sights now set on a career in national government, secretly confided that he was not overly disappointed by the loss—he even believed that the presidency might someday be within his reach. At a minimum, he now thought he had a marker on the president for performing the political favor.

In early October 1933, Roosevelt reengaged on the drafting of securities exchange legislation, asking his secretary of commerce, Daniel Roper, to produce a set of recommendations for a securities exchange bill. In March of 1933, after Samuel Untermyer prepared his draft bill, contemplating the postmaster general as market regulator, Roosevelt had deflected confrontation with Untermyer by assuring him that his proposal, though not ideal for securities offering legislation, would be considered as a basis for an exchange regulation bill, the third and final piece of Roosevelt's financial reform legislative package. Roper essentially ignored the Untermyer bill, given its obvious inadequacies, and established a committee to propose its own stock exchange legislation.[35]

To the relief of Whitney, the Committee on Stock Exchange Regulation, as Roper named it, well represented Wall Street interests. It was chaired by John Dickinson, the assistant secretary of commerce and a former Sullivan & Cromwell attorney, and also included Sullivan & Cromwell partner Arthur Dean and Henry T. Richardson, a conservative corporate attorney not sympathetic to stock exchange regulation. Representing the reform interests were

James Landis, then a newly appointed commissioner of the Federal Trade Commission, and Columbia University law professor and Roosevelt brain truster Adolf A. Berle. From the outset, the ideological split on the committee doomed any consensus, and Landis and Berle, knowing they were outvoted, were not going to lend their names to any watered-down compromise legislation simply to preserve harmony. Competing proposals were put forth by Landis, on behalf of the reformers, and by Richardson, on behalf of Wall Street interests.[36]

Early in November, Landis delivered to the committee his ultimatum regarding the minimum requirements for his support of a stock exchange bill. They included publicly filed periodic financial reports by listed companies; public reporting of stock transactions by officers, directors, and the listed companies themselves; regulation of specialists, brokers, and dealers; prohibition of pool operations, "wash sales" (selling a security to an affiliate to create the appearance of price movements or trading volume), and "matched orders" (placing buy-and-sell orders contemporaneously to also create such appearances); and regulation of the over-the-counter market.[37]

On November 16, at Dickinson's request, Richardson prepared his own draft legislation, which would establish an independent seven-member stock exchange commission appointed by the president; it was comprised of two members representing the general investing public, two members from a stock exchange or a commodity exchange, one member engaged in agriculture, one member representing business, and the president of the Federal Reserve Bank of New York, who would serve as chairman. The commission suggested by Richardson would have limited power, effectively restricted to approving the exchange rules and ensuring they were adhered to. "This bill is drawn," said Richardson, "on the theory that in so far as possible, each exchange will discipline its own members and conduct its own affairs."[38]

Landis had heard enough. Convinced that the Committee on Stock Exchange Regulation was stacked against meaningful reform, he effectively abandoned it and sought approval from President Roosevelt to draft his own securities exchange legislation separate from the Committee on Stock Exchange Regulation. Roosevelt gave Landis his blessing. The president then instructed Raymond Moley to reach out to Thomas Corcoran and Benjamin Cohen, asking that they assist in the preparation of securities exchange legislation outside the Department of Commerce process. Frankfurter's hot dogs were now back in action.[39]

Much of Roosevelt's time that fall was consumed by efforts to aid the ailing farmer by raising agricultural commodity prices. A risk of FDR's "try anything" pragmatism was that he might, quite literally, try anything, and relative to the farm income issue he had fallen under the sway of an oddball professor from the Cornell School of Agriculture named George F. Warren. Roosevelt's friend and sometime adviser, Henry J. Morgenthau Jr., was a student of Warren's; and through Morgenthau, Roosevelt was exposed to Warren's unorthodox theories of agricultural price movements. Warren's theory was that prices of farm products were tied directly to the price of gold, so all that was needed for crop prices to go up was for the price of gold, relative to the dollar, to increase. And now that Roosevelt had taken the dollar off the gold standard, all that had to be done was to buy gold in large quantities to raise its price, and, voilà, crop prices would rise. Roosevelt bought it. He decided to cause the Reconstruction Finance Corporation to buy gold in large quantities to raise its price.

Traditional economists thought the president had gone bonkers. Warren's half-baked theory mistook correlation for causation—of course, dollar inflation raised the price of gold, crops, and everything else. It didn't follow that buying gold would raise farm prices. Hard-money men were furious. The scheme wasn't likely to raise agricultural prices for very long, but it sure was inflationary. Glass was apoplectic. So too was Secretary Woodin's deputy, Dean Acheson, who resigned in protest. Roosevelt replaced him with Morgenthau.

Henry Morgenthau Jr. was a textbook example of what we today call a slacker. The son of a wealthy New York real estate developer, Morgenthau had all the advantages money could buy: a prep school education at Phillips Exeter Academy in New Hampshire, an opportunity for Ivy League education at Cornell University, frequent overseas travel, and political contacts. He dropped out of Cornell after a year of study in 1911 and failed at a number of jobs his father arranged for him.[40] In 1912, he decided he would become a farmer and went back to the agricultural school at Cornell. He dropped out again. Next he convinced his father to buy him a 1,000-acre farm in Dutchess County—Henry decided he wanted to be a Christmas tree farmer. It was a money-hemorrhaging disaster throughout the 1920s. He thought he might do better as editor of a farming magazine—the *American Agriculturalist*—it too lost a pile.[41]

What Morgenthau was unquestionably good at was cultivating Franklin Roosevelt. As luck would have it, his farm in Dutchess County was near Roosevelt's, and the two hit it off splendidly. He was an advance man on Roosevelt's 1928 campaign for governor and was appointed to an essentially ceremonial position as chairman of Roosevelt's Agricultural Advisory Commission (the commission did not exist by statute, had no state financing, and members served pro bono).[42] During the 1932 campaign, Morgenthau again served as a campaign advance man.[43] As a reward for his support, on May 27, 1933, President Roosevelt appointed his friend governor of the Farm Credit Administration.[44] Needless to say, grave doubts were expressed about Morgenthau's qualifications to be secretary of the Treasury of the United States.

His principal qualification was unquestioned: his caninelike loyalty to FDR. During his first year in office he pioneered using the IRS as a weapon of political dirty tricks, poring through the tax returns of prominent citizens to develop dossiers that might be used against them if they crossed the administration. When William Randolph Hearst gave an interview critical of the National Recovery Administration in early August 1934, Morgenthau went through not only Hearst's tax returns but also those of his mistress, Marion Davies. Foolish enough to record his crimes in his diary, Morgenthau wrote that he "found that there was plenty there; also plenty on Marion Davies. I told the President on Tuesday that we thought it would be better to proceed at once on Hearst's and Marion Davies' income tax before he attacked because if we started something after he attacked, he would say that we were doing it to revenge and spite. The President agreed."[45] Despite his ethics issues, inexperience, and his belief in the madcap monetary theories of Professor Warren, Morgenthau would turn out to be a fiscal moderate and a skillful financier of the government's debts.

Roosevelt went on national radio with a fireside chat, "On the Currency Situation," on October 22, to announce the gold-buying plan. The RFC would buy all the newly minted gold in the United States and, if necessary, buy it in world markets. For the next seven weeks, Roosevelt, Professor Warren, and Morgenthau would meet every morning for breakfast with the RFC's Jesse Jones and set the price of gold, at first just buying from the captive U.S. mine operators, but later in the free market in London. While gold prices certainly rose, to Roosevelt's great embarrassment, crop prices didn't. They fluctuated, seemingly unrelated to his binge buying. By the second week of December, Roosevelt quickly shelved the whole program. On January 30, 1934, Roosevelt signed the Gold Reserve Act, which returned the country to a modified gold standard, setting the nominal price at $35 per ounce—an inflationary 59 percent increase—but continuing to curtail convertibility of dollars into gold.

By early December, Corcoran, Landis, and Cohen had enlisted a young Federal Trade Commission attorney, I.N.P. Stokes, to assist in the drafting. Stokes was soon joined by Telford Taylor, a 1932 Harvard Law School graduate working at the Department of the Interior. (Taylor would later be best remembered for his service as chief counsel for the prosecution at the Nuremberg trials—his character is portrayed by Richard Widmark in *Judgment at Nuremberg*.)[46]

Meanwhile, the Wall Street attacks on the Securities Act of 1933 continued. At the annual convention of the Investment Bankers Association of America, Arthur Dean was the featured speaker. He encouraged the assembled bankers to speak to the press in detail about their objections to the Securities Act: "If investment bankers can convince the public that they are really anxious to get a workable law and are not yelping for modifications for selfish interests, public sentiment can be enlisted to support reasonable changes. The law obviously was not adequately considered by Congress before it was enacted, but in this connection it is fair to consider the position of the Congressmen. With Congressmen called up one day to pass laws affecting railroads and laws for public utilities the next, it is hardly surprising that no continued study of the securities bill was possible before it was enacted. Investment bankers must organize a forceful campaign to educate the public through the press."[47]

Frank M. Gordon, president of the Investment Bankers Association of America, issued a statement at the convention linking the Securities Act's chilling effects on capital raising with the continued high unemployment nationwide. "A reservoir of money that can be translated into jobs for millions of people is held back by the need for clarification of the liability sections of the Federal Securities Act," he said. "All over the United States, corporations are ready to undertake the necessary financing, but no corporation director in his senses is going to risk existing resources by putting his name on financing under a law that makes him personally liable for the next 10 years and adopts the un-American principle that he is to be judged guilty unless he can be proven innocent. It is time for some plain speaking. This law is a hindrance to national recovery. Personally, I do not believe that anyone ever intended to pass a law which makes a securities dealer who handles $10,000 worth of a $10,000,000 issue liable for the entire $10,000,000."[48]

All over Washington preparations were being made for the battle over an exchange regulation bill. There were the two competing administration-sanctioned bill-drafting teams—Roper's committee and the Corcoran, Landis, Cohen team. There was also a major private sector effort to propose a bill undertaken by the Twentieth Century Fund, a pioneer think tank organization founded by department store magnate and liberal philanthropist, Edward A. Filene. And watching all of these efforts, and planning his counter all the while, was Richard Whitney. There was no question which of the three Whitney favored—he kept in close contact with Roper's group. On December 4, Whitney met with the Committee on Stock Exchange Regulation chairman, John Dickinson, hopeful that his proposal for a new stock exchange commission dominated by business interests might be workable.[49]

Whitney was still girding for a public battle if the exchange legislation introduced by Roosevelt were to come from the Frankfurter-Filene contingents. Whitney was significantly strengthening the Exchange's publicity and lobbying capabilities. His efforts were leaked to *The New York Times* on December 15. Knowing that opposition to federal legislation would need to appear to be generated by Main Street and not Wall Street, Whitney issued an immediate denial: "My attention has been called to an article published in this morning's press to the effect that the New York Stock Exchange had approved an extensive publicity and advertising program for the alleged purpose of enlisting public support against Federal regulation of the Exchange. No such program has been approved or even considered. It is true that frequent misstatements in regard to the functions of the Exchange have disturbed many of its members and some of them submitted to the law committee of the Excha nge plans for publicity campaigns designed to inform the public of the facts regarding its operations. At a meeting of the law committee held yesterday morning, a plan for a series of talks over the radio of a historical nature or purely descriptive of the functions of the Exchange was submitted, but was not adopted or approved, though subject, of course, to further consideration."[50]

J.P. Morgan Jr.'s man at the New York Stock Exchange and the hero of Black Thursday, Richard Whitney placed the single most celebrated order in stock market history. But intervention by Morgan could not halt the Crash of 1929.

(BELOW) Election Night, 1932. Roosevelt awaits returns with his campaign manager, Democratic Party Chairman James A. Farley. It would be a rout—Roosevelt took 473 Electoral College votes to Hoover's 59. Contrary to later conventional wisdom, Roosevelt's election actually made the banking crisis worse.

Ferdinand Pecora (left) chatting with J.P. Morgan & Co. attorney John W. Davis of the Davis Polk & Wardwell firm. Pecora, an unknown former prosecutor in New York City, won the job of chief counsel to the Senate Stock Market Practices Subcommittee, and was catapulted to national fame with his disclosures of Wall Street avarice and unfair dealing.

National City Bank chairman Charles E. Mitchell (left, in white hat), and his lawyer after his acquittal on criminal tax evasion charges. "Sunshine Charlie," as he was derisively nicknamed after his cheery post-crash prognostications, was Pecora's first casualty after it was revealed that he used paper losses from a sham stock sale to his wife to avoid paying taxes in 1929.

Carter Glass of Virginia was an unlikely advocate for the big banks. Born in the antebellum South and with little formal education and no experience in finance, he sat on both the House and Senate Banking and Currency Committees and served as Secretary of the Treasury. He would become the single most important lawmaker in the history of American finance.

Raymond Moley (left, with Congressman Sam Rayburn) was Roosevelt's most trusted White House aide on financial matters during the early days of his administration. He was instrumental in the selection of William Woodin as Treasury Secretary, advocated for Joe Kennedy as Chairman of the SEC, and oversaw the drafting of the Emergency Banking Act, the Securities Act of 1933, and the Securities Exchange Act.

Roosevelt signs the Emergency Banking Act with Treasury Secretary Woodin looking on. It was the largest grant of peacetime power to a president over the US financial system. *The New York Times* headline read: "Roosevelt Gets Power of Dictator."

(BELOW) Roosevelt delivering his first "fireside chat," explaining his reasons for bailing out the nation's ailing banks.

Louisiana Senator Huey P. Long was a champion of alienated rural, small town Americans and a thorn in Roosevelt's side. Despite his demagoguery, he was considered a threat to challenge Roosevelt for the presidency in 1936.

Representative Henry Steagall of Alabama had been introducing deposit insurance legislation in Congress since 1923. Despite opposition from President Roosevelt and Senator Glass, Steagall prevailed and the FDIC was born.

William Woodin (center) was Roosevelt's second choice for Treasury Secretary and was thought by many to be an amiable lightweight. Here he smiles for the cameras with bales of the new currency that was his brainchild: the Federal Reserve Bank Notes

Harvard Law School Professor Felix Frankfurter was the intellectual godfather of the cadre of young lawyers staffing New Deal agencies. Despite his misgivings about Roosevelt, the President would frequently turn to him for advice. When the securities bill floundered, Frankfurter was called in to save the day.

As Chief Counsel to the 1913 Pujo Committee investigating the "money trust" and interrogator of J.P. Morgan Sr., Samuel Untermyer was the Pecora of his day.

Representative Sam Rayburn of Texas, a staunch Roosevelt ally and Chairman of the House Committee on Interstate and Foreign Commerce, shepherded both the Securities Act of 1933 and the Securities Exchange Act through the House.

President Roosevelt signs the Glass-Steagall Banking Act of 1933 with Carter Glass (third from left), Comptroller of the Currency J.F.T. O'Connor (to Glass's left), Henry Steagall (to Roosevelt's immediate left), and others looking on.

Arthur Dean was John Foster Dulles's junior partner at Sullivan & Cromwell in the battle against the Securities Act, but his methodical, deliberate approach impressed even the act's authors. He went on to an illustrious career in public service. He is pictured here in Korea, after negotiating an end to the Korean War.

(BELOW) Middleton Beaman (far right, back row) receiving an honorary degree from Columbia University in 1949. Beaman was the first legislative counsel for the House of Representatives in 1916. Sam Rayburn insisted that the exacting, methodical Beaman oversee revisions to the securities bill.

Thomas "Tommy the Cork" Corcoran was Frankfurter's most beloved protégé. Frankfurter would choose Corcoran to lead the team attempting to salvage Roosevelt's securities legislation. Together with James Landis and Benjamin Cohen, they were nicknamed "Frankfurter's Hot Dogs" by the press.

Future Secretary of State John Foster Dulles as a young partner at Sullivan & Cromwell. He would lead the law firm to unparalleled influence both on Wall Street and in Washington, but his lobbying against the Securities Act of 1933 was a rare miscue in Dulles's sterling career.

Senator Key Pittman (right) with Congressman Samuel McReynolds (left), and Secretary of State Cordell Hull setting sail from New York to England for the London Economic Conference. The conference was a disaster and Pittman, chairman of the Senate Foreign Relations Committee, nearly caused several international incidents with his drunkenness, gunplay, and generally obnoxious behavior.

J.P. Morgan Jr.'s popularity increased after testifying at the Pecora thanks to Lya Graf (pictured on Morgan's knee), a performer with the Ringling Brothers, Barnum & Bailey Circus. When she was placed on his lap by a press agent, Morgan's kind, good-natured response softened his public image. Ms. Graf would return to her native Germany where her life met a tragic, violent end at the Auschwitz extermination camp.

Senator Duncan Fletcher of Florida, chairman of the Senate Committee on Banking and Currency, pictured here with J.P. Morgan Jr. after his testimony in the Pecora hearings. In 1933, Fletcher was tasked with oversight of the hearings, as well as the Glass-Steagall Banking Act and the Securities Act. But his most challenging task was managing the personalities in his own caucus.

Pool operators Bernard "Sell 'em Ben" Smith (center) and his sidekick Thomas Bragg (right) chatting with Carter Glass in April 1932 during early hearings of stock market practices subcommittee. When Pecora came calling for them, Bragg left the country for "vacation" in Hawaii and Smith ended up in Australia.

Arthur Krock, *New York Times* bureau chief and dean of the White House correspondents was initially Joe Kennedy's only ally in the press. The two men would become close friends, with critics alleging that Krock effectively functioned as Kennedy's in-house public relations man.

Press Baron William Randolph Hearst. Hearst was the stumbling block to FDR's nomination at the 1932 Democratic Convention in Chicago, controlling the California and Texas delegations. When FDR's men desperately tried getting through to Hearst, he refused—until Joe Kennedy intervened and convinced him to back Roosevelt.

Richard Whitney testifies before the Senate Committee on Banking and Currency in 1934 in opposition to the Fletcher-Rayburn securities exchange bill. Whitney mounted the most sophisticated lobbying effort Congress had ever seen against the bill. He failed in preventing federal regulation but succeeded in moderating many of its provisions.

Joe Kennedy (seated, middle) was FDR's choice for SEC chairman, but Ferdinand Pecora (seated, left) challenged Kennedy for the top job, incredulous that the president preferred someone who months earlier Pecora investigated for stock manipulation. The New Deal left agreed, but it would turn out to be Roosevelt's best appointment of the New Deal.

Joe Kennedy worked tirelessly to rebrand himself from upstart market plunger to elder statesman of Wall Street. He worked the press equally hard to cultivate his image as a dedicated public servant.

Firebrand Wall Street critic John T. Flynn was a former investigator for Pecora who had become Kennedy's most prominent critic in the press. But Flynn would later acknowledge being wrong about Kennedy, praising his administration of the SEC.

Michael J. Meehan (standing, right) was the first "big fish" Kennedy's SEC went after. In 1928, Meehan had operated the most spectacular pool in history, making over $200,000,000 (in today's dollars) in four days trading RCA shares. At Kennedy's urging, the SEC's general counsel, John Bums (seated, left), was ruthless in pursuing Meehan over suspicious stock trades in 1935.

Babe Ruth with the Boston Braves, shaking hands with Yankees owner and general manager Col. Jacob Ruppert at the Polo Grounds on Opening Day 1935. Babe's decline during the Depression from his super-human home run production to a broken down curiosity making less than half his peak salary, resonated with an America also down on its luck.

Whitney was also ever-vigilant to enforce strict discipline among the Exchange membership. In early December, Henry Goldman Jr., whose father had been a founding partner of Goldman, Sachs & Co., wrote a letter to Richard Whitney suggesting reforms in New York Stock Exchange practices. He sent a similar letter to the Senate Committee on Banking and Currency. For years, Henry Goldman Jr. had been the sole specialist in three stocks: Celotex, Ohio Oil, and United Piece Dye Works. After word of the Goldman letter reached the Exchange leadership, four members sprang forward announcing themselves to be specialists in the three stocks previously serviced only by Goldman. It had long been an unwritten rule of the Exchange that members didn't horn in on each other's business, but Whitney was enraged by Goldman's disloyalty. Other Exchange members followed the lead and threw their business to the new specialists, with Goldman losing a substantial part of his business in the process. Richard Whitney was taking no prisoners.[51]

December also witnessed a brief break in the "capital strike." While to date about $100,000,000 of securities had been registered with the Federal Trade Commission under the Securities Act, most of the issues had been Repeal stocks, investment trusts, and a few mining and industrial issues. No old-line company had registered under the Securities Act until Mathieson Alkali Works, then the world's largest maker of chlorine, filed to register $7,000,000 of new common stock in mid-December, to be underwritten by Hayden, Stone & Co. Conservative *Time* magazine, partially owned by a number of J.P. Morgan & Co. partners, commented that "Mathieson will not know whether its plunge was fatal until after the stock has been issued and shyster lawyers have had an opportunity to start nuisance suits."[52]

On New Year's Eve 1933, the Twentieth Century Fund announced that it was nearing completion of its survey of securities markets and would soon be publishing a report containing "concrete, practicable, and constructive recommendations for the elimination or restriction of abuses."[53] The announcement was likely motivated by a fear that Roosevelt might soon present a bill to Congress before their final report was issued. "In the case of certain particularly important subjects," the announcement said, "the staff has conducted extended original research using hitherto unavailable statistics as well as the existing general survey of information."[54]

In January 1934, while Whitney and the rest of Wall Street anxiously awaited an exchange regulation bill from Roosevelt, Babe Ruth signed a contract with the New York Yankees for the 1934 season. He was to be paid $35,000—$17,000 less than he'd been paid for the 1933 season and less than half of the $80,000 he'd been paid in 1930 and 1931—but he was still the highest paid player in baseball.[55] In Ruth's decline was a metaphor for the end of the era he so perfectly embodied—the Roaring '20s, the Jazz Age, a time when great fortunes were made virtually overnight on Wall Street, and great celebrations of good fortune were carried on all night in the speakeasies with smuggled booze and flapper girls, with corrupt police looking the other way and New York Mayor Jimmy Walker joining in on the fun. The larger-than-life Babe, the onetime sensitive, vulnerable Baltimore orphan who now swatted home runs by day and led the carousing at night, had won America's heart. But the party was over. And like the country, Babe Ruth was paying the price.

On January 23, 1934, Commerce Secretary Roper submitted to Roosevelt the final report of the Committee on Stock Exchange Regulation. It recommended that all securities exchanges obtain a license from the federal government to operate. And, that a federal stock exchange authority, composed of at least three members, including one representative of the exchanges, be established, with broad discretionary powers to adopt rules and regulations to revoke or suspend an exchange's license, fine an exchange, or require a change in its governing personnel. The report recommended that the form and content of exchange rules governing such matters as pools, margin trading, specialists, short selling, listing requirements, reports, and accounting not be set forth in detail in legislation, but be prescribed by the authority. The report also proposed that the authority would engage in the collection of statistics upon which it would base its rules and regulations. And it also identified a number of powers that the authority should not exercise, including not requiring the licensing of individual brokers and not regulating the over-the-counter market.[56]

The same day Roper submitted his report to the White House, a draft of the Corcoran, Landis, and Cohen bill was delivered to Senator Duncan Fletcher and Ferdinand Pecora.

Once again, Roosevelt would cleverly sidestep the unpleasant task of rejecting a legislative proposal solicited by him. Rather than telling Roper his proposal was unacceptable, he punted it over to Congress, where Pecora and the Senate Committee on Banking and Currency would obviously take the lead. Yet again, Roosevelt would keep his options open as long as possible.

On January 25, President Roosevelt forwarded Roper's report to Senator Fletcher and Representative Sam Rayburn to "assist them" in developing the proposed legislation. However, the White House made clear in a public statement that it was not endorsing the report's recommendations. "In transmitting these reports to the committees," a White House press release stated, "the president called especial attention to the fact that the reports were submitted for the inspection and consideration of the committees and were not intended as recommendations either to the committees or to the Congress."[57]

Fletcher and Pecora were shocked by the lack of teeth in Roper's proposed legislation. After reviewing the report, Corcoran, Landis, and Cohen, in consultation with Pecora, took a harder line in their draft bill to compensate for those compromises they thought would be required when negotiating with supporters of Roper's approach. In addition, Fletcher wanted to introduce the Corcoran bill as soon as possible, hoping to prevent Roper's recommendations from gaining traction.[58]

A week after the Roper report was delivered, Fletcher met with the press to discuss timing of the legislation. "We will begin immediately the drafting of stock exchange legislation," said Fletcher, "and we will proceed with all speed possible so as to hasten the beginning of the final inquiry into the stock exchange phase of the problems involved in these hearings. Whether the legislation will follow along the lines suggested in the report of the President's committee, which was filed with the Committee last week, is a question for the Committee to decide."[59]

Richard Whitney was angling for a delay. In a meeting with Ferdinand Pecora on January 29, Whitney proposed a series of conferences at which stock exchange reform would be debated. The Senate Banking and Currency Committee immediately rejected Whitney's delaying tactic, indicating that it would decide the issue in public hearings with specific legislation under consideration. Pecora also suggested that the draft legislation the Senate committee was preparing would recommend that exchange members be required to declare that they were either dealers (dealing for their own accounts) or brokers (dealing for customers). But they could not be both. He told reporters that answers to his questionnaire demonstrated that the practice of acting in both roles was widespread and resulted in broker-dealers taking advantage of their clients.[60]

Pecora went to New York on February 3 to advocate for a tough exchange bill. At the annual Real Estate Board of New York dinner at the Hotel

Commodore in Manhattan Pecora was one of the two keynote speakers (the other was Fiorello La Guardia, the newly sworn in forty-ninth mayor of New York). Pecora devoted his entire speech to the stock exchange legislation. "The investigation has now reached the stage where it is expected to produce one of its most important results—the bringing of the New York Stock Exchange and all other security markets under the control or regulation of the people of the United States," Pecora stated. "The New York Stock Exchange for more than a century has opposed and defied any form of public regulation or control. How that control will be exercised and how far it will go is, of course, important, but of greater importance is the fact that the government, in my opinion, will for the first time assert its authority over this powerful institution. No city, no state, can deal with the New York Stock Exchange. The State of New York has frequently been criticized for not regulating the New York Stock Exchange. If New York State were to attempt it, the Exchange would threaten to move to New Jersey; and if New Jersey attempted to do anything about it, the Exchange would move to Delaware; and if Delaware tried to deal with it, it would move to Canada or perhaps to Mexico. Only the United States Government can reach it, and this the United States Government is undoubtedly prepared to do."[61]

Pecora's speech was met with polite applause, mixed with boos.[62]

On Wednesday, February 7, 1934, a conference was held at the White House to brief the president on the terms of the securities exchange bill that would be introduced to the House and Senate that Friday. Meeting with the president were Senator Fletcher, Representative Rayburn, Secretary Roper, FTC Commissioner Landis, and Ferdinand Pecora. At the meeting, Roosevelt expressed a desire for speedy passage of a bill. "We are going right ahead with this legislation," Senator Fletcher declared, "and I will probably have an explanatory statement of its principal provisions ready for publication in the next day or two."[63]

The following day, Edward A. Filene forwarded to President Roosevelt the specific recommendations prepared by the Twentieth Century Fund. Filene's recommendations centered on a federal incorporation statute, pursuant to which all corporations engaged in interstate commerce would be required to be chartered by the federal government. That statute would set forth minimum standards of accounting and reporting and require public disclosure by

officers and directors of transactions in company securities. Filene also proposed licensing securities exchanges, brokers, dealers, and investment advisers under federal statute. Filene's proposed law would require specialists to
be either dealers or brokers, but they could not be both, and would prevent a
broker from trading for his own account. The proposed law would also enact
limitations on the size of short positions and require weekly public disclosures of all short positions. Filene also proposed an "intrinsic value"–based
limitation on margin loans. They would be limited to an amount not exceeding twice the aggregate projected net income per share of stock pledged for
the next five years. And in no event would a margin loan exceed 60 percent of
the current market value of the stock.[64] Filene's proposal, however, was delivered too late to serve as the basis for the legislation about to be introduced.

As planned, Senator Fletcher and Representative Rayburn introduced the
securities exchange bill drafted by Corcoran, Landis, and Cohen in the Senate and House of Representatives on Friday, February 9.[65] Concurrent with the
introduction of the bill, President Roosevelt delivered a message to Congress
urging exchange regulation legislation but stopping short of endorsing the bill:

> "In my message to you last March proposing legislation for federal su-
> pervision of national traffic in investment securities I said, 'This is but one
> step in our broad purpose of protecting investors and depositors. It should
> be followed by legislation relating to the better supervision of the purchase
> and sale of all property dealt with on exchanges.'
>
> "This Congress has performed a useful service in regulating the invest-
> ment business on the part of financial houses and in protecting the investing
> public in its acquisition of securities.
>
> "There remains the fact, however, that outside the field of legitimate in-
> vestment, naked speculation has been made far too alluring and far too easy
> for those who could and for those who could not afford to gamble.
>
> "Such speculation has run the scale from the individual who has risked
> his pay envelope or his meager savings on a margin transaction involving
> stocks whose true value he was wholly unfamiliar, to the pool of individuals
> or corporations with large resources, often not their own, which sought by

manipulation to raise or depress market quotations far out of line with reason, all of this resulting in loss to the average investor, who is of necessity personally uninformed.

"The exchanges in many parts of the country which deal in securities and commodities conduct, of course, a national business because their customers live in every part of the country. The managers of these exchanges have, it is true, often taken steps to correct certain obvious abuses. We must be certain that abuses are eliminated and to this end a broad policy of national regulation is required.

"It is my belief that exchanges for dealing in securities and commodities are necessary and of definite value to our commercial and agricultural life. Nevertheless, it should be our national policy to restrict, as far as possible, the use of these exchanges for merely speculative operations.

"I therefore recommend to the Congress the enactment of legislation providing for the regulation by the Federal Government of the operations of exchanges for dealing in securities and commodities for the protection of investors, for the safeguarding of values, and so far as it may be possible, for the elimination of unnecessary, unwise, and destructive speculation."[66]

The bill ran fifty pages long, covering a wide range of market activities going well beyond securities exchanges. It required all securities exchanges to register with the FTC; regulated margin loans; prohibited manipulative trading practices; regulated short sales; prohibited all exchange members from trading for their own account or acting as an underwriter; prohibited brokers from also acting as dealers; required the registration of all securities listed on a securities exchange; required issuers of listed securities to file periodic reports; regulated proxy solicitations; enabled the FTC to regulate the over-the-counter market and trading by U.S. persons of securities of U.S. issuers on foreign exchanges; regulated insider trading; provided for mandatory record-keeping requirements by exchanges, their investors, and brokers; and provided for the ability to criminally prosecute individuals for violating of the act.[67]

The FTC would determine the details of the registration statement for exchanges, but the bill mandated that it at a minimum contain an undertaking requiring the exchange and its members and issuers of securities listed thereon to comply with the act and the rules and regulations promulgated by the FTC thereunder; copies of the exchange's constitution, articles of incorporation, by-laws, rules, and related instruments; data regarding membership; and an undertaking to furnish the FTC with amendments and updates to the foregoing documentation. The bill also provided that no registration would be granted unless the rules of the exchange provided for the expulsion and suspension of a member for conduct inconsistent with just and equitable principles of trade, including violations of the act or any rule or regulation promulgated by the FTC thereunder.[68]

The margin provisions would make it unlawful for any member of an exchange or any person transacting securities business through any member of an exchange to extend or maintain credit on securities not registered on a national securities exchange. In addition, it would be unlawful for any member to extend, maintain, or arrange credit on any securities registered on a national securities exchange in an amount exceeding 80 percent of the lowest price at which such securities sold during the preceding three years or 40 percent of the current market price. The FTC was given the power to lower these loan values for any period of time or in respect of any specified class of securities.[69]

Exchange members and those transacting securities business through exchange members were to be prohibited from borrowing on securities other than through a member of the Federal Reserve System. They would also be prohibited from incurring aggregate indebtedness in an amount exceeding ten times their net current assets. Brokers were to be prohibited from using capital to finance the carrying of securities for their own accounts. Hypothecation of a customer's securities in an amount exceeding the debt of that customer would also prohibited, and commingling customer securities with those of others (or lending a customer's securities to others without the written consent of that customer) was to be made unlawful.[70]

A number of manipulative trading practices were to be made unlawful: wash sales; matched orders; "churning" (placing buy and/or sell orders to create the appearance of public interest in a stock); creating rumors of a pool or other unusual trading activity in a stock; disseminating false or misleading market rumors regarding a security; paying another person to disseminate rumors regarding a security; engaging in transactions to peg, fix, or stabilize the price of a security; "cornering" a security by acquiring substantial control of the public float of a security; trading any put, call, straddle, or other option or similar transaction on an exchange.[71] The bill also made it unlawful for any person to effect a short sale or a stop-loss order of securities except in accordance with the rules and regulations promulgated by the FTC.[72]

The bill provided for the segregation of the functions of brokers, specialists, and dealers. It made it unlawful for any member of an exchange or any broker to act as a dealer in or underwriter of securities, whether or not registered on any national securities exchange. It also made it unlawful for any specialist to effect transactions in securities except on fixed-price orders or to disclose any information about the specialist's order book unless that information was available to all members of the exchange.[73]

Securities listed on a securities exchange would be required to be registered with the FTC. The information required in the registration statement was substantially similar to the requirements provided for in the Securities Act of 1933.[74] The bill also provided for periodic reports of issuers to be filed with the FTC and the relevant exchanges. Issuers would be required to file annual and quarterly reports with a balance sheet and income statement certified by an independent public accountant and monthly reports showing sales and gross income.[75]

Any person soliciting proxies would be required to file with the FTC a proxy statement disclosing the purpose of the solicitation, the persons holding the proxy and their relationship to the security subject to the solicitation, and the names and addresses of the persons being solicited. It was also made unlawful for any exchange member or broker to give a proxy on a customer's security without the written authorization of the customer.[76]

The bill would give the FTC authority to prescribe rules and regulations governing trading in the over-the-counter market. Officers and directors of an issuer with a security registered on a national securities exchange would be required to file forms with the FTC disclosing all securities of the issuer owned by them. It also would make it unlawful for any such person to sell short securities of its related issuer and for any insider to disclose confidential information affecting a registered security not necessary or proper to be disclosed as part of the insider's corporate duties. Any profit made by a tippee in transactions in such securities within six months of receipt of the information was required to be paid over to the issuer.[77]

Every national securities exchange, every member thereof, and every broker and dealer would be required to preserve accurate records in accordance with rules and regulations prescribed by the FTC.[78] In addition, any person making a statement in any document or report filed with the FTC pursuant to the act that was false or misleading and sufficiently important to influence the judgment of an average investor would be liable to those who did not know the statement was false or misleading and who purchased or sold a security affected by the statement. Any person who willfully violated the act or any rule or regulation made thereunder would be guilty of a crime and subject to a fine of up to $25,000 and up to ten years' imprisonment and, in the case of an exchange, a fine of up to $500,000.[79]

Senator Fletcher issued a lengthy public statement following the bill's introduction. "Honest brokers have nothing to fear from the bill," he said. "Indeed, they are likely to gain by the cleaning out process that will follow and by the elimination of unsavory practices and perhaps by the elimination also of those who have engaged in such practices." Fletcher also laid down a challenge directly to Whitney: "Economic bosses can no longer seek in the name of private enterprise to misuse positions of power and trust. The provisions of the bill on this subject strike the first blow at a system that has given a small and willful group of men control over the properties and savings of the great mass of investors. The stock exchanges will be given opportunity to enforce the standards of conduct laid down in this legislation and such other standards consistent with it as they may deem proper. But if the exchanges fail in the future as they have failed in the past to maintain proper standards, the penalties of the criminal law and effective civil liabilities attach in order to ensure that the standards laid down by the bill will be living standards and not a mere dead letter of the law. When this legislation goes into effect, privileged insiders who unjustly got money from the general public can be compelled to restore that money to those who lost it. The financial market places of this country will be cleansed and made safe for honest investors."[80]

Both proponents and opponents of the bill agreed that a battle over the legislation would be hard fought. *The New York Times* called the Fletcher-Rayburn bill "one of the most drastic regulatory measures ever submitted to

Congress."[81] The White House reiterated its position that the bill was strictly a congressional measure and had neither the approval nor disapproval of the president. On February 11, a worried Thomas Corcoran telegraphed Felix Frankfurter in Oxford, England, urging him to lobby the president to publicly come out in favor of the Fletcher-Rayburn bill and against Roper's proposal to create a Wall Street–dominated securities exchange commission: "Exchange bill well received by press but indications terrific fight in which skipper's position doubtful to remove exchanges from administrative jurisdiction of Federal Trade Commission per bill to new Commission dominated by exchange members . . . urge all possible help this point particularly soon as possible and the suggestion to skipper of Ben for Federal Trade Commission."[82]

Richard Whitney wasted no time implementing his well-rehearsed battle plan. The Fletcher-Rayburn bill was as close to a worst-case scenario as Whitney thought possible. On February 11, he held a special meeting of the governing committee of the New York Stock Exchange, also inviting the heads of the thirty most important brokerage houses, to unveil his plan for opposing the Fletcher-Rayburn bill.[83] There were constituencies beyond Wall Street that would find parts of the bill objectionable; mobilizing Main Street opposition would be possible. Most obviously, securities registration and periodic reporting requirements would impose a burden and expense on all listed companies nationwide. Same for the restrictions on insider stock transactions. The bill's margin provisions affected banks, brokers, and investors everywhere, but hit hardest would be those accounts with a larger proportion of unlisted securities, which were overrepresented in the western regions of the United States. The provisions segregating brokers from dealers and underwriters disproportionately affected small-town America, where the local brokerage office often performed all three functions, with barely enough profit in the Depression years to keep the lights on.

Whitney had a four-prong plan of attack against the Fletcher-Rayburn bill. First, he would send letters mobilizing all 1,375 New York Stock Exchange members, warning them of the dangers the legislation posed to business. Those members, together with their affiliates, had offices in all forty-eight states and in nearly every congressional district. Second, similar letters would be sent by Whitney to executives of eighty large companies with securities listed on the exchange. Third, in order to demonstrate the effectiveness of self-regulation, the governing board immediately adopted new rules—prohibiting members and their firms from participating in stock pools organized or used intentionally for the purpose of unfairly influencing the market price of any security; prohibiting members acting as a specialist from acquiring or granting an option on a stock they were acting as a specialist for; and preventing any specialist from disclosing information in his order book to unauthorized persons. Fourth, Whitney would take the counteroffensive to Washington by testifying against the bill in front of both the House and Senate committees and personally organizing the lobbying effort there on behalf of other exchanges, brokerage firms, and corporations opposing the bill.[84]

At a press conference nominally called to announce the new rules (but actually the opening public salvo of the war against the Fletcher-Rayburn bill), Whitney said: "The three rules have been adopted as a result of a careful study by officials of the Exchange which has extended over many months. In August of last year, the Exchange called upon all members to report all pools and options in which they were interested or of which they had knowledge. As a result of the examination of these records it was felt that a specific rule should be adopted prohibiting pool and option transactions which are intended or actually used to influence unfairly the course of prices. The final drafts of those rules were completed last week and submitted to the governing committee on Thursday, February 8, but action was deferred until today so as to allow the Governing Committee ample opportunity to consider them."[85]

When asked about the Fletcher-Rayburn bill, Whitney argued that "in many respects it deals with matters which are already covered by the rules of the New York Stock Exchange which is conclusive evidence that the purpose of the Exchange and the purposes sought to be achieved by the bill are in many respects identical."[86]

Continuing on this theme, Whitney said: "In general, the bill is aimed at eliminating from the stock market manipulative practices which might unfairly influence the course of prices. It attempts also to prevent excessive speculation. For many years the Exchange by changing its rules, has sought to accomplish the same result. For instance, we have rules prohibiting fictitious transactions and 'wash' sales and also matched orders. The rule adopted today in regard to the manipulative operations strengthens the provision of the constitution which prohibits members participating in transactions intended to bring about a condition in which prices would not fairly reflect market values. The dissemination of rumors by members of the Exchange has long been forbidden and we have considered the issuance of false or misleading statements to induce the purchase or sale of securities as nothing short of fraud. We have likewise forbidden all payments for the purpose of securing inspired publicity and have not only prohibited corners but have vested in the Governing Committee of the Exchange power to fix the price at which contracts affected by a corner should be liquidated. While we have not prohibited options, except when granted to or acquired by a specialist, we have for many years prohibited members trading in 'puts' and 'calls' which are the commonest form of options."[87]

Whitney then outlined his argument against the proposed legislation: "In many respects, I think the bill contains rigid and unworkable provisions which will impair the liquidity of American securities. The margin requirements contained in Section 6 fix certain mechanical minimums which, depending upon the course of prices, will allow brokers to carry securities at anywhere between a 25 percent and a 150 percent margin. The lower of these figures is actually less than the margin now required as a minimum by the Exchange. The 150 percent provision is, obviously, excessive and might force the liquidation of many accounts. The worst feature, however, of these rigid margin requirements is that they are made mandatory upon our entire banking system in respect of loans made to persons who have purchased listed securities within thirty days.[88]

"Another bad feature," Whitney continued, "is the prohibition against brokers advancing credit against securities other than those listed on an exchange. This will deprive people owning unlisted securities of the right to use them as the basis of credit in brokerage accounts. While the securities of our largest and most important companies are listed on exchanges, there are literally hundreds of thousands of sound small companies operating in the United States which are not listed on an exchange. By arbitrarily treating all of the securities of small local enterprises as being worthless in brokerage accounts, a great hardship will be imposed upon the vast number of persons who have invested in these securities."[89]

Whitney went on to criticize the segregation of brokers and dealers: "The flat prohibition against a member of an exchange buying or selling securities as a dealer is a harsh rule which will operate particularly against members doing business in our small financial centers. It will also destroy the odd-lot business which now affords the only market to investors holding less than a hundred shares of stock."[90]

Next, Whitney spoke to the listing and periodic reporting requirements: "Probably the worst features of the bill are those which purport to regulate corporations and corporate practices by imposing conditions upon the listing of securities upon exchanges. The bill requires every corporation listed on an exchange to register its securities with the Federal Trade Commission. The minimum requirements set forth in the bill are so burdensome that corporations may be unwilling to keep their securities listed on any exchange. Furthermore, the Federal Trade Commission is given unlimited power to require additional information in regard to corporate affairs which, like all other reports or information furnished to the Commission, must be made available to the public. These powers are so extensive that the Federal Trade Commission might, in effect, control the management of every listed company and, if these powers should be used unwisely, might result in the publication of confidential statistics which would be destructive of American industry, because it would furnish vital information to foreign competitors. The provisions affecting corporations and likewise the responsibilities of officers, directors and stockholders have no proper place in a bill regulating stock exchanges. Regulations of this character belong in a national corporation law where they can be made applicable not only to companies which are listed upon Exchanges, but all American companies which are publicly owned and are engaged in interstate commerce or the use of United States mails. The inclusion of these provisions in the stock exchange bill results in making them applicable only to securities dealt in on exchanges. Corporations which are not listed upon exchanges will not be subject to this form of Federal supervision, nor will the directors, officers or stockholders of such unlisted companies be subject to the very severe criminal and unheard of civil penalties contained in the bill. This fact will furnish a potent reason why large and important companies will prefer to have their securities dealt in 'over the counter' rather than on exchanges."[91]

The following day, Whitney sent a letter to members of the New York Stock Exchange outlining the concerns he presented at the press conference. "This bill is the most important legislation affecting the stock exchange and its listed corporations which has ever been introduced in Congress," Whitney wrote. "It contains sweeping and drastic provisions which affect seriously the business of all members and which may have very disastrous consequences to the stock market resulting in great prejudice to the interests of investors throughout the country."[92]

The brokerage houses that met with the governing committee of the Exchange also sent telegrams to their branch offices that day. "This proposed National Securities Act is a matter of grave concern to every owner of real estate or securities, to all officials of corporations or banks and to every policy holder. It is no exaggeration to say that very few of your friends and clients can afford to disregard this new menace to national recovery. We are mailing you a copy of the bill. Please study it. The more you study it, the worse it seems. Please discuss it with others and urge them to acquaint themselves with some of these vicious provisions. I am confident that if the country understands the bill, an overwhelming protest will arise."[93]

On February 15, Whitney also sent a letter to the presidents of the eighty large listed companies warning them of the bill. "These powers are so extensive," Whitney said, "that the Federal Trade Commission might dominate and actually control the management of each listed corporation. I have taken the liberty of addressing you because the prevalent belief that the bill applies only to stock exchanges and dealers in securities has led many people to overlook the provisions which it contains directly affecting corporations and subjecting them to the control of the Federal Trade Commission." Whitney had hundreds of copies of the bill printed and distributed, along with a copy of his critical letter, encouraging members to give copies to customers.[94]

To establish a physical presence in Washington, Whitney rented a town house in Georgetown (nicknamed the "Wall Street Embassy") and decamped his general staff there for the duration of the Securities Exchange Act legislative battle. Whitney's careful planning in advance of the bill, however, came up short on one critical point: maintaining the loyalty of the exchange's broker members. The Fletcher-Rayburn bill drove a wedge in between their interests and those of the specialists and dealers. Without informing Whitney, the brokers sent their own man to Washington, E.A. Pierce. Pierce secretly established a "shadow" command center at the Carlton Hotel and had already reached out to Sam Rayburn to moderate the bill behind the scenes away from the center of the action in the Senate. When Whitney found out about this disloyalty, he became enraged, instructing his attorney Roland Redmond to call Pierce—at 3:00 a.m.—to let him know there would be retribution. But known only to Whitney and Pierce, there were ancillary dealings between the two men that made it most unlikely that Whitney would take any acts of vengeance against Pierce. Whitney was in no position to alienate any of his many personal creditors.[95]

Rayburn determined that he would promptly begin hearings on the bill before the House Interstate and Foreign Commerce Committee. Hearings began on February 14, with James Landis as the first witness. Fearing the proposal for a new, independent securities regulator as recommended by Commerce Secretary Roper might garner support, Landis advocated vesting the FTC with regulatory power to oversee the act and suggested a reorganization and enlargement of the commission to enhance its securities market expertise.[96] (He had in mind Ben Cohen for one of the new commissionerships.) Rayburn determined that the first week of hearings would elicit testimony favorable to the bill. Corcoran appeared on February 21, advocating strongly in support of segregating brokers and dealers. Corcoran referred to New York Stock Exchange dealers as "chiselers." "They are like sea birds following ships," Corcoran said. "They simply follow the market and pick up what they can."[97]

After the bill's proponents had dominated the first week of hearings, Rayburn invited Richard Whitney to testify on February 22. By all accounts, Whitney was highly effective. Staying on message, he highlighted how the bill would affect local markets away from Wall Street. Whitney spent a great deal of the day criticizing the margin provisions of the bill. "In the last analysis," he said, "the problem of fixing the loan values of particular securities is a local one which must be dealt with by persons who are thoroughly familiar with the local market conditions and who are in constant daily touch with all the trading on which loan values depend." At the end of his testimony that day, Whitney proposed creating a federal stock exchange authority separate from the FTC, comprised of seven members: two appointed by the president; two cabinet officers (likely, the secretary of commerce and the secretary of the Treasury); one appointed by the Federal Reserve Open Market Committee; and two stock exchange representatives, one chosen by the New York Stock Exchange and the other chosen by the other exchanges. "Such an authority," Whitney said, "would not only represent the interests of the public, but would have the benefit of the opinions and advice of two cabinet officers, and through its connection with the Open Market Committee of the Federal Reserve System, would be in close contact with credit conditions throughout the United States. It would also include men who had detailed technical knowledge of Exchange operations."[98]

As for the powers of the new authority, Whitney said: "We believe that they should include the power to fix the requirements for the listing of securities; the control of pool syndicates and joint accounts and also options intended or used to influence market price; the power to control the circulation of rumors or statements calculated to induce speculative activity, the use of advertising and the employment of "customers' men" or other employees who solicit business; to the end that all practices which may tend to create unfair prices may be diminished. This Authority should also have power to study and if necessary adopt rules in regard to those cases where the exercise of the function of broker and dealer by the same person is not compatible with fair dealing and to adopt rules in regard to short selling, if it should become convinced that regulation of this practice is necessary."[99]

While the Federal Trade Commission was the most logical existing agency to be the federal regulator of the securities industry, its limitations were apparent even to those friendly to reform. It already had a broad mandate, and few of the commission members, save Landis, knew very much about the securities industry or had any practical experience in it. As the Pecora Hearings demonstrated, subtle but critical differences masked fair play from foul in stock market operations, and the creativity of market professionals in swiftly readjusting to new market rules could not be overestimated. On February 7, two days before the Fletcher-Rayburn bill was filed, Senator William H. King, a Utah Democrat, introduced a bill to establish a Federal Stock Exchange and Securities Commission, comprised of three commissioners appointed by the president, with not more than two commissioners from the same political party and at least one of whom would be "thoroughly experienced in stock-exchange practices." King's securities commission would have licensed all stock exchanges, had the power to set margin requirements in conjunction with local Federal Reserve Banks, and would have been given administrative authority over the Securities Act of 1933. The bill received little attention from either his fellow senators or the press, but it was the first legislation introduced to create a separate federal securities and exchange commission.[100]

Pecora was convinced that despite revelations from Wiggin and others during the Chase hearings and despite the breakaway by E.A. Pierce and the "customers' men," Whitney maintained enough personal credibility (and the New York Stock Exchange enough resources) to muster an effective lobbying attack against the Fletcher-Rayburn bill—perhaps not enough to kill it but certainly enough to minimize its effectiveness. Pecora and Fletcher decided that rather than hold hearings on the bill immediately, as Rayburn had done, which would necessitate granting Whitney a second national audience to agitate against the bill, they would hold hearings showing the New York Stock Exchange at its worst: stock pools, ineffective oversight, and sham transactions running roughshod over shareholder rights. From February 14 through February 26, Pecora investigated the manipulative practices in Repeal stocks during their run-up and subsequent collapse in the spring and summer of 1933.

The first witness was Russell R. Brown, chairman of the board of American Commercial Alcohol Corporation. During the spring of 1933, Brown correctly thought it an opportune time to form a pool in his company's stock, given the general interest in Repeal stocks. American Commercial Alcohol stock was then trading at around $20 per share. By July 18, it had run up to nearly $90 per share. Within three days, however, it would fall sixty points and trade at $30 per share.[101] Brown, of course, had safely cashed out by then.

The operation of a stock pool is relatively simple to explain. First, the pool operator needs to acquire a supply of stock with which to conduct the trading activity. Since secrecy and cost are the crucial components to the success of a pool, it is optimal to obtain the stock by way of an option either from the company whose stock is to be the subject of the pool or by the company's insiders, as purchases in the open market might garner unwanted attention and raise the price of the stock. Second, the pool operator needs to effect a pattern of trading to convince the trading public that there is genuine, benign interest in the stock supporting an increase in its price. Third, the pool needs to sell its shares—quickly—at the inflated price, before the public figures out it has been duped.

On May 2, 1933, Brown granted an option to purchase 25,000 shares of American Commercial Alcohol stock at $18 per share ($2 below market) to Thomas E. Bragg, a stock market operator affiliated with the W.E. Hutton Co. brokerage firm. The account at W.E. Hutton Co. opened for the pool was named

"B.E. Smith no. 296"; Thomas E. Bragg was essentially a bag carrier for one Bernard E. Smith, legendary pool operator and short seller.[102]

"Sell 'Em Ben" Smith would enjoy the irony that it was shenanigans in alcohol stocks that revealed the bad behavior of the Irish American rascal kings of Wall Street. Smith had grown up in the Hell's Kitchen neighborhood on the west side of Manhattan. Purely by luck (or was it through cultivation?), Smith made friends with Percy Rockefeller, John D. Rockefeller's nephew, while working as a car salesman. Principally because of his ability to make the young Rockefeller laugh, the uneducated Smith was transformed into a trader by his patrician friend. This allowed Smith a veneer of respectability when the two would socialize together at Rockefeller's clubs. Stuyvesant Fish Jr., a Rockefeller friend and scion of one of New York's oldest and most respected families, had sponsored Smith for his seat on the New York Stock Exchange. It was easy to see why the blue-blooded swells liked having the Irishman around—he was one of the funniest, most outrageous characters in a business amply stocked with them. According to one tale, Smith was once staring intently at a young junior Ivy League broker at Hutton on a sales call with an important customer. "Hang up the phone," Smith barked at the young man. The young man, hand over the mouthpiece, whispers, "Why?" "HANG UP THE FUCKING PHONE! NOW!" Smith screamed. The young man shook his head no, with a look of abject terror in his eyes. Smith ripped the young man's phone cord out of the wall, holding it up with a wide Celtic grin. "Why did you do that?" the young man asked incredulously. Smith shrugged, smiled, and quipped, "I'm short AT&T."[103]

What Smith was deadly serious about was making money. And when it came to running a pool, he had instincts and nerve second to none. His ribald humor masked an intense discipline and ambition. Smith neither smoked nor drank and also was devoid of the stereotypical Irish sentimentality. He might have made the Rockefellers and the Fishes laugh, but he also made them much richer—and loyally cut them in on his pool operations.[104]

Smith was the most prominent of a troika of hugely successful Irish American traders of the Jazz Age. The second most prominent was Michael J. Meehan. Meehan, three years Smith's junior, was born in Blackburn, England, but like Smith, had grown up in Manhattan. Meehan's rise also mirrored Smith's. While working as a theater ticket broker at McBrides Theatrical Ticket Agency,

Meehan met and befriended a number of white-shoe Wall Street bankers who helped him lease a seat on the New York Curb Exchange in 1918. Two years later, the baby-faced, horn-rim-bespectacled Meehan was successful enough to buy his own seat on the New York Stock Exchange. Eight years later, his firm owned eight NYSE seats, more than any other brokerage firm, and he lived in the Sherry-Netherland hotel, where he counted among his friends Governor Al Smith and Democratic National Committee Chairman John Jacob Raskob.[105]

Meehan pulled off the greatest stock pool of all time, making himself $15,000,000 (more than $200,000,000 in today's dollars) over four days in early 1928, when he drove the stock of RCA up from 85¼ to 147 before pulling the plug. He was also a visionary who foresaw the public's seemingly insatiable desire to trade stocks. His firm was the first to place brokerage offices on ocean liners like the *Bremen,* the *Leviathan,* and the *Berengaria,* and in the lobbies at grand hotels like New York's Waldorf Astoria.[106]

With his RCA pool millions, Meehan launched himself into New York society. The following year he moved into a fourteen-room, six-bath co-op at 856 Fifth Avenue, one of the city's premier WASP buildings, whose residents also included J.P. Morgan & Co. partners Henry P. Davison, Harold Stanley, and Thomas Cochran, as well as Averill Harriman, founding partner of Harriman Brothers & Company, and William H. Woodin, future secretary of the Treasury. He threw grand parties, renting out hotel ballrooms for private gatherings with four hundred of his closest friends. He contributed $100,000 of his RCA windfall to his friend Al Smith's 1928 presidential campaign.[107]

The third Irishman—and a distant third in the eyes of Wall Street at the time—was Joseph P. Kennedy. Kennedy made his bones on Wall Street by successfully defending Hertz's Yellow Cab Company from a bear raid in 1924 but spent a larger part of the 1920s in Hollywood restructuring the motion picture industry—and making his first fortune in the process. He was also a frequent participant in pool operations, like Ben Smith and Mike Meehan.

Kennedy took all of his chips off the table before the Crash. It was the critical decision that made his family's future success possible. During the summer and early autumn of 1929, Kennedy got out of the stock market completely, quietly liquidating his substantial equity holdings and instead investing in high-quality government securities and cash. He never explained what really prompted this fateful decision. Despite his unquenchable ambition and hunger for acceptance and recognition by the gatekeepers of the financial, political, and social establishments, Kennedy never aggrandized his remarkably prescient, fortune-saving market exit. Instead, he masked his shrewd, cold calculation in a benign and irresistible folksy tale.

At the time of the Crash, Patrick Bologna was a skinny twenty-two-year-old Italian kid from the Bronx with a shoeshine stand at 60 Wall Street, one of the many colorful characters who inhabited the financial canyons of lower Manhattan. Bologna was the self-appointed "Bootblack to Wall Street" and a minor celebrity among the hard-bitten brokers and traders for his dispensing of unsolicited investment advice along with a shine.[108] As Kennedy told it, he had gotten a shoeshine from Bologna in the summer of 1929, and as it happened, his calls on the stocks that he was touting that morning turned out to be surprisingly accurate. "When the time comes that a shoeshine boy knows as much as I do about what is going on in the stock market . . . it's time for me to get out," Kennedy said.[109]

Kennedy was also prescient in seeing that panic would soon turn to resentment, and that a fortune saved by a lucky hunch would attract less public anger. Pat Bologna would, not surprisingly, forever corroborate Kennedy's version of events, telling newsmen—and still giving shoeshines and stock tips—into his late seventies about how he'd saved the Kennedy family fortune.

During the year following the Crash, Kennedy added millions more to his fortune by shorting the market discreetly from a desk loaned to him by the Halle & Stieglitz brokerage firm on Madison Avenue. At some point during that first year of the Great Depression, Joe Kennedy's professional energies became less focused on making more money and more on exerting influence in the political realm—motivated in equal parts by a desire to bring status and prominence to his family and a fear that ideological extremism might take hold in America, perhaps violently redistributing his wealth. Kennedy would later write that in "those days I felt and said I would be willing to part with half of what I had if I could be sure of keeping under law and order the other half."

In 1930, at the invitation of Henry J. Morgenthau Jr., Joe Kennedy made a trip to Albany to have lunch with Franklin D. Roosevelt, then governor of New York, and a contender for the Democratic nomination for president in 1932. Republicans significantly outnumbered Democrats when it came to wealthy donors, so whatever misgivings FDR had about Kennedy, he kept to himself. "I think I was the first man with more than $12 in the bank who openly supported him," Kennedy recalled, with only slight exaggeration.[110]

Kennedy worked tirelessly to raise money for Roosevelt. He personally contributed today's equivalent of $750,000 to the campaign, loaned the campaign another $1,250,000, and raised millions more from wealthy friends.[111] But Kennedy's most valuable service to Roosevelt came at the 1932 Democratic National Convention in Chicago. With Roosevelt having failed to secure the two-thirds vote necessary for nomination after three ballots, many on the convention floor were in favor of seeking an alternative candidate—especially the Texas and California delegations, who had withheld their votes from Roosevelt in favor of House Speaker John Nance Garner. Garner had the support of a key media and financial backer: publishing magnate William Randolph Hearst. Ensconced at Hearst Castle in San Simeon, California, Hearst wasn't taking Roosevelt's calls. Kennedy, who knew Hearst from Hollywood, was a favorite of the news baron; he would take Kennedy's call. If the convention deadlocked, Kennedy told Hearst, there was no hope Garner would be nominated and there was a real risk that a candidate more liberal than Roosevelt would snatch the nomination. Hearst gave his blessing to Garner to hop onto the Roosevelt bandwagon; and on the next ballot, the candidate would get his two-thirds majority.[112] Kennedy was now quite a bit more than just a rich young Irish trader in Roosevelt's eyes (and Kennedy would rarely again make an important decision without soliciting the advice of W.R. Hearst).

Unlike the WASPs and Jews on Wall Street, the Irish formed few of their own investment houses. Most were lone wolves like Kennedy and Smith. One exception was McDonnell & Company, which was the market leader in underwriting and trading stock purchase rights. McDonnell & Company was formed in 1905 by James McDonnell, with capital from his father-in-law, the inventor and utilities executive Thomas Murray.

In 1923, some well-heeled families of Southampton, New York, organized a beach club on the Atlantic shore, on a strip of land across from Agawam Lake. Around that time, Thomas Murray bought a large parcel of oceanfront property in Southampton, building himself a big house with all the modern amenities, including two saltwater swimming pools, one for the adults and one for the children. And as a good Catholic, Murray had plenty of children and even more grandchildren. Being a talented inventor he designed and developed a water filtration system that recirculated saltwater from the Atlantic and back without any residue of sand remaining in the pools (this was a problem that had bedeviled people of a certain class in those days).

Not long after Murray established himself at Southampton, his son-in-law, James McDonnell of McDonnell & Company, followed, buying an equally large house. Next came three more of Murray's children and their families. Eventually, the Murray-McDonnell clan owned eight houses over thirty acres of Southampton waterfront—plus garages, stables, boathouses, more saltwater pools, and even a polo field. On Sunday mornings in the summer, a caravan of limousines would take the extended family to Mass at the Sacred Hearts of Jesus and Mary Church.[113]

Not all of the old-line Protestant families of Southampton were thrilled by the Irish invasion, though local shopkeepers were not displeased with the enormous business of feeding, clothing, and bejeweling the enormous Murray-McDonnell family, who paid their equally enormous bills on time. When they got to know their Irish neighbors, though, many of the older families actually liked the Murray-McDonnells—who were hardly the shanty types their neighbors had feared they might be.

The Southampton Bathing Corporation, as the beach club was formally named, had an unwritten but strict "no Irish need apply" policy and to this day is the most exclusive beach club in the country.[114] While more progressive members thought that someday the younger Murray-McDonnells might be invited to join, all assumed that was many years off.

The members of the Bathing Corporation decided that the club ought to have a pool. When the problem of the sand was brought up, a member mentioned having swum in the Murray pool. When Tom Murray was asked how he managed to keep his pools clean, he excitedly showed off the complicated filtration system, along with documents from the U.S. Patent Office granting him a patent on the system.

The following summer, the Southampton Bathing Corporation had a brand new saltwater pool, without sand, making use of Thomas Murray's patented filtration system; and three generations of Murray-McDonnells swam, as full members, in that pool.[115]

One problem that Russell Brown faced in granting the option to Ben Smith's pool was where to get the 25,000 shares to satisfy its exercise. Normally, this would be a simple matter: the company would issue the option to the pool operator. However, American Commercial Alcohol's charter gave its shareholders what are known as preemptive rights, whereby existing shareholders have a right to subscribe proportionately for shares issued by the company before they can be sold to non-shareholders. Those "rights" were exactly the type of securities McDonnell & Company made a fortune underwriting and trading. An exception to this right existed, however, for shares issued in connection with the acquisition of another corporation. It was by using this exception that Brown would obtain the needed 25,000 shares.[116]

Brown had two of his cronies form a new corporation, capitalized by assets of little or no value, save for the personal promissory notes of the cronies, aggregating $450,000 in principal amount. Brown then caused American Commercial Alcohol to issue 25,000 shares of stock to his two conspirators in exchange for the stock of the new corporations under the exception to the preemptive rights charter provision. These 25,000 shares were then sold to Brown under the option agreement at $18 per share—or $450,000 in total—the proceeds of which were immediately applied to repay the promissory notes.[117]

On May 3, 1933, Ben Smith commenced pool operations that continued until July 24, 1933. Approximately 29,000 shares of American Commercial Alcohol were purchased and approximately 44,000 were sold. Smith drove the stock price over this period from a low of $20 to a high of $89⅞, and back to below $30 when he terminated the pool.[118]

All of the transactions were approved by the board of directors of American Commercial Alcohol. Of course, those directors, including Brown, were granted secret interests in the pool. Together with the two cronies of Brown who created the dummy corporations, these same fiduciaries were also given a hidden interest in underwriting fees in connection with a public offering by American Commercial Alcohol to its existing shareholders, entered into on May 31, 1933, and undertaken while the stock was being manipulated by Smith. All told, the officers, directors, and cronies pocketed today's equivalent of approximately $4,000,000 with no capital risk of their own and no disclosure to their public shareholders.[119]

There was, however, one independent gatekeeper Brown had to circumvent—the Listing Committee of the New York Stock Exchange, where the American Commercial Alcohol stock traded. But the Listing Committee was asleep at the switch. Under questioning by Pecora, Frank Altschul, chairman of the Listing Committee, revealed that he hadn't even bothered to review basic financial statements of the two companies American Commercial Alcohol was acquiring, even a cursory review of which would have revealed the sham.

On August 1, 1933, a special meeting of shareholders of American Commercial Alcohol was held to ratify the issuance of the 25,000 shares. All of the shares represented at the meeting were voted by proxy. The statement used to solicit the proxies took the form of a letter disclosing only the mechanics of the issuance to acquire the two corporations. No mention was made of the secret interests of Brown and the others in the underwriting fees; no disclosure was provided as to the value of the assets of the two dummy corporations, or that they were organized at the direction of Brown; no mention was made of the option granted for the benefit of Ben Smith's pool; and, of course, nothing was said regarding the participation of Brown and the others in Ben Smith's pool. Pecora was never given the chance to question either Bragg or Smith. In advance of the hearings, Bragg had decided to take a vacation to Hawaii. Smith went farther west; he was "on vacation" in Australia.[120]

When Pecora finished with the drama of American Commercial Alcohol on February 21, 1934, he turned to the pool operations in Libbey-Owens Ford Glass Co. stock. In truth, the company wasn't even remotely a Repeal stock. It didn't make bottles; it made shatterproof glass for windows and windshields, principally for General Motors automobiles. That wouldn't matter, thought Elisha Walker of Kuhn, Loeb & Company: the public could be convinced that its stock, too, would skyrocket after Prohibition's end. Many unsuspecting investors might confuse it with Owens-Illinois, a large bottle maker. And to the detriment of investors, Walker was proven correct.

Walker was able to locate a block of 145,000 shares of Libbey-Owens Ford stock for sale by an investment group headed by Gordon Auchincloss and obtained an option to purchase the shares.[121] With the option in hand, Walker assembled his pool participants. Kuhn, Loeb would hold a 13½/65ths share in the pool; Redmond & Co., the firm that would control the pool-trading operation, would hold a 10/65ths interest; Bell & Beckwith, a Toronto brokerage firm, was granted a 10/65ths interest; the brokerage firm Wright & Sexton was given a 5/65ths interest; Lehman Brothers held a 6½/65ths interest; an entity controlled by Harry Sinclair, called Hyva Corporation, held a 5/65ths interest; Walter P. Chrysler, the automobile magnate, held a 5/65th interest; and Joseph P. Kennedy held a 10/65th interest.[122]

It was that last participant in the pool that drew the most attention, given Joe Kennedy's close ties with the Roosevelt administration. Pecora did not let the opportunity to highlight Kennedy's involvement pass by. He questioned Henry Mason Day, a partner in the Redmond & Co. firm, about the pool's well-connected participant:

MR. PECORA: Who is Joseph P. Kennedy?

MR. DAY: Mr. Kennedy is a capitalist or well-known private citizen.

MR. PECORA: Do you know what his business is?

MR. DAY: I don't think he has a business.

MR. PECORA: When you say he is a capitalist, does that cover your understanding of what his business is?

MR. DAY: Well, I do not know. My understanding of a capitalist is somebody who has considerable funds and does not have to work.

MR. PECORA: I am not a capitalist.

MR. DAY: Neither am I, sir.[123]

The Senate hearing room broke out in laughter. No one in the hearing room that day—certainly not Ferdinand Pecora—would have guessed that in a little more than four months, Pecora would be working for Joseph P. Kennedy.

Prior to the formation of the pool, Libbey-Owens Ford was a thinly traded stock. Once the pool commenced operations, trading volume in the stock skyrocketed, with price movements that were difficult to comprehend. This practice, known as "jiggling," drew attention to a stock. But the pool proved only moderately successful. During the four months of its operation, the stock of Libbey-Owens Ford rose from $27 per share to $37 per share, with resulting profit to the pool of about $7,000,000 in today's dollars.[124]

The Repeal stock investigation had accomplished what Fletcher and Pecora had hoped. Whitney's pronouncements on the efficacy of self-regulation were now openly lampooned. The Senate Banking and Currency Committee was now ready to commence hearings on the Fletcher-Rayburn bill.

On February 21, Senator Fletcher took to the floor of the Senate and harshly criticized Richard Whitney and the New York Stock Exchange's lobbying campaign against the bill. "The propaganda released by the Exchange officials is intended," said Fletcher, "to persuade the people that regulation of that Exchange and the other exchanges by the federal government will hurt business. Whose business? Only that of bankers who have lined their pockets by disregarding the interests of their customers. Government regulation certainly will hurt the market operators and speculators who have used the facilities of the stock exchanges of the country to mullet the public out of millions and in sum total out of billions of dollars. But regulation will not hurt the investor or the business man."

Two days after Fletcher's floor speech, Whitney gave an exclusive interview to *The New York Times* to answer the charges. "I think the charge is unfounded," said Whitney. "I summarized the provisions of the bill and asked the presidents of the corporations having stock listed on the New York Stock Exchange to give the matter their personal consideration. I think every citizen has the right to call to the attention of other citizens the provisions of pending legislation which would affect them. In this case, I feel the Exchange was under a duty to do so. The corporations listed on the Exchange had paid a fee to secure a public market for their securities. The pending bill would destroy this public market and would force many corporations to withdraw from listing. I think we would have been derelict in our duty if we had not called the bill to their attention. If this is propaganda, then the right of free discussion of public questions has gone and the constitutional right of free speech no longer exists."[125]

Then, without explanation, Fletcher decided to go easy on Whitney. During the first week of Senate hearings, Fletcher allowed hostile witnesses to present a nearly unrelenting attack on the legislation. Even the testimony of Tommy Corcoran—a moment that should have been a high point of the hearings for the bill's supporters—was marred by a misstep by Fletcher. Immediately before Corcoran was to testify, the New York Stock Exchange requested that its attorney, Roland Redmond of Carter Ledyard & Milburn, be permitted to cross-examine Corcoran. Inexplicably, Fletcher allowed the request, dampening the effectiveness of Corcoran's testimony.[126]

Whitney's allies had not abandoned him. The arbitrage firms came out against the Fletcher-Rayburn bill on the first day of the Senate hearings. The Chicago and Boston exchanges opposed it on the second day. A number of smaller exchanges publicly announced their opposition later that week. Even the president's cousin Archibald Roosevelt testified against the bill on behalf of the New York City Municipal Bond Dealers Committee, stating that "if the bill goes through, we will be out of business."[127]

The high drama of the first week of hearings was the appearance of Whitney himself before the Senate Banking and Currency Committee. Whitney's testimony was substantively a repeat of his performance before the House committee, but with more emphasis given to his counterproposal for an industry-represented federal stock exchange authority with broad rulemaking powers. Again, Whitney was unflappable under questioning. "We should be glad," he said, "to see a regulatory body constituted under federal law to supervise the resolution of these grave problems with authority to require the Stock Exchange to adopt rules and regulations designed to prevent dishonest practices which unfairly influence the pricing of securities or unduly stimulate speculation; authority to control pools, syndicates and joint accounts and options intended or used to unfairly influence market prices."[128] Whitney's idea for a separate federal agency was publicly endorsed by the U.S. Chamber of Commerce on the following day and by John Dickinson the following week.[129]

It was clear by the end of February that the Fletcher-Rayburn bill would not pass in its current form. There was simply too much opposition. Rayburn acknowledged as much. "There seems to be a shying away from the Federal Trade Commission. There will be government action of some sort. What these are for is to find out what they should be. In the long run the committee will be called upon in executive session to enact something. I don't think there is anyone here who intends to put the exchanges out of business."[130] On March 5, Senate Majority Leader James Robinson took Rayburn's admission even further: "As to whether the stock exchange regulation bill may be ready during this session of Congress, no assurance at this time can be given."[131] Against the odds, Whitney had won the first round.

Once again, it turned out that Roosevelt had played his cards wisely. He hadn't publicly endorsed the original Fletcher-Rayburn bill, knowing that such sweeping legislation would face stiff opposition. After the first round of congressional hearings, Roosevelt had a better idea of what to defend and what required compromise. Given Roosevelt's February 9 letter demanding a law in the present session, the prestige of the administration was at stake. On March 7, the president publicly announced that he still expected legislation in the present session. He then tasked Corcoran, Landis, and Cohen with redrafting the bill with input from both the Treasury Department and the Federal Reserve Board (who had opposed certain provisions of the bill, particularly the margin limitations).[132]

Eight round-the-clock drafting sessions were held in the Federal Reserve building. Corcoran, Landis, and Cohen prepared ten revised drafts prior to the bill's reintroduction to the House on March 19.[133]

Although it moderated many of the controversial provisions, the revised bill retained the basic architecture and scope of the original. The margin limitations were relaxed, and government-backed securities were exempted from the requirements. With respect to the initial extension of margin credit, credit was limited to greater than 40 percent of current market price or 100 percent of the lowest trading price in the last three years, but not to exceed 75 percent of the current market price. With respect to maintaining margin credit, credit levels were to be limited to 60 percent of current market price or 100 percent of the lowest trading price in the last three years, but not to exceed 85 percent of the current market price. The Federal Reserve Board was given the power to reduce permitted credit levels or, under extraordinary circumstances, allow more margin credit. Credit extended by persons other than exchange members, brokers, and dealers could also be limited to those amounts, if the Federal Reserve Board so determined. Existing margin loans would not be subject to the provisions until January 31, 1939. In addition, the revised bill required that the Federal Reserve Board and the FTC study the feasibility of fixing maximum loan values on the basis of the projected earnings of an issuer, as proposed by Edward Filene's Twentieth Century Fund.[134] The revised bill modified the broker-dealer borrowing limitation by permitting brokers and dealers to borrow not only from Federal Reserve member banks but also from exchange members, other brokers, and dealers, or non–Federal Reserve member banks in localities where no Federal Reserve member bank existed.[135]

A new provision was added making it unlawful to receive payment from a broker, dealer, or person selling or purchasing a security for disseminating any information regarding a security registered on a national securities exchange, unless the information was being published as an advertisement. Options trading was to be permitted and subject to the rules therefor adopted by the FTC.[136] The provisions relating to the segregation of brokers, dealers, and specialists were significantly liberalized. Instead of being confined to being brokers, specialists would be permitted to be either brokers or dealers, but not both. Exchange members could act as both brokers and dealers, so long as they didn't offer margin on newly listed securities, notified customers in what capacity they were acting, and traded for their own account only through other exchange members.[137] To avoid a rush of new registrations upon the act's effectiveness, the revised bill allowed the FTC to grant provisional registration until April 1, 1935, for securities already listed. And with respect to ongoing periodic reporting requirements, only annual financial statements were required to be audited.[138] The provisions relating to insider trading in the original bill were eliminated. The liability provisions for misleading statements were confined to actual damages sustained in reliance upon such statements. Liability for controlling persons was limited to those persons not acting in good faith. And the statute of limitations for actions would be two years after accrual of the cause of action instead of two years after discovery of the violation.[139] The revised bill contained a new provision enlarging the FTC from five to seven members, contemplating that two new members with securities industry expertise would be added. The president was authorized to divide the membership of the FTC into as many divisions as he saw fit, each to consist of no less than three commissioners.[140]

Richard Whitney's response to the revised bill was swift and unequivocal, calling it "destructive" on the day of its introduction. "While the introduction of the Federal Reserve Board as an agency which may exercise some control over credit and the inclusion of provisions limiting the unfair civil penalties contained in the original Fletcher-Rayburn bill represent steps in the right direction," Whitney said, "it is apparent from even a hasty reading of the new bill that its underlying purpose is to carry out the social theories of those who believe that the Federal Government should control not only credit and the operation of the stock exchanges but also all commerce and industry. This new bill will have as serious effects upon the security market as the original Fletcher-Rayburn bill. In my opinion, it will inevitably bring about declining prices and will interfere with and delay the economic recovery of the nation. This bill is destructive and not constructive."[141]

Ferdinand Pecora responded immediately to Whitney's criticisms: "I do not believe that Mr. Whitney's criticism of the revised Fletcher-Rayburn bill is sincere. He asserts that the revised bill does not meet the objections to the original draft voiced before the Senate and House Committees. Of course, if all of Mr. Whitney's objections were met, there would be no bill at all."[142] After summarizing the revisions to the bill, Pecora continued his counterattack on Whitney: "The bill does not seek to enact the social philosophy of any special group. It seeks rather to make certain that the wildcat speculation which was fostered and encouraged by the New York Stock Exchange prior to October, 1929, and the results of which were so baneful as to dislocate American industry and to throw 13,000,000 breadwinners out of employment, will not again afflict our people and imperil their prosperity. The American businessman who reads this bill with an honest and open mind will not shiver with fright at the scarecrows and ghosts which Mr. Whitney pretends to see."[143]

On March 20, the House Interstate and Foreign Commerce Committee called Thomas Corcoran to testify about the revised bill. Corcoran said that every objection to the original measure had been "honestly weighed," and that, while he did not speak for them, he was of the opinion that the revised bill was approved by the Treasury Department and the Federal Reserve Board, a claim later confirmed by Chairman Rayburn.[144]

The following day, Tom K. Smith, assistant secretary of the Treasury, directly contradicted the assertions of Corcoran and Rayburn. He asserted that the Treasury would express "neither approval nor disapproval" of the bill. And with that statement, Rayburn's hope that the bill would be reported with limited, cursory additional hearings evaporated. Opponents of the bill were granted additional days of testimony. It was clear Roosevelt wanted to test-run the bill one more time through the congressional hearing process before further staking his credibility with a full-fledged endorsement.[145]

On March 22, Richard Whitney appeared again before the House Interstate and Foreign Commerce Committee. "Our basic objections to the old bill," he said, "apply with equal force to the new one. I do not believe that sound legislation can be based on the framework of this redrafted bill." Whitney offered a series of amendments to the revised bill. First, he proposed that all margin regulation be delegated to the full discretion of rules adopted by the Federal Reserve Board. Similarly, he would have broker-dealer debt limits determined by the Federal Reserve Board. He proposed allowing members and specialists to act as both brokers and dealers, subject to rules adopted by the exchanges and approved by the new stock exchange commission. These and a number of other proposed amendments were set forth in a formal memorandum he submitted to the committee.[146]

Whitney's lobbying effort continued in full force. He enlisted Paul V. Shields, a Democrat close to the administration, to participate in the letter-writing campaign in opposition to the revised bill. Writing to his friend, Democratic Party chairman and postmaster general James Farley, Shields stated, "I wish to God I could impress upon you the seriousness of this whole thing. Just as sure as we are alive, you have another airmail situation on your hands in this bill. Frankly, I feel that these smart young birds, commonly referred to as the Frankfurter Fellows, are going way too far, and it is high time that we appreciated that they have nothing to lose and no thought of the effect on the administration. You and ourselves are the ones who are holding the bag. Please do not take offense at my putting this thing bluntly, but I think it is vital."[147]

Whitney was more nasty than Shields in his attacks on the "Frankfurter Fellows" and not above resorting to appealing to ethnic and religious prejudices. He returned to New York and made the rounds on Wall Street telling all who would listen that the bill had been written "by a bunch of Jews out to get Morgan."[148]

The day after Whitney testified, the hearings in the House Interstate and Foreign Commerce Committee took a turn for the bizarre. Appearing before the committee was James H. Rand Jr., the chairman of an organization called the Committee for the Nation. Rand was founder of an office equipment company that later became Sperry-Rand, one of the earliest large computer-manufacturing companies in the United States. He cofounded the Committee for the Nation with Frank Vanderlip, a former president of National City Bank, in January 1933. The Committee for the Nation was dedicated to economic recovery and advocated measures such as abandoning the gold standard. Briefly, it enjoyed a measure of influence in the national economic-recovery debate.

Rand declared to the House Interstate and Foreign Commerce Committee that he was in possession of a letter from distinguished educator Dr. William A.

Wirt of Gary, Indiana. Wirt claimed that several unnamed members of Roosevelt's administration had told him that a cabal of brain trusters planned on overturning the government by gaining control of the press, industry, labor, and education, replacing Roosevelt with a Stalin-type dictator after he'd served his purpose as dupe and front man. Rand read Wirt's letter to the committee. "Last summer," Wirt wrote, "I asked some of the individuals in this group what their concrete plan was for bringing about the proposed overthrow of the established American social order. I was told that they believed that by thwarting our then evident recovery, they would be able to prolong the country's destitution until they had demonstrated to the American people that the government must operate industry and commerce. I was told that, of course, commercial banks could not make long-time capital loans and that they would be able to destroy, by propaganda, the other institutions that had been making capital loans. Then [they said] we can push Uncle Sam into the position where he must make these capital loans. And, of course, when Uncle Sam becomes our financier he must also follow his money with control and management."[149]

Rayburn pounced on Rand first. "Are you here making a direct charge or by inference that President Roosevelt has surrounded himself with men advocating the overthrow of this government?" Rand responded by suggesting that Rayburn call Dr. Wirt as a witness. When other congressmen asked Rand why he hadn't obtained the names of the supposedly traitorous brain trusters, he replied that Wirt had told him, "Everyone knows them."[150]

Rand next attacked Corcoran, Landis, and Cohen, saying that the revised bill had been drafted by "a group of radical young lawyers who hold no elective office." "Here in Washington," Rand added, "a group of theoretically trained young men, sincere but totally inexperienced in government and business, wield great influence."[151]

Over in the Senate Banking and Currency Committee, the second round of hearings on the revised bill commenced. Richard Whitney testified. Likewise, Tom K. Smith of Treasury, who gave lukewarm support for the bill: "The Treasury has been consulted on certain parts of the bill which are of direct concern to it. Within the limited time available those have been studied to determine whether they would have an unduly adverse effect on the marketing of government securities or on the national financial structure. Changes which were regarded as necessary within the framework of a general regulatory measure were suggested to the counsel for the committees of the Senate and the

House, and were, in all material respects, incorporated in the bill. The Treasury has not considered those provisions in the bill which relate strictly to technical matters of stock exchange practice and regulation. Failure to comment on those provisions does not mean that Treasury is opposed to them, but only that they have not been objects of our study. The Treasury is, therefore, not in a position to express an opinion on them."[152]

By contrast, Eugene R. Black, governor of the Federal Reserve Board, in his testimony before the Senate Committee, gave a wholehearted endorsement of the revised bill. "It is fair, workable and right in principle and will accomplish the purpose of regulating the Exchanges under fair practices. The board is prepared to approve it as revised."[153]

On March 24, Representative Alfred Bulwinkle of North Carolina, a strong Roosevelt ally, announced that he would introduce a resolution calling for inquiry into Dr. William Wirt's allegations of communist disloyalty by unnamed members of the president's brain trust. Both Chairman Rayburn and Speaker of the House Rainey announced that they had no objection to the resolution. Bulwinkle was clear that his intentions were to acquit the president and his advisers of any suspicion. "I don't believe anyone did make those statements," he said.[154]

On March 26, President Roosevelt finally publicly endorsed the bill and encouraged a rapid push toward closure of the committee-level legislative process. He sent identical letters to Chairman Fletcher and Chairman Rayburn requesting a strong stock exchange bill:

My dear Mr. Chairman:

Before I leave Washington for a few days' holiday I want to write you about a matter which gives me some concern.

On February 9, 1934, I sent to the Congress a special message asking for Federal supervision of national traffic in securities.

It has come to my attention that a more definite and more highly organized drive is being made against effective legislation to this end than against any similar recommendation made by me during the past year. Letters and telegrams bearing all the earmarks of origin at some common source are pouring into the White House and to Congress.

The people of the country are, in overwhelming majority, fully aware of the fact that unregulated speculation in securities and commodities was one of the most contributing factors in the artificial and unwarranted "boom" which had so much to do with the terrible conditions in the years following 1929.

I have been definitely committed to definite regulation of exchanges which deal in securities and commodities. In my message I stated: "It should be our national policy to restrict, as far as possible, the use of these Exchanges for purely speculative operations."

I am certain that the country as a whole will not be satisfied with legislation unless such legislation has teeth in it. The two principal objectives are, as I see it:

First, the requirement of what is known as margins so high that speculation, even as it exists today, will of necessity be drastically curtailed; and

Second, that the government be given such definite powers of supervision over Exchanges that the government itself will be able to correct abuses which may arise in the future.

We must, of course, prevent in so far as possible manipulation of prices to the detriment of actual investors, but at the same time we must eliminate unnecessary, unwise and destructive speculation.

This bill as shown to me this afternoon by you seems to meet the minimum requirements. I do not see how any of us could afford to have it weakened in any shape, manner or form.

Very Sincerely,

FRANKLIN D. ROOSEVELT[155]

The following day, the Senate Banking and Currency Committee held its last day of hearings with Richard Whitney and his counsel, Roland Redmond, testifying about their proposed amendments. The key development of the hearings was not Whitney's testimony but the statement by Senator Glass that he would oppose any bill giving the Federal Reserve Board authority over determining margin requirements. "I do not think the Federal Reserve Board should be mixed up in it at all," said Glass. "In my opinion not one of the eight board members knows anything about it. The Federal Reserve Board was set up to respond to the requirements of credit, not to control credit." To curb speculation, Glass proposed a federal tax on any purchases and sales of a security within six months of each other.[156]

The margin-lending question became the vortex of the competing interests working to influence the final bill. Without question, excessive borrowing for securities speculation was the proximate cause of the stock market bubble. Much of this money came, directly or indirectly from Federal Reserve member banks, enabled by an easy-money policy by the Federal Reserve Board, which kept reserves plentiful and interest rates low. Financial conservatives like Carter Glass believed that banks should be prohibited from financing securities market activities and that, accordingly, the Federal Reserve Board, a bank regulator, should have no role in regulating margin levels. Glass would have limited such lending to brokers and dealers, whose loans would be regulated by either the FTC or a new federal securities regulator. The "bring Wall Street to heel" reformers wanted low margin levels, rigidly set. They believed that to prevent future bubbles, buying stock with borrowed money should be strictly limited. Wall Street, joined by many from the pro-inflation contingent, argued that margin levels should be flexible: equity prices had collapsed—it was a long, long way from a bubble market—and limiting the ability to purchase stock would only depress prices further; and banks, awash in reserves, would lose a lucrative lending market and a safe one; margin loans proved to be easy to liquidate after the Crash with banks nearly always recovering their money.

On April 4, Rayburn formally appointed a subcommittee to make final modifications to the bill. The unresolved margin question dominated the agenda. The subcommittee consisted of Rayburn as chairman, Democrats Clarence Lea of California and George Huddleston of Alabama, and Republicans Myers Young Cooper of Ohio and Carl Mapes of Michigan.[157]

The same day the House subcommittee was appointed, Samuel Untermyer, unable to resist the limelight, testified before the Senate Banking and Currency Committee. Untermyer proposed nationalizing New York Stock Exchange membership and having the proceeds of any sales of exchange seats transferred to a trust to finance the expenses the FTC incurred in regulating the exchanges.

He showed himself to be a peddler of unrealistic, sensationalist proposals. Once again, Untermyer was ignored by the president and the congressional leadership.[158]

Between April 9 and 11, the Senate Banking and Currency Committee adopted three significant modifications to the bill, all drafted by Carter Glass. First, Glass proposed the creation of a three-member Securities and Exchange Commission to replace the FTC as the agency overseeing both the exchange legislation and the Securities Act of 1933. It was passed by the committee by a vote of ten to eight, with five Democrats joining five Republicans in approving the resolution. Next, he required that the new commission determine the margin limitations for credit provided by brokers to their customers, but with the Federal Reserve Board maintaining authority over the margin loans by banks to brokers and with no statutory formula in either case. And he proposed that the entire subject of segregating the functions of broker, dealer, and specialist be left to the discretion of the new commission.[159]

The approval of these amendments was widely regarded as a victory for Richard Whitney. Glass vehemently denied advancing Whitney's cause, calling the bill a "sweeping defeat" for the Exchange. "I had never read a word of Mr. Whitney's testimony," Glass said. "I had had no communication with him either direct or indirect. My idea in the amendment was to prevent the Federal Reserve Board from being mixed up with stock gambling. I examined the record today and found that Mr. Whitney's ideas and mine were as different as night from day."[160]

On April 11, Senator Fletcher referred the remaining issues on the bill (relating to registration of listed securities, periodic reports, insider stock sales, and proxies) to a subcommittee consisting of himself, fellow Democrats William Gibbs McAdoo and James Byrnes, and Republicans Frederick C. Walcott and Phillips Lee Goldsborough.[161]

On April 12, Richard Whitney reached out directly to President Roosevelt, seeking a meeting to discuss the exchange bill. In his letter, Whitney wrote that "the stock exchanges of the country are not opposed to effective legislation. They are, however, united in opposing the Rayburn bill because they know that the immediate and necessary effect of its enactment will be a renewed deflation of securities prices and a dislocation of business which will unquestionably interfere with your program for recovery. I sincerely trust that you will accord me an interview so that I can explain to you fully and frankly the dangers which are inherent in the adoption of a rigid and inflexible regulatory statute like the one now under consideration. I trust you will believe me when I say that in making this request I am actuated solely by a desire to see sound legislation enacted and I earnestly hope you will arrange to see me."[162]

Roosevelt declined the meeting request.

Rayburn's subcommittee significantly watered down the statutory formula for the margin loan limitations. The formula, which the Federal Reserve Board could override essentially at its discretion, would apply to initial extensions of margin credit only, not maintenance of margin credit, the limitations on which would be completely within the discretion of the Federal Reserve Board. Under the revised provision, initial margin loans would be limited to the greater of 55 percent of the current stock price or 100 percent of the lowest price of the stock in the last three years, but not more than 75 percent of the current stock price. On April 14, the House subcommittee presented its bill to the full Interstate and Foreign Commerce Committee.[163]

On April 17, the Senate subcommittee presented its revised bill to the full Senate Committee on Banking and Currency, with the principal changes being the expansion of the size of the new securities and exchange commission to five members and an increase in the amount of stock ownership triggering the limitation on insider securities trading to 10 percent from 5 percent.[164]

On April 20, the Senate Banking and Currency Committee adopted the bill as presented by the subcommittee, reporting it to the full Senate by a vote of eleven to eight, with two Republicans joining nine Democrats in favor.[165]

On April 25, the House Committee on Interstate and Foreign Commerce voted to report its bill to the full House with minor revisions.[166]

On the eve of the House committee vote, Rayburn charged Whitney with directing "the most powerful lobby ever organized against any bill which ever came up in Congress" by a "campaign of misrepresentation and fright." Whitney replied with alacrity: "The attempts of Chairman Rayburn to attribute industry's position in this legislation to propaganda from the Stock Exchange groups is fully unwarranted. Industry's interest in this legislation is more vital, if possible, than that of the Stock Exchange itself, and its viewpoint has been reached as the result of its own investigation and analysis."[167]

On April 30, debate began on the House floor. Rayburn expanded on his charge that the New York Stock Exchange was conducting a propaganda campaign against the bill. "There is no use trying to write a bill that will be effective, that will protect the public in general and investors in particular which will please also the great exchanges of this country," he told the House. "These stock exchange amendments were offered in the committee. We were able to vote them down. They will be offered on the floor of this House, and I intend to brand every one of them as they come." He called to the attention of the House the stock exchange members present in the gallery. "I am glad to see them here. They are engaged in a business that ought to go on if it can go on legitimately. We should have a market for the exchange of securities but it should be a clean market place."[168]

The second day of debate was principally concerned with a description of the bill's provisions and a recital of key testimony from the committee hearings. On May 2, floor debate became contentious when Republican House members called the bill a communist measure and Democrats retaliated with an outlandish demonization of Wall Street. The Republican attack was led by Congressman Fred Bitten of Illinois:

"Only the day before yesterday, when the distinguished chairman was addressing the House, he paid compliment to his visitors in the gallery from the stock exchange. Today I pay compliment to my visitors in the gallery, the youthful legislative wizards from the little red house in Georgetown. The Scarlet-fever boys have written into the Rayburn bill an unusual section which in itself is in the nature of an argument for doing unconstitutional things which the bill itself is intended to circumvent. The popular demand for stock exchange regulation has given the Prof. Felix Frankfurter cheerleaders a vehicle to control all credit and corporate practices such as not even Russia can boast of today. The boys in the little red house breathed easier when their child was finally deposited in the hopper by Chairman Rayburn. I am told that Telford Taylor, a young and recent graduate from Harvard, now in the Interior Department, was the father of the very first Fletcher-Rayburn child, but it was soon kidnapped by Landis (FTC) and Frankfurter (H.U.) who immediately proceeded with the advice of Pecora, Tommy Corcoran (RFC) and Benjamin Cohen (P.W.A.), to put the finishing touches on what was intended to be the second child; too much vodka and too little cream made it too hot for even the red-letter boys, and it was again rewritten only to be drowned in the sea of publicity. If the present unhappy child should be adopted by the Congress, the Federal Trade Commission could restrict almost every industry in the United States and could regulate it out of existence by the control of credit and other restrictions without having to give its reasons for doing so. Lenin and Trotsky never envisioned such far-reaching possibilities for strangulation."[169]

Democratic representative Charles Traux of Ohio was even more vitriolic in response:

"I am for this bill because it is doing something to Wall Street instead of doing something for Wall Street. I am for this bill because it will do something to the bloodiest band of racketeers and vampires that ever sucked the blood of humanity, John "Pirate" Morgan & Co. If all the tears and the blood he has caused to flow could be gathered together into a pool it would be deep enough and large enough to float his $3,000,000 yacht, the *Corsair*, and the private yachts of all his fellow pirates. Something has been said about teeth and tusks in this bill. Both of them are too light for me. I would equip this bill with triple-plated, copper-riveted, razor-honed spear points steeped in the poison of the deadliest snakes of India. . . . Under the sharp questioning and pointed barbs of Ferdinand Pecora, whenever Morgan the Magnificent's memory was bad, it was his able aide, Lamont, who refreshed his memory. Such swindlers as the suave, blasé, perfectly manicured Whitney who, when asked a pointed leading question would tilt his aristocratic head with all of the nonchalance and composure of a Webster declaiming messages that would be written in the immortal tablets of history. 'The answer will be ____.' Elegant and arrogant though Whitney was, his own admissions convicted him of being one of the coldest and cruelest of all the Bluebeards. Then there were the Kuhn Loebs, the Dillon Reads, leaving a slimy trail of legalized burglary, rotten riggings of markets and feculent odors of grand larceny that led from coast to coast and Gulf to Lakes, and smelled to high heaven. An army of 5,000 is chasing Dillinger. Yet the Wall Street bandits still run at large, feeding on the hard earned savings of honest American citizens. So the more stringent Government supervision made of the operations and dealings of these hijackers, that much better the interests of the country generally will be secured."[170]

After Representative Traux's colorful denunciations, Republican representative Hamilton Fish offered a measured defense of Wall Street—after blaming large commercial banks with securities affiliates (already broken up by Glass-Steagall) for the economic crisis:

> "If there are any guilty people in this country it is the American public led on by the big international bankers; not by the stock exchange, but by the big international bankers with their securities affiliates. They are the people who led us on, encouraged and urged us to buy foreign bonds and a lot of worthless securities. They are the people who, after the inflation collapsed, said that the wages of the American laborers must be reduced, that the compensation of the veterans must be sliced, and that the civil service employees of New York must have their pay cut. Mr. Mitchell and Mr. Wiggin, if you want to blame anybody by name, are the ones responsible more than anyone else. They kept telling the Congress in 1929 to keep hands off business and not to interfere with business, that they knew what was best for the public; and we, I am ashamed to say, listened to them, while they continued to mullet the public and even ruin their own depositors and stockholders. The individual members of the stock exchange are simply in business to handle transactions in stocks and bonds listed on the exchange. I do not think it is fair for any Member to attack either Mr. Whitney or any other member of the stock exchange for transacting legitimate business. If we speculate and lose, we must expect to pay the piper and not blame anyone except ourselves."[171]

Freshman Representative Everett Dirksen of Illinois (the future Republican Senate majority leader) criticized the bill for its constricting effect on credit at a time when banks were already reluctant to extend it to customers:

> "In light of the fact that there are now one and a half billion in excess reserves and that the immense gold reserves would permit credit expansion of unlimited proportions, this diminution of loans was estimated at $4,604,000,000 which is actually $99,000,000 less than a year ago. Loans on securities as of April 25 were $3,516,000,000 which is $122,000,000 less than a year ago. Remembering that one year ago the Nation was at its lowest ebb

the fact that all loans, including security loans, is around $100,000,000 less than at that time. The conclusion is obvious, that in addition to the restrictions imposed by the F.D.I.C., the Banking Act, and other measures, there is a distinct fear and apprehension in the air which continues to freeze bank credit. This is singular enough in the light of the clamor that has been going up for weeks for legislation, such as the Glass Bill or the credit industry bill to expand bank credit and investment credit. Here we have a bill to do what? By its very language to control credit, to curtail the excessive use of credit, to offset what will be attempted later in some kind of credit measure, and the psychological effect on the Nation might be disquieting indeed. Has anyone advanced a reason why this particular bill should be created at this time? Is a boom at hand that needs curbing before it is born? By such measures as this that boom may die aborning. I wish I shared the optimism that foresees an immediate boom, particularly when relief rolls are heavier and unemployment greater than it has been at any time since last October. Conceding that there is an upward momentum in business, the stability of such momentum is precarious enough and why imperil it with a bill that is overly drastic?"[172]

The most substantive development of the day was the announcement by Democratic representative Alfred Bulwinkle of North Carolina that he intended to offer an amendment to the bill eliminating the Federal Trade Commission as the administrative agency and substituting it with a three-member commission appointed by the president, with the advice and consent of the Senate.

With general debate over on May 3, the House considered various amendments formally offered from the floor. Seventeen amendments were offered but only three minor amendments—all supported by Rayburn—passed.[173] On May 4, Representative Bulwinkle moved to create the three-member commission overseeing the act, but his amendment was rejected by a vote of 145 to 102. Shortly after the vote on the Bulwinkle's amendment, the full bill was called for a vote: 281 voted in favor with eighty-four opposed and ninety-nine not voting.[174]

The day the bill passed the House, Senator Fletcher introduced an amendment to the Senate liberalizing a number of the provisions of the Securities

Act and clarifying a number of its ambiguities. The amendment reflected many of Arthur Dean's recommended changes. Fletcher proposed to limit the liability of underwriters to only losses relating to that portion of the offering actually underwritten by each underwriter, not all losses. He also proposed requiring that plaintiffs prove they actually relied on the alleged misstatement or omission when purchasing the securities at issue. Fletcher demanded the reduction of the statute of limitations for actions under the Securities Act and the limiting of liability for controlling person to only those circumstances where controlling persons had knowledge of (or reasonable grounds to believe) that a material misstatement or omission occurred. Lastly, Fletcher proposed disclosure requirements for bondholder protective committees.[175]

The bill was similar to one previously introduced by Republican senator Daniel Hastings of Delaware. But the Hastings bill had gone further, requiring that a plaintiff prove that his losses were caused by the alleged misstatement or omission.[176]

On May 7, the Senate began floor debate on the bill, with Senator Fletcher recounting the highlights of the Pecora Hearings and explaining the key points of the legislation. During the course of the nearly weeklong Senate debate on the bill, numerous amendments were offered, but none of substance were passed.[177] On Saturday, May 12, the Senate passed the bill, including Fletcher's amendments to the Securities Act of 1933, by a vote of sixty-two to thirteen, with twenty-one senators abstaining.[178]

On May 14, the House and Senate conferees were announced: representatives Rayburn, Huddleston, Lea, Cooper, and Mapes and senators Fletcher, Alben W. Barkley, Byrnes, Goldsborough, and Couzens.[179] The principal differences between the House and Senate versions were whether a new commission (Senate bill) or the FTC (House bill) would administer the federal securities laws; whether there would be any statutory goal posts for margin requirements (House bill) or left to regulation (Senate bill); and whether the Federal Reserve Board would set margin requirements for all lenders and brokers (House bill) or just Federal Reserve member banks (Senate bill).[180]

Noticeably absent from the Senate conferees were Carter Glass and his ally Democratic senator Robert Wagner of New York. This omission was interpreted by the press and Glass himself as a lack of support by Senator Fletcher and the

Democratic leadership for Glass's commitment to limit the Federal Reserve's involvement in the stock market through margin regulation and the desire for a new commission. "It was a direct affront and a gratuitous indignity, and deliberately intended to be," said Glass. On May 15, he resigned from the Senate Banking and Currency Committee. "I named Senators Barkley and Byrnes as Democratic conferees," Fletcher said. "And I named them because they had been active supporters of the legislation and had worked hard on the bill and were sympathetic to the legislation. They helped me when I needed help most, and I put them on the committee. That is all there is to it. I love Carter Glass and Bob Wagner and there was no ill will involved in my action." Senate Majority Leader Joseph Robinson refused to accept Glass's resignation. "There will be no changes in the Democratic membership of that committee," he said, when asked about Glass's resignation.[181]

Glass's fears proved to be well-founded when on May 16 President Roosevelt revealed that he favored the House bill.[182]

The conferees first met on the afternoon of May 17 and decided to deal first with the less substantive, technical differences in the two bills, deferring the larger issues of margin and administration until a later date.[183] On May 24, the conference committee agreed to the provisions of the bill amending the Securities Act of 1933. The most controversial provision of the Securities Act amendments was a proposal to regulate the activities of bondholder protective committees. Senator Fletcher agreed to leave these committees unregulated by the act.[184]

On May 25, word of a compromise on the margin and administrative issues reached the press. It was reported that the conferees had agreed to accept the House proposal on margin regulation in exchange for agreement on the Senate bill's provisions for a new securities and exchange commission. "All I can say is that we are making progress and we expect to agree on a completed bill tomorrow," said Senator Fletcher. "It will be a constructive measure and one that I think both houses will accept."[185] The following day, the conferees announced they had agreed on a bill consistent with those reports.[186] The conference bill was formally submitted to both houses of Congress on May 30. Votes were scheduled in both the House and Senate on June 1.

After a brief discussion of the conference report, both the House and Senate approved the bill by an unrecorded voice vote.[187]

The Securities Exchange Act established the Securities and Exchange Commission, to be composed of five commissioners, appointed by the president with the advice and consent of the Senate, serving for a term of five years.

The Federal Reserve Board was authorized to prescribe margin rules both for initial extensions of credit and subsequently maintained credit. The margin rules would not become applicable to already-existing loans until July 1, 1937.

Immediately upon the bill's passage, Richard Whitney released a statement:

"The National Securities Exchange Act of 1934, which was passed by Congress today, differs in many important respects from the original Fletcher-Rayburn bill. The New York Stock Exchange opposed the original bill because it contained rigid and inflexible provisions which would have proved unworkable in practice. Many of these objectionable features have been eliminated, and the present act creates a new administrative commission of five persons to be appointed by the President and gives the commission broad powers to protect investors in the security markets of the country. The Exchange has always advocated these fundamental purposes of the Act. Although it still contains provisions that may prove impracticable, I am truly hopeful that if wisely and judiciously administered, the Act will be a constructive measure. For these reasons, and because national recovery and revival of business are of paramount importance, the Stock Exchange intends to do everything in its power to cooperate with the commission in the administration of the Act."[188]

Whitney also sent a letter to President Roosevelt offering the full assistance of the New York Stock Exchange to the new commission in preparation for the July 1, 1934, effective date of the act.

"As the New York Stock Exchange has every desire to cooperate with the commission, it occurred to me that the period between now and the 1st of July might profitably be used by the experts and other persons who will advise the new commission in studying the operations of the Exchange. . . . I would only be too pleased to extend to those persons every facility of the Exchange to study its operations. As you undoubtedly know from Colonel

McIntyre, I have on several occasions during the last few months endeavored to see you. I did so because there were so many provisions of the original drafts of the bill which were entirely unworkable that I felt I should discuss them with you. There are still many problems involved in some of the provisions of the bill, just reported to the Senate, and I trust you will be willing to see me at some time in the near future so that we may discuss how the Exchange can assist in the administration of this new and important piece of legislation."[189]

Whitney's hope for a Main Street rebellion against the bill never fully materialized, but his lobbying efforts were nonetheless effective in moderating a number of provisions of the bill to the advantage of the Exchange's members and listed companies. Exchange members were not required to be brokers only; dealers were permitted to continue to be members. The issue of the separation of the broker and dealer roles was deferred pending further study. Margin requirements were not rigidly set by law, but rather left to regulation by the Federal Reserve Board, a regulator much more sympathetic to Wall Street than the Federal Trade Commission. Quarterly reports by listed companies no longer required auditing, and the threshold for reporting equity ownership was set at 10 percent rather than the previous 5 percent. The prohibition against insider tipping and forfeiture of insider trading profits was eliminated. Perhaps most important, Whitney got his new agency—the Securities and Exchange Commission—and was no longer subject to the perceived anti-business prejudice of the Federal Trade Commission staff.

The Securities Exchange Act gave the federal government broad powers to regulate not only securities markets but also the corporations seeking to access capital by issuing securities in the public markets. However, most specifics were left to the Securities and Exchange Commission. The law would, in effect, be what the commissioners said it was. The SEC commissioners would have the power to seek a truce between Washington and Wall Street, if they so desired, or to intensify hostilities. All concerned were now looking for clues as to which course Roosevelt would direct.

At noon on June 6, President Roosevelt held a signing ceremony in the White House for the Securities Exchange Act of 1934. Alongside him were Senator Fletcher; representatives Rayburn, Lea, and Mapes; Ferdinand Pecora;

Tommy Corcoran; and Benjamin Cohen. When asked prior to the signing who he would appoint to the Securities and Exchange Commission, Roosevelt said he had received the names of more than fifty persons, but he hadn't yet given any consideration to appointees. But this was untrue: Roosevelt had long since settled on one man to head the new Securities and Exchange Commission.[190]

SEVEN

"YOUR FRIEND, JOE K. IN BOSTON":

The Creation of the Securities and Exchange Commission

Before it was certain there would even be a Securities and Exchange Commission, Franklin Roosevelt knew who he wanted to head it. In early April 1934, Roosevelt finally reached out to Joseph P. Kennedy regarding a possible position in the administration. The timing appeared right to Roosevelt to reward Kennedy for his support in the 1932 campaign. The Pecora Hearings were essentially over, and although the disclosures regarding Kennedy's participation in the Libbey-Owens-Ford pool were embarrassing, Kennedy had been shown to be, at worst, an opportunist. He had violated no laws nor any duties to any investors or counterparties. Nothing had come out that would disqualify him for high office. Many other equally prominent officials, including Treasury Secretary Woodin, who gladly accepted IPO allocation payoffs on J.P. Morgan's "preferred lists," were equally opportunistic or worse.

Through his son, James, Roosevelt first offered Kennedy a diplomatic post in South America, where it was thought he would be useful in negotiating trade treaties.[1] He then offered him the ambassadorship to Ireland.[2] Kennedy declined both, uninterested in either negotiating trade treaties in Uruguay or in being the "Irish" ambassador to Ireland. (Sixty years later, his daughter Jean would accept the ambassadorship to Ireland without a thought of ethnic condescension, her brother's presidency having eliminated practically all remaining sense of Irish social inferiority in America.)

Now twice rebuffed, the president was eager to come to terms with Kennedy on an acceptable post. During the second week of April, while both were on vacation in Florida, Roosevelt requested that Kennedy meet his train at the Palm Beach station for a quick chat. After exchanging pleasantries, Roosevelt invited Joe and Rose Kennedy to spend the following weekend at the White House. Kennedy accepted.[3]

Joe and Rose Kennedy arrived at the White House at 11:05 a.m. on April 14. That afternoon James Roosevelt and his wife, Betsey, took them to the racetrack, and that evening, Kennedy accompanied the president to the Willard Hotel for the annual Gridiron Dinner. Throughout the four-hour dinner, the president said nothing about his reason for inviting Kennedy. After returning to the White House around midnight, the president asked Kennedy to join him in his study for a talk. They ruminated on a wide range of topics for over three hours. At 3:15 a.m., Roosevelt retired to bed—still not having told Kennedy why he had been summoned. But as Kennedy was undressing for bed, James Roosevelt knocked on the guest bedroom door and informed Kennedy that the president wanted to speak with him again at 11:00 a.m.[4]

Kennedy rose early, attended 9:00 a.m. Mass, returned to the White House at 10:00 a.m., and packed for the trip home to New York. At 11:00 a.m., Kennedy met Roosevelt, who was still in bed and was being treated for a cold by a Navy doctor. When Roosevelt asked him why he'd declined offers of a diplomatic post, Kennedy expressed his annoyance at having been frozen out of the administration for over a year. The president blamed Kennedy's Wall Street connections, but Joe, expecting the response, presented him with a memo showing that the bulk of his money had been made in Hollywood, not on Wall Street. Roosevelt replied that he wasn't interested in how Joe had made his money and wanted him to come to Washington and serve on the securities commission contemplated by the Senate bill. Kennedy was non-committal. At 2:30 p.m., Joe and Rose left the White House for New York.[5]

In a letter to his eldest son, Joseph P. Kennedy Jr., Kennedy remained indifferent to the possibility of serving on the new commission, writing that he would "probably not be interested" in the job.[6] In a May 11, 1934, letter to Felix Frankfurter, Tommy Corcoran discussed the president's views on the composition of the commission, as relayed to him by Roosevelt adviser Raymond Moley: "The ticket for the Stock Exchange Commission on which the Skipper has secretly smiled is Jim – Democrat, Ben – Democrat, Judge Healy – Republican, Mathews – Republican, and your friend, Joe K. in Boston – Democrat. The last is particularly 'deep well,' comes straight from the Skipper through Ray."[7]

On June 15, 1934, Moley prepared a memorandum for the president regarding eight possible nominees to the five-member commission. At the top of the list was Joseph Kennedy, who was also Moley's choice for chairman. Next was Jim Landis, followed by George C. Mathews, a liberal Republican from Wisconsin, who Roosevelt had appointed to the Federal Trade Commission. Fourth was Benjamin Cohen. The fifth was the moderate Democrat banker Paul V. Shields, followed by Gordon Wasson, a thirty-five-year-old banker at Morgan Guaranty Trust Company who'd acted as Morgan's liaison with Corcoran, Landis, and Cohen and was well liked by both the reformers and the Wall Street community. Rounding out the list were Frank C. Shaughnessy, president of the San Francisco Stock Exchange, and Judge Robert E. Healy, a Vermont Republican and Federal Trade Commission member. At the bottom of the memorandum, Roosevelt added his preferences for the commission— Kennedy, Landis, Shaughnessy, Mathews, and Healy. Curiously absent from Moley's list was Ferdinand Pecora, who had great popular support and a strong patron in Senator Fletcher.[8]

The New York Times was reporting that Landis and Mathews were nearly certain to be nominated to the commission, while also floating the names of Tommy Corcoran and Benjamin Cohen; New York bankers James C. Auchincloss and William Freiday; Goldman Sachs partner Sidney Y. Weinberg; and Frank Shaughnessy and fellow San Francisco banker Dean Witter.[9]

On June 24, James Roosevelt called Joe Kennedy requesting that he come to Washington later that week. Kennedy was laid up in Hyannis Port with a broken leg after being thrown from a horse but was swayed by James Roosevelt's strong urging to travel to New York, so as to be halfway to Washington if he was called upon by the president.[10]

On June 25, *The New York Times* reported that James Landis would be selected as chairman of the commission.[11] The following day, Kennedy was called by journalist and friend Herbert Swope, who speculated that Pecora would be offered the chairmanship, with the understanding that he would resign after a year to make way for Kennedy. Swope said that Roy Howard, the influential publisher of the Scripps-Howard newspaper chain, had objections to Kennedy and wanted Pecora. Kennedy told Swope he wasn't even sure he wanted to serve on the commission and had no desire to serve unless it was as chairman.[12]

Notwithstanding the apparent movement in favor of Pecora, Kennedy agreed to go to Washington the next day. Despite his playing hard to get with the president, Kennedy wanted to be the first chairman of the SEC.

Kennedy spent most of his first day in D.C. with Raymond Moley, who tried to convince him to serve on the commission even if he was not chairman.[13] *The New York Times* was now reporting that Pecora would accept a one-year term as chairman and that Landis and Mathews would be appointed, with the remaining two positions likely to be filled by Baldwin Bane and Robert E. Healy.[14] Kennedy reiterated his position to Moley: it was the chairmanship or nothing.[15]

Kennedy received a call at his hotel from the White House requesting that he meet with the president at 5:00 p.m. Before leaving for the White House, Kennedy called upon the man he most admired and respected: press magnate William Randolph Hearst. It should be the chairmanship or nothing, Hearst advised.[16]

Kennedy arrived at the White House promptly at 5:00 p.m. but sat with the president for an hour while Roosevelt attended to other business. By 6:00 p.m., he still hadn't mentioned the Securities and Exchange Commission. The president invited Kennedy to join him for a swim in the White House pool. As they swam, Roosevelt signed a bill, discussed a radio speech he would make that night, but avoided any discussion of the SEC situation. After the swim, they dressed and had a cocktail in the president's study. Still, nothing about the SEC. Dinner was served at 8:00 p.m., with Mrs. Roosevelt, financier Bernard Baruch, and several others joining. At the end of dinner, Eleanor Roosevelt asked, "Franklin, when are you going to talk to Joe?" "About two o'clock tomorrow morning," the president joked.[17]

Shortly after his radio speech, Roosevelt sent for Kennedy and Baruch. Moley was with the president when they arrived. "Joe, sit down and just pretend you are not here while we discuss the make-up of committees I have to appoint before I leave on my vacation tomorrow." Roosevelt then read a telegram from Pecora indicating he would be willing to take the chairmanship for a year. He then handed Kennedy a sheet of paper with a list of names in the following order: Kennedy, Mathews, Landis, Healy, and Shaughnessy. "This is a list I made up two weeks ago, and I see no reason to change it except to put Pecora in Shaughnessy's place," Roosevelt said. "Because I have a sort of agreement with Fletcher to give Pecora one of the places. I think you can be a great liberal on that, and I think you would do a great job running it." The four men continued talking until about 2:00 a.m.[18] Kennedy left the next day to spend the weekend in Hyannis Port.

On Friday, June 29, Roosevelt casually tipped off reporters that rumors of Kennedy's appointment shouldn't be discounted. "I sat up and drank beer with Barney Baruch and Joe Kennedy. I did not do any work at all, it was awful— two o'clock and I have no excuse for it."[19]

On Saturday night, Marvin McIntyre, President Roosevelt's personal secretary, called Kennedy in Hyannis Port to inform him that Roosevelt had released to the press his nominees for the Securities and Exchange Commission. And though the president did not have the statutory authority to name its chairman, he indicated that Kennedy was his choice. McIntyre told Kennedy he would have to be in Washington on Monday morning to be sworn in. Roosevelt left it to James Farley to tell Pecora that Kennedy would be the choice for chairman. "Ferdie took it pretty well," Farley reported back to the president.[20]

Pecora was taking it well because he wasn't ready to concede the chairmanship quite yet, or at least not without some concession from Kennedy. He bore no ill will toward Joe; Roosevelt was a different matter. The president had now put him, the champion of the small investor who had brought down the malefactors of great wealth, in a position of near supplication to Kennedy, who had barely escaped disgrace at Pecora's hands just a few months earlier. And this after Pecora did the president a favor by entering the Manhattan D.A.'s race. Quite a change in fortune.

On July 1, Kennedy traveled to New York and met with Herbert Swope, Bernard Baruch, and Raymond Moley to discuss the next day's showdown with Pecora. Moley told Kennedy he had a letter from Roosevelt ready to give to Landis, Mathews, and Healy instructing them to elect Kennedy chairman.[21]

When Kennedy arrived in Washington on Monday morning, he went straight to the White House to meet with McIntyre and discuss the day's events. As word leaked to the newspapermen that a fight was brewing between Kennedy and Pecora for the chairmanship, the press gaggle gathered at the Federal Trade Commission building.

In the early afternoon, in ninety-three-degree heat, Kennedy arrived at the FTC's gray stucco building on Connecticut Avenue, wandered through the waiting journalists, and went to George Mathews's office. Pecora arrived shortly after Kennedy and headed for Landis's office. For the next hour, Landis shuttled between his office and Mathews's, acting as go-between for Kennedy and Pecora.[22]

Kennedy and Landis left Mathews's office and walked four doors down to Landis's, where Pecora awaited. The two men conferred face-to-face for another hour. Pecora told Kennedy that he felt poorly treated by Roosevelt and wanted to return to private law practice if he could not be chairman. Pecora offered that if he was made chairman, he would step down in sixty days, allowing Kennedy to assume the chairmanship. Kennedy rejected the offer, countering that Pecora be awarded primary responsibility for the supervision of the trading and exchange division of the commission—if he would agree to forgo the chairmanship.[23]

He agreed.

Kennedy, Pecora, and Landis emerged smiling, and returned to Mathews's office, where the swearing-in and press conference were to be held. Healy had returned to his office on the floor above and had to be called to come downstairs for the proceedings. He arrived, in shirtsleeves, and with all five commissioners present, Mrs. Edna B. Vincel, a notary of the Federal Trade Commission, administered the oath. A brief executive session of the commission followed, during which Kennedy was formally elected chairman unanimously. When asked by reporters what had transpired in the closed-door meetings, Kennedy responded, "We were simply discussing policies and matters like that. We discussed a dozen different things." When asked if the chairmanship was one of the topics discussed, all of the commissioners answered with silence and a smile.[24]

The first working session of the Securities and Exchange Commission was held the following day and was devoted principally to coordinating the hiring of senior staff. Speaking to reporters, Kennedy announced: "The days of stock manipulation are in the past now. There will be little of this 'buy today and out Thursday business' from this time on. Times have changed and things that seemed right four or five years ago are now out of the picture. The commission will operate to protect legitimate investors, big and little, and this applies to the whole field covered by the new law."[25]

Kennedy was well aware he had a past to live down and wasted no time trying to get out in front of the accusations that he was a Wall Street wolf put in charge of the henhouse: "Any success I ever achieved was in administrative work and not in market operations. Of course, I know something about the Exchanges and my experience is that money made in speculation is negligible when compared to the returns received by those who invest their money in gilt-edge securities and hold on to them. Few who know the facts will deny the accuracy of this statement."[26]

At lunch that day, Kennedy met with Corcoran, Landis, and Cohen at the Tally-Ho Tavern Coffee House to begin the process of winning over the reformers. "Why the hell do you fellows hate me?" Kennedy asked the shocked young men. They assured the new chairman that he had it wrong.[27]

But he didn't have it wrong. Kennedy was the most unpopular major appointment to date among the liberal New Dealers. Journalist John T. Flynn, previously a Pecora investigator, wrote that "had FDR's dearest enemy accused him of an intention of making so grotesque an appointment as Joseph Kennedy to the Chairman of the SEC, the charge might have been laid to malice, yet the President has exceeded the expectations of even his most ardent ill-wishers."[28]

In his diary, Secretary of the Interior Harold Ickes wrote regarding Roosevelt's appointment of Kennedy: "I am afraid I do not agree with the president as to the chairman he is going to name for the Securities Commission. He has named Joseph P. Kennedy for that place, a former stock market plunger. The president has great confidence in him because he made his pile, has invested all his money in Government securities and knows all of the tricks of the trade. Apparently he is going on the assumption that Kennedy would now like to make a name for himself for the sake of his family, but I have never known many of these cases to work out as expected."[29]

Jerome Frank, general counsel of the Agricultural Adjustment Administration (and a future SEC chairman), said naming Kennedy was "like setting a wolf to guard a flock of sheep."[30] Tommy Corcoran quipped to Ray Moley: "Oh well, we've got four out of five anyhow."[31] Roy Howard wrote in an editorial in his *Washington News* that the president "cannot with impunity administer such a slap in the face to his most loyal and effective supporters as that reported to be contemplated in the appointment of Joseph P. Kennedy."[32]

Roosevelt's choice of Kennedy for the SEC chairmanship was indeed difficult to explain. He was, in truth, a relatively minor figure on Wall Street. Although he'd been associated over the course of his career with a number of brokerage and investment houses, the associations were always loose ones and the houses (such as Hayden, Stone & Co., Halle & Stieglitz and Redmond and Company) were second-tier institutions. Kennedy had never held a senior-level position in any banking institution other than at the tiny Columbia Trust Company, controlled by his father. He was the consummate lone wolf. He had made his fortune—and would continue to grow it manyfold after his government service ended—essentially by himself, with a telephone and small cadre of loyalists, like Edward Moore (for whom his youngest child was named). If Roosevelt was looking to appease Wall Street, Kennedy was not a logical choice. The list of executives up for consideration for the Securities and Exchange Commission contained a number of men much more respected and trusted on Wall Street: Sidney Weinberg, Paul V. Shields, Gordon Wasson, Frank C. Shaughnessy, and the Auchincloss brothers. Others explained the appointment as Roosevelt repaying his political debt to Kennedy for his assistance during the 1932 campaign. But there were dozens of posts Roosevelt could have offered Kennedy that would have met with less resistance and criticism. Indeed, offering Kennedy the ambassadorship to Ireland was sufficient to repay the political debt. The most plausible explanation for why Roosevelt chose Kennedy is that he believed him the best available man for the job.

The job awaiting Kennedy was daunting. All of the country's dozens of securities exchanges had to be either registered with the Securities and Exchange Commission or granted an exemption from registration because of a low volume of trading. All of the securities traded on the exchanges needed to be registered as well. Forms for those registrations needed to be created and rules governing registration adopted. Forms for annual and quarterly reports by issuers of registered securities needed to be created, as well as forms for disclosing ownership of equity securities of listed companies.

The commission was also required under the Securities Exchange Act to adopt rules and regulations governing an enormous portion of the activity in the securities markets. These included a "net capital rule" limiting leverage at brokerage firms, rules governing hypothecation of customer securities and stabilization of trading prices for securities in distribution, rules for permissible options trading on exchanges, rules limiting short selling and stop-loss orders, rules defining manipulative trading activities and excessive off-floor trading.

The Securities Exchange Act and Securities Act amendments also directed the commission to undertake four major studies and reports to Congress with recommendations for legislation. The first, due by January 3, 1935, was a study of the rules of national securities exchanges with respect to governance and disciplining of members. The other three, due by January 3, 1936, were studies concerning the feasibility and advisability of the complete segregation of the functions of brokers and dealers, the trading in unlisted securities on exchanges, and the activities of protective committees in reorganization and liquidation proceedings.

Kennedy's most important duties were enforcing the new laws in an aggressive manner so that the nation's investor base would regain confidence in the fairness of the securities markets, while at the same time encouraging Wall Street and corporate America, fearful of the liability under the new laws, to raise needed funds in the securities markets to stimulate economic growth and get Americans back to work.

Kennedy was never fully accepted or trusted by either the inner circle of the brain trust or the power elites on Wall Street. Louis M. Howe, Roosevelt's de facto chief of staff, had a near obsession with keeping Kennedy away from the president.[33] And the Wall Street establishment had long been skeptical of him. Fresh off his enormous success in reorganizing Hollywood studios, Kennedy visited the offices of J.P. Morgan & Co. one day in 1929 to schedule a meeting with Morgan to discuss some business opportunities. Morgan must have thought Kennedy's overture a bit too presumptuous and concluded that he needed a dose of humility. On the appointed day, Morgan had Kennedy cool his heels, then dispatched a clerk to tell Kennedy he was sorry but

Mr. Morgan was too busy to meet.[34] (The relationship between Kennedy and Morgan would change dramatically by the end of the decade. When Kennedy was ambassador to the Court of St. James, he lived in the Morgan's London mansion, which J.P. Morgan Jr. had donated to the British government in 1920. Morgan also gave Kennedy use of his country estate in England, Wall Hall, during the German blitz in 1940.)[35]

On the same day Kennedy was rebuffed by Morgan, he had scheduled a second appointment with another Wall Street power player to discuss business opportunities. This meeting with legendary trader Michael J. Meehan at the office of M.J. Meehan & Co. was nearly as disastrous for Kennedy as the non-meeting with Morgan. Kennedy was barely through his pitch when Meehan cut short the meeting, showing Kennedy the door. To be stood up by the legendary J.P. Morgan Jr. was certainly disappointing, but to be given the bum's rush by a fellow trader (and fellow Irishman) like Meehan—on the same day no less—was humiliating. This was not the kind of snub the proud Joe Kennedy would soon forget (or forgive).[36]

Roosevelt knew what made Kennedy tick—wealth, which he had already obtained in great measure, and political power and social acceptance, which he had yet to obtain. Despite the enormous risk that the Securities and Exchange Commission would fail in its ambitious agenda, Kennedy was willing to take on the task, provided its success (or failure) would be personally linked to him. Success would mean being an equal to Morgans and Whitneys on Wall Street and a savior to the little investor on Main Street. Failure would surely mean he would forever be known as Roosevelt's folly.

Despite a complicated personal relationship—the yearlong exile from the administration, Kennedy's relentless bad-mouthing of the president for his apparent ingratitude, Kennedy's turning down of the Irish ambassadorship, and Roosevelt's cruel toying with Kennedy at his White House visits—Kennedy needed Roosevelt, and Roosevelt needed Kennedy.

It wasn't only Kennedy's unique one-foot-in-the-door relationship with both the New Dealers and Wall Street and his remarkable administrative skills that made him attractive. Roosevelt's gravest political risk was an "Irish rebellion" within the ranks of the Democratic Party. He had neutralized Al Smith in 1932 with the help of James Farley, Bronx leader Ed Flynn, and Joe Kennedy, but there remained the ever-present threat of an urban machine Irish–populist farmer alliance that could undo his New Deal coalition. This seed was already germinating in 1934 in the curious friendship between Senator Huey Long and Father Charles Coughlin of Michigan, a radio evangelist popular among Irish Catholic Democrats nationwide. Roosevelt would continually weigh the political risks to himself of elevating the profile of potential rivals like Kennedy and Farley versus alienating them. Many thought the appointment of Kennedy as ambassador to Great Britain in January 1938, an offer no Irish American of his social ambition could possibly refuse, was motivated principally by Roosevelt's desire to get him out of the way—literally out of the country—while he plotted an unprecedented third term. When a threat to Roosevelt materialized in 1940 with James Farley's challenge for the Democratic nomination, Roosevelt had so skillfully diluted the opposition, including by tacitly encouraging both Farley and Vice President John Nance Garner to run in order to avoid a united opposition, that he was able to orchestrate a "Draft Roosevelt" movement at the convention.

Kennedy knew a key to his success as SEC chairman would be an ability to convince Wall Street, Congress, and the public that he had broad powers and would be acting as the president's proxy in exercising those powers. "It's not what you are," Kennedy would say to his children, "it's what people think you are."[37] Kennedy would maintain a close relationship with the president throughout his tenure and then exaggerate that closeness by way of his allies in the press. Throughout his career, he made cultivation of the press a top priority. Arthur Krock, The New York Times Washington bureau chief, would become Kennedy's off-the-books public relations man.

On July 4, 1934, Krock profiled Kennedy for the Times, asserting that Kennedy "has never been in a bear pool in his life."[38] Other contemporaneous articles from The New York Times were equally positive: "When Mr. Roosevelt won, Mr. Kennedy was mentioned prominently for the Cabinet. He was not named. Next, he was mentioned as possible successor to the late Secretary Woodin. Again he was not named."[39] Most of the mentioning of Kennedy for those posts was likely by Kennedy himself. But Kennedy's brilliant use of the press served the national interest in establishing the Securities and Exchange Commission.

Kennedy knew that with the controversy surrounding his past on Wall Street there would be no tolerance for any impropriety under his watch. Accordingly, the first rule adopted by the Securities and Exchange Commission was a prohibition on speculative securities transactions by employees of the commission. Commission staff would lead by example, avoiding even an appearance of conflicts. On July 6, Kennedy announced the rule:

"The Commission voted that no employee of the Commission shall participate directly or indirectly in any transaction concerning a security subject to the jurisdiction of the Commission, except that such prohibition shall not be construed to prevent the sale or purchase of a security for bona fide investment purposes. To the end that this regulation shall be properly observed, it is ordered that (1) no employee shall carry any securities on margin, and (2) every employee shall report every transaction in any security whether exempted or otherwise to the Commission within forty-eight hours after making of such transaction exclusive of Sundays and holidays. Violation of this regulation shall be regarded as instant cause for dismissal."[40]

Despite his desire to leave his personal imprint on the new commission, Kennedy did not have a free hand in choosing his top deputies. Four of the five top staff positions had been bargained away by Kennedy during his horse-trading for the chairmanship. He had promised Pecora that David Saperstein would be named chief of the Trading and Exchange Division. Landis was promised that Baldwin Bane would be named head of the Administrative Division and that Donald Montgomery would be named chief of the Registration Division. It was also agreed with Landis that Yale professor William O. Douglas would be named chief of the Protective Committee study. Douglas brought with him as his top assistant a young lawyer named Abe Fortas. It was a study undertaken by two future U.S. Supreme Court justices.[41]

The remaining senior staff appointment—and probably the most important—was that of general counsel, head of the Legal Division. Landis, Corcoran, Frankfurter, and the rest of the New Dealers strongly advocated for Benjamin Cohen, believing he had been denied a seat on the SEC because Roosevelt feared a backlash against the appointment of a Jewish commissioner.[42] Many in the Wall Street establishment viewed the securities reform movement, led for two generations by Jewish professors Louis Brandeis and Felix Frankfurter, and aided prominently by Jewish lawyers Samuel Untermyer and Benjamin Cohen, as Jewish revenge visited upon Christian bankers who excluded them from boardrooms and social clubs. In early 1934, Morgan partner Russell Leffingwell, discussing the separation of investment banking and commercial banking mandated by Glass-Steagall with fellow partner Thomas Lamont, openly expressed the anti-Semitism many others privately harbored: "The Jews do not forget. They are relentless. . . . The reason why I make so much of this is that I think you underestimate the forces we are antagonizing. . . ."[43]

Kennedy was unmoved by pleas for a consolation prize for Cohen. He wanted an ally—a Boston Irishman—for general counsel. It was a paradox in Kennedy. He would get visibly angry if referred to as an Irishman. One time, he exploded at a newspaperman who referred to him as Irish: "Goddamn it! I was born in this country! My children were born in this country! What the hell does someone have to do to become an American?"[44] Curiously, most, if not all, of his important mentors were WASPs, not Irish Catholics—Gordon Abbot, Guy Currier, Galen Stone, William Randolph Hearst, Franklin Roosevelt. Yet throughout his career, nearly all of his closest, trusted lieutenants were Irish Catholics.

John J. Burns was born in Cambridge, Massachusetts, in 1901, the son of Irish immigrants. He attended parochial school in Cambridge and Boston, graduating from Boston College and then Harvard Law School. He, too, was a protégé of Felix Frankfurter and was invited to join the Harvard Law School faculty in 1929. In 1934, Burns became a full professor at Harvard Law School and, shortly thereafter, was named an associate justice of the Superior Court of Massachusetts. All before his thirtieth birthday.[45]

Kennedy met Judge Burns for the first time on July 15, 1934. Kennedy was so impressed with Burns he announced his appointment as the SEC's first general counsel the very next day.[46]

The new chairman gained a reputation as a taskmaster. When he called around to several staffers one morning early in his tenure and found that no one was yet in the office, he sent a memo to all commission employees: "From now on everybody must be at his desk at 9:00 unless he received my personal permission to the contrary. Joseph P. Kennedy, Chairman."[47]

Shortly after issuing his directive, Kennedy received a call at home at 3:00 a.m. Eddie Moore answered the phone: "I've got to speak to Mr. Kennedy personally," said the caller, a young commission staffer. "He's sleeping," replied Moore. "I've got to speak to him personally," the young man insisted. A reluctant Moore awakened Kennedy. "Mr. Kennedy, I'm down in the library at the office. I've just finished up a memorandum that the general counsel wants first thing in the morning. It's 3:00 a.m., I'm awful tired, and I'm wondering whether, pursuant to the memorandum, I could have your personal permission to come in at 9:30 a.m. tomorrow."[48]

The commission staff was unquestionably hardworking and efficient. At times, they grew weary of the workload. One staffer, after spending hours reviewing the disclosure in a registration statement with Commissioner Healy, grew tired of Healy's mantra about "sufficient information to protect the average prudent investor" and snapped: "Judge, in my humble opinion, the average prudent investor is a greedy son of a bitch."[49]

On July 16, 1934, the Senate Banking and Currency Committee released Pecora's final report from the two-year investigation of the securities markets. Kennedy's investment in the Libbey-Owens-Ford Glass Company pool was prominently featured in press accounts of the report. The reaction was bruising.

Leading the attack against Kennedy was Pecora's friend John T. Flynn. Writing in the July 18, 1934, issue of *The New Republic,* Flynn again excoriated Kennedy. Flynn began with the pool:

> "This is indeed an impossible world. Last summer Ferdinand Pecora was busy probing the sins of Wall Street. At the same time Joseph P. Kennedy was busy with a group of his pals—Mason Day, Harry Sinclair, Elisha Walker, of Kuhn, Loeb and Company and two or three others—putting over a pool in Libby Owens Ford Glass Company stock. The pool was inspired by Walker of Kuhn, Loeb in whose office at the time Pecora was drilling for facts. It was managed by Mason Day of Redmond and Company, stock brokers, where Joseph P. Kennedy had his office."[50]

Moving on to the Kennedy appointment, Flynn continued:

> "Of course, I did not in my wildest dreams imagine he would appoint a speculator as Chairman of that body. There are various groups in Wall Street. There are commission brokers who scrupulously refrain from speculation, will not let their employees speculate, operate no pools, believe in market reform and who, in accordance with their lights, operate their brokerage business in a civilized manner. I thought perhaps Roosevelt would appoint such a man, though I thought this would be a grave error. I did not think he would

go to the bottom of the heap—I speak of the Wall Street operators. Below the commission brokers in civilized rating would be the floor traders, who would be excluded from the Exchange. Below them are the specialists who speculate for their own account and who should be whipped off the floor. And below them are the outside speculators, fellows like Mathew Brush, Jesse Livermore, Percy Rockefeller, Arthur Cutten, Tom Bragg. They frequently have desks in brokers' offices where they play the game close to the ticker and close to their shirt fronts. Who, I ask, would have believed, as Pecora last February unfolded the sorry tale of the repeal pools, that the President of the United States would have gone to this class?"[51]

Flynn then attacked Kennedy's record as an executive in Hollywood, pointing to the income statement of Pathé Exchange, Inc., a company Kennedy ran between 1927 and 1930:

"Beginning with Kennedy, sales increased very little, but costs rose rapidly. In the three years before the coming of the wizard, the company's sales exceeded costs each year. In the four years after Kennedy, the company's costs exceeded sales every year.... The common stock went from around $12 to $1.50 a share. Finally, the company was sold to R.K.O. to escape complete dissolution.... He has gone from a desk in a broker's office to the headship of the commission that will manage Wall Street for the New Deal. I say it isn't true. It is impossible. It could not happen."[52]

Kennedy refused to let the fallout from the Pecora Hearings report affect his agenda or effectiveness. In the week following its release, Kennedy kept a visibly busy schedule. On July 19, he met with representatives of the American Institute of Public Accountants and the American Society of Certified Public Accountants to solicit their recommendation regarding financial statement preparation under the Securities Act and Securities Exchange Act.[53] On July 24, Kennedy met with Frank Altschul, chairman of the NYSE Listing Committee, J.M.B. Hoxsey, secretary of the exchange, and Roland Redmond, the exchange's outside counsel, to discuss the process of registering the exchanges. "It was just an informal talk during which the members of the Commission and the representatives of the New York Stock Exchange discussed some of the more important matters facing the Commission," Kennedy said. "There will be further conferences of the same kind in the near future."[54]

The following afternoon, Kennedy delivered his first nationally broadcast radio address, a speech before the National Press Club in Washington, D.C. The address was widely anticipated as the Roosevelt administration's unveiling of the SEC's philosophy. It was also Kennedy's best opportunity to defuse his critics after the Pecora report revelations. Would the speech set a tone of conflict or cooperation with Wall Street? Kennedy took the occasion to reassure Wall Street and corporate America that they had a partner in the Securities and Exchange Commission:

> "We at the S.E.C. do not regard ourselves as coroners sitting on the corpse of financial enterprise. On the contrary, we think of ourselves as the means of bringing new life into the body of the security business. We are not working on the theory that all men and all women connected with finance, either as workers or investors, are to be regarded as guilty of some undefined crime. On the contrary, we hold that business based on good will should be encouraged so that it may be helpful."[55]

Kennedy went on to explain his mission:

> "I conceive it to be an important part of the job we are trying to do here in the S.E.C. to reassure capital as to its safety in going ahead and to reassure the investor as to the protection of his interests, by restricting certain practices which have proved to be detrimental to their interests and by making available adequate information to the public upon which it can act intelligently. We regard ourselves as the President has said, as partners in a cooperative enterprise. We do not start off with the belief that every enterprise is crooked and that those behind it are crooks."[56]

Kennedy's words had the desired effect. They were, in essence, the announcement of a truce, a new phase in the relationship between New Deal Washington and Wall Street. Richard Whitney was quick to praise the speech: "I think Mr. Kennedy has shown that he is approaching his job carefully and from a sane and sound point of view. It is unnecessary to reiterate that we shall do everything to help the Commission achieve the results they desire. What Mr. Kennedy said is just good common business sense, and to my way of thinking, most reassuring."[57]

Equally important, the speech was also widely praised by members of the brain trust. In a letter dated July 20, 1934, Columbia law professor and Roosevelt adviser Adolf A. Berle wrote Kennedy: "I am writing particularly because there are people whose idea of stock exchange regulations is to civilize stock exchanges with fire and sword. I understand why they feel that way about it, but it is not a fruitful approach, and I am glad that you spoke the way you did in your first public statement on behalf of the new Commission."[58]

Kennedy used the opportunity presented by the successful national radio address to procure another favorable profile from *The New York Times* in order to mitigate any lingering negative fallout from the Pecora report. The piece, written by S.J. Woolf of the Washington bureau, describes Kennedy on the job in almost fawning words:

"Sitting in a scorching room in a temporary wooden building which the government erected hastily during the war, Mr. Kennedy expressed his views concerning past abuses and future reforms. It was no visionary or theorist who spoke."

"Tall, broad-shouldered and athletically built, Mr. Kennedy lounged in his chair. There is nothing formal or foreboding about him. He answers good naturedly questions about former activities—questions which might never had been asked had he been less free and candid in his manner. He has operated in stocks, but he has done it with his own money. He has never been in a bear pool. He says whatever success he has achieved has been the result of administrative work and not of market operations. He does not deny, however, that he knows the Wall Street game."

"There is a certain fanatical fervor about him when he describes his present job. He regards it almost as a mission. He feels sure that the Commission will eradicate the evils which attended the securities market. There is an engaging candor about Mr. Kennedy. And an impression of capability. Moreover, he has great personal charm. These qualities account for much of his early success in business."[59]

The piece closed with a quote from Kennedy.

"'Since the war, a great number of our citizens have been investors. The country taught them to put their money into bonds and they have increased their
holdings in different forms of securities. The millions of policy holders in
our life insurance companies are moreover indirectly invested in securities.
It's the job of our Commission to help all those people. The days of stock manipulation are over. Our ideas have changed. Things that seemed all right a
few years ago find no place in our present-day philosophy. Big and little investors are going to be protected and malefactors of great wealth will not have
an opportunity to ply their nefarious trades.'"[60]

It had been less than a month since the Pecora report had been released,
but its disclosures regarding Kennedy's Wall Street past seemed to have been
completely forgiven, if not forgotten.

In the heat of the Washington summer, Kennedy began grinding out the
particulars of the SEC's regulatory regime. On August 13, 1934, after a frenetic
six weeks of meetings and conferences, the commission approved and published the final forms and rules for the registration of the country's forty-three
exchanges under the Securities Exchange Act, as well as the regulations and
forms for the temporary registration of securities listed on those exchanges. In
addition, on that day, the commission published the rules and regulations
implementing the reporting of stock ownership by officers, directors, and ben-
eficial owners of more than 10 percent of the stock of a listed company. The
filing of stock ownership reports would commence in November 1934.[61]

Commenting on the new rules and forms, Kennedy said: "We don't tell
him what's a good buy; all we do is give information on the details of the stock.
We hope to eliminate practices which have caused undue fluctuations, but even
by eliminating these manipulative practices, you cannot control all of the rises
or falls of the market."[62]

On August 29, the commission issued more regulations, relating to permitting the continued trading on an exchange of unlisted securities. The application for permission to continue such trading was to be filed by the
exchanges with the commission no later than September 16, 1934.[63]

On September 13, the SEC held a meeting with representatives of the stock
exchanges on the issue of short selling, which would only be permissible after

October 1, 1934, the effective date of the Securities Exchange Act, if the SEC allowed it. During the Crash, as in 2008, short selling was blamed in part for the collapse of stock prices. The short sellers themselves, then as now, argued that they serve a useful market function—bringing inflated prices down to earth and providing liquidity in the market by purchasing to cover short sales. In the aftermath of the Lehman collapse, short sales of stocks of financial companies were temporarily banned by the SEC. Representatives of seven exchanges were present at the meeting with Kennedy in Washington. Kennedy announced that pending promulgation of rules, short-selling transactions would be permitted as they were presently allowed. In explaining the difficulties involved in formulating a rule, he noted that, all told, the commission had heard the views of twenty exchanges on the short-selling issue, and none had the same rules on when it was permitted.[64]

On September 18, Kennedy, along with the other commissioners and top aides, were given a tour of the New York Stock Exchange by Richard Whitney. Part photo op, part working session, the event gave Kennedy the opportunity to press the flesh with rank-and-file exchange members and apply his considerable charm to his constituents. When the press asked whether he intended to crack down on the exchange, Kennedy replied: "We haven't started off on that premise. The commission is going to make rules as well as it can, and if they are interpreted in that light, the commission can't help it."[65]

When asked about the looming effective date of the act, Kennedy reiterated that trading rules would not be complete by October 1: "Final rules and regulations on stock exchange operations will be promulgated by the commission only after due consideration is given to all factors. Because of the tremendous amount of work involved, present indications are that the task cannot be completed by October 1, the date on which the commission can begin to regulate the securities exchanges."[66]

Asked what he thought the floor brokers made of the commission's visit, Kennedy, referencing the fact that they were there on a day with very low trading volume, joked that the "brokers seemed to be looking to their telephones to see whether or not any business was coming over the wire."[67] The members appreciated Kennedy's outreach and humor. There was a growing feeling among them that federal regulation might not be altogether bad for business.

As the effective date of the Securities Exchange Act approached, Yankees fans again faced the prospect of no World Series in New York. The team again finished second in the American League—and again seven games back, but this time to the Detroit Tigers (who would lose the World Series to the St. Louis Cardinals in seven games). On September 24, the Yankees played their last home game against the Boston Red Sox. Ruth announced mid-season that 1934 would possibly be his last. Yet only 2,000 fans came out to watch the Babe's final game in Yankee Stadium. He played only one inning, making an error in the outfield and was then pulled for a pinch runner after walking. The Yankees lost five-to-zero. For the season, Ruth was down significantly in all batting categories. His average slipped to .288; he hit only twenty-two home runs but batted in a respectable 104.[68]

On September 26, the Securities and Exchange Commission took its first adverse action against Wall Street when it denied the temporary registration of bonds of the Brooklyn-Manhattan Transit Corporation. The bonds had recently been issued pursuant to the intrastate offering exemption from registration under the Securities Act—all bonds, the subway operator claimed, were offered and sold only in New York. However, in connection with the offering, the bonds were required by the underwriters to be listed on the New York Stock Exchange. Kennedy took the view that, notwithstanding the fact that all of the underwriters and dealers were exclusively in New York, the distribution of the bonds had not "come to rest" until they were in the hands of purchasers who held them for investment purposes. And the simultaneous listing of the bonds on an exchange indicated an intent to further distribute the bonds to purchasers not necessarily residing only in New York. Accordingly, the SEC denied temporary registration because it believed the New York Stock Exchange listing violated the Securities Act. By refusing to register the bonds under the Securities Exchange Act, the SEC effectively delisted them from the New York Stock Exchange. Kennedy believed that if exempt offerings with subsequent exchange listings were permitted, the Securities Act would be gutted and the authority of the SEC subverted.[69] An important message was relayed: regulation would be reasonable, but circumvention would not be tolerated.

On September 27, the SEC certified the registration of twenty-one exchanges under the Securities Exchange Act. Twenty-four exchanges had submitted applications for registration. After investigation by the SEC, one exchange, the New York Mining Exchange, discontinued operating entirely and another, the New York Produce Exchange, closed its facilities to securities trading. The third exchange not registered—the Los Angeles Curb Exchange—merged with the Los Angeles Stock Exchange.[70]

In addition, nineteen stock exchanges were granted exemptions from registration. Fifteen such exchanges were granted exemption for low volume, and four exchanges agreed to discontinue operating altogether—the California Stock Exchange, the Boston Curb Exchange, the Hartford Stock Exchange, and the Philippine Stock Exchange of Manila.[71]

On October 1, 1934, most provisions of the Securities Exchange Act became legally effective. The best compliment that could be paid to Kennedy's SEC was the one given it by the market that day—indifference. The Dow Jones Industrial Average closed at ninety-two on September 1, 1934, at ninety on October 1, and at ninety-three on November 1. As Kennedy had hoped, it was a non-event to the financial markets. It was a historic event nonetheless. What might have been a day of revolt on Wall Street became a milestone of a new era of improved capitalism.

The temporary registration of securities listed on national securities exchanges became effective that day. Two thousand nine hundred and ten stock issues were registered, along with 1968 bond issues with a total principal amount of nearly $29,000,000,000. The temporary registrations were valid through June 30, 1935. The development of the forms and rules for the permanent registration of listed securities would be a primary focus of the commission through the fall and winter. These forms, prepared by the officers, attorneys, and accountants of the thousands of companies with listed securities, needed to reflect a balance between disclosure of sufficient information so that investors had a reasonable basis on which to make investment decisions, but not be so burdensome to prepare that management resources would be monopolized in processing them or that the costs of the preparation would be prohibitive. Corporate management had companies to run, and the challenges of doing so during the Depression were daunting enough. The last thing needed was more responsibilities when managements were already doing more work with less pay. And these forms needed work in tandem with the Securities Act registration forms and the forms for ongoing periodic reporting by public companies. A lack of coordination could result in duplicative or inconsistent reporting obligations.

In the process of developing the forms and rules, Kennedy sought out and received direct input from many of the most important business executives in the country. Those working most closely with Kennedy were Gerard Swope, president of General Electric, William J. Filbert, vice chairman of U.S. Steel, and Thomas C. McCobb, controller of Standard Oil of New Jersey.[72] Once he had sign-off on the forms and rules from his informal advisory group of business leaders, Kennedy was comfortable that the requirements were reasonable.

In November, Kennedy shifted the message of the commission from re-assuring capital to prodding it out of malaise. The so-called capital strike— the unwillingness of large companies and Wall Street to raise capital in the public securities markets purportedly for fear of liability under the Securities Act—had continued. Kennedy had spent the first four months of his tenure communicating to the market that business and capital had a reliable partner in the newly created SEC. But now, Kennedy concluded, was the time for busi-ness to step up and raise capital under the registration provisions. Although it was perfectly legal for companies to limit their fund-raising to non–public offerings not requiring registration—"private placements" in the parlance of Wall Street—Kennedy thought this was subverting his goal of establishing the legitimacy of the SEC and demonstrating the ease and flexibility of the registration process under Kennedy's SEC, as opposed to the previously more burdensome and less accommodating approach to registration with the FTC. Since July, $63,000,000 of debt issues had been privately placed by Stan-dard Oil of New Jersey, Consolidated Gas and Electric Company of Balti-more, and Consumers Power Company of Michigan. Kennedy viewed this as an unfair vote of no confidence against the SEC by corporate America.[73]

On November 15, Kennedy made his first major public address since his July 25 National Press Club speech. Kennedy talked about the dearth of new securities issuances in the public market and described the registration pro-cess as "a road without difficulties, except those made by unnecessary timidity." Kennedy attacked head-on the four main charges made against the Securities Act: that the liability provisions were unduly severe, registration was overly expensive, irrelevant information was required and the information re-quirements were burdensome, and the registration process was unduly time-consuming.[74]

Kennedy noted that the liability provisions were based on the English Com-panies Act and were not much different than existing common law with re-spect to fraudulent misrepresentation. "Directors, officers, underwriters and experts may avoid liability," Kennedy noted, "if they can sustain the burden of proof that they exercised the standard of care and investigation of reasonable persons under the circumstances. In a word, negligence and dishonesty are penalized, as is true in every walk of life."[75]

Responding to the excessive costs of registration charge, Kennedy said: "The total items of expense which, by any stretch of the imagination, are chargeable to new legislation amount to 38/100 of 1 percent of the gross proceeds of the finances involved, and there can be no doubt that an appreciable amount of legal expenses and accounting expenses which are included in these costs would have had to be incurred even if there were no Securities and Exchange Commission and no registration."[76]

Concerning the "burdensome" information requirement allegation, Kennedy noted that the forms and rules he put in place had eliminated much of the burden. "One of the most prominent lawyers in the field of corporate finance has stated categorically that when the few proposed amendments to forms and rules have been adopted, there will be nothing in the way of inconvenience or expenses which should deter the American businessman from seeking new capital in accordance with the requirements of the act."[77]

Finally, regarding time delay, Kennedy stated: "This criticism, I venture to say, is grossly exaggerated. The largest financing under the Act—all of you gentlemen have heard of it—the Edison Electric Light Co. public offering, required but 20 days between the original application and the final clearance permitting floatation."[78]

Prodding alone, however, would not be enough. Kennedy knew he had to make compliance with the SEC's registration and reporting requirements more user-friendly.

On December 20, 1934, the SEC approved the general form (Form 10) for the permanent registration of listed securities under the Securities Exchange Act. Form 10, which Kennedy had previously vetted with the business leaders, applied to the great majority of industrial companies and utilities but not to common carriers regulated by the Interstate Commerce Commission, companies under jurisdiction of the Federal Communications Commission, foreign issuers, banks, insurance companies, or companies in receivership. Eleven additional forms for these types of companies and special types of securities were subsequently issued. In the press release announcing the adoption of Form 10, the SEC stated: "An outstanding characteristic of the requirements is that corporations and their accountants are given a wide latitude in the manner of presenting the required data. The Commission's emphasis in this respect has been on substance rather than form. The criterion set by the Commission is that it must secure the facts about which 'an average prudent investor ought reasonably to be informed.'"[79]

Again, markets were pleased with the flexibility and sensitivity to issuer concerns contained in Kennedy's new forms.

At the start of 1935, Chairman Kennedy found himself in a budget fight with the House Appropriations Committee, having first requested an appropriation of $4,227,000 for the commission for the July 1, 1935, to June 30, 1936, fiscal year. He was beaten back by the administration to $2,370,000 in the budget Roosevelt submitted. The House Appropriations Committee was seeking to cut it further to $1,649,000. On January 12, Kennedy appeared before the committee to plead his case. He followed up with weeks of detailed correspondence with Representative James Buchanan, the chairman of the committee, justifying the salary of every employee. Ultimately, Kennedy prevailed and was given a budget of $2,300,000.[80]

Meanwhile, Kennedy continued his efforts to simplify the registration process to encourage new capital raising in the public markets. On December 5, 1934, Kennedy had instructed John Burns to study revisions of the basic registration form (Form A-1) under the Securities Act. Throughout December and early January, the commission staff discussed the development of new forms with Tommy Corcoran, Benjamin Cohen, and Arthur Dean. On January 11, 1935, Kennedy told President Roosevelt that the revised form would be ready the following Monday. "That is where we hope to get private capital back into industry," he told the president.[81]

On Monday, January 13, the commission announced that it had approved Form A-2, a simplified document for the registration of securities of "seasoned issuers" under the Securities Act. Form A-2 was available for corporations with three years of audited financial statements and which either had available to its security holders financial reports for at least ten years or had net income in any two of the five most recent fiscal years preceding the date of the latest balance sheet filed with the registration statement. Other prospective issuers were required to continue to use the more cumbersome Form A-1, but Kennedy indicated he also intended to simplify that form.[82]

Kennedy simplified disclosure for seasoned issuers not only because these companies were better known to the investing community but also because having blue-chip companies sell securities through the registration process would cure fears of liability and facilitate acceptance of SEC review. "This is our answer," Kennedy said, "to our pledge to make less onerous, less expensive, and more practical the registration of securities. We have tried this out with the most vociferous opponents of the Securities Act and with accountants. We believe that this form can be filed without unreasonable delay or expense. They feel there is nothing in it which is unreasonable and will advise their clients to go ahead. The charge has been made that the Act has been holding back the flotations. Well, this is our answer and many of the most hostile critics now say that it is not impractical."[83]

Kennedy noted that there were about $3,000,000,000 in securities of seasoned corporations that were callable for redemption and were selling in the market at above their call price. "Experience has taught us," said Kennedy, "that the refunding operation is the forerunner of new financing. I don't see why there cannot now be a substantial amount of refunding."[84]

To illustrate the reduction in disclosure burden brought about by Form A-2, Kennedy had an aide show reporters the registration statement recently filed on Form A-1 by Republic Steel Corporation, which was over 2,000 pages long. Kennedy explained that the patent disclosure alone was more than one hundred pages, nearly all of which was eliminated by Form A-2. "Concise and fair summaries of essential information" was all that was required in the prospectus in Form A-2.[85]

Immediately after the release of Form A-2, Kennedy had commissioners Landis and Mathews, as well as John Burns, make speeches to important industry associations explaining the new, simplified form and reiterating that circumventing registration through an aggressive reading of the private-placement exemption would not be tolerated. On July 14, Landis addressed the New York State Society of Certified Public Accountants at the Waldorf hotel in New York City. "Form A-2 is, I believe, a distinct advantage over the early Form A-1," said Landis. "Not only does it materially lighten the difficulties and expenses that were entailed by meeting the earlier requirements, but it also furnishes the investor with more valuable and more current information. This, I feel sure, is bound to result in a more informative and less cumbersome prospectus, and very much less hesitancy on the part of business executives and accountants of accepting the obligations of the Securities Act."[86] On January 18, Commissioner Mathews addressed the Illinois Society of Certified Public Accountants to the accounting profession's technical disclosure questions about Form A-2 and Form 10.[87]

On January 15, John Burns addressed a meeting of the chairmen of the Investment Bankers Regional Code Committees in Washington, D.C., and expressed the commission's displeasure with financing by means of private placements rather than registered offerings:

"There has been an alarming tendency of late in the direction of private financing, which it seems to me would have serious implications for you gentlemen in the investment banking business. It has also great evils from the point of view of the average small investor; the investor who became an investor as a result of the tremendous drive during the Liberty Loan campaigns and who now sees the great companies, such as Standard Oil and Swift & Company, selling their bonds only to insurance companies and other institutions. The small fellow who has held a refunded obligation must pick a bond or a stock from a list of decidedly inferior types of securities. This development has been brought about largely, but not directly, by the Securities Act. Even causation in a strictly philosophical sense—I may say occasioned by the Securities Act, but more properly this situation has been caused by the reaction of the large issuers to what they conceive to be the dangers of the Securities Act, dangers I submit in all honesty are grossly exaggerated.

"In order to make it more difficult for that type of financing to be followed, the Commission has labored very diligently for some months, with aid of the most expert accounting and legal criticisms available and has produced a form which has been widely acclaimed. The new form was unanimously agreed upon by the leading accountants and lawyers familiar with registration problems in carrying with it a minimum of liability and designed to furnish a form of questionnaire which could be answered expeditiously and with comparatively little expense. That has been the first act.

"We have compromised insofar as we possibly could under the Act to furnish the investor protection and at the same time avoid any undue burden on the issuer, the officers, the directors, or on the underwriters."[88]

On January 16, 1935, the Senate formally confirmed Kennedy as chairman of the SEC and George Mathews, James Landis, Robert Healy, and Ferdinand Pecora as commission members.[89] A vacancy, however, would soon arise as Ferdinand Pecora had been nominated by New York governor Herbert Lehman to the New York Supreme Court. On January 18, Pecora officially resigned, effective January 21, 1935.[90] The early speculation was that Roosevelt would appoint either Baldwin Bane or Benjamin Cohen to fill the vacancy. He would ultimately choose neither man. On October 5, 1935, the president appointed James Delmage "J.D." Ross, a pioneer in the municipal power ownership movement and the father of Seattle City Light (in part because the SEC had just begun administrative authority over the Public Utility Holding Company Act of 1935).[91]

The Senate confirmation gave Kennedy another opportunity to meet the press. On January 20, *The New York Times* ran yet another profile, highlighting Kennedy's work ethic:

"Marwood, a twenty-five room mansion, a show place of Rockville, Maryland, is twelve miles from Washington. At present, its only occupants are Mr. Kennedy and Eddie Moore, his secretary, also of Boston. The nine Kennedy children are in Florida. Mr. Kennedy commutes weekly to Miami by air. Even if the family were living in Washington, it wouldn't see much of the father. One of the office clerks said, with a bit of a sigh, that 'the Chairman' is always at his desk at 8:30, which is a very early hour indeed for Washington workers, under any administration. He remains on the job until anywhere from 6 to 8 o'clock."[92]

Kennedy also used the interview to announce his idea for a branch office system at the SEC: "Just as soon as funds are available, we should establish offices in New York, Boston, Chicago, San Francisco and two or three other points. Our force at present numbers about 350, all experts in their lines, selected because of their knowledge of the work to which they are assigned."[93]

Kennedy told the press that he rented the large Marwood estate because he needed the space when Rose and the children visited. His life there was remarkably ordered. He rose early and rode his horse every morning before setting off to Washington. Most nights Kennedy would return from the city with dinner guests, which on several occasions included President Roosevelt, who enjoyed lobster dinners flown in from Boston and movie screenings of Hollywood's latest offerings, which Kennedy was somehow able to get hold of even before public release. James Farley, Tommy Corcoran (who would bring his accordion for sing-alongs), and Arthur Krock were also frequent guests.[94] Kennedy neither smoked nor drank and was careful about his diet and his sleep. While he would screen popular comedies and westerns to entertain his guests in Marwood's basement theater, his personal tastes ran more high-brow. He loved nothing more than to sit on the terrace at Marwood and listen to classical music. When Eddie Moore and his other Irish cronies asked for a change of pace, Kennedy always refused. "You dumb bastards don't appreci-ate culture," he'd growl.[95]

An invitation to Marwood became a coveted prize among the status-conscious New Deal elite. Roosevelt himself would pass out invitations to overnights at Kennedy's estate as rewards to loyal officials or to cajole sena-tors and congressmen whose votes were needed.

On January 20, Kennedy formally implemented the commission's branch office system. "To deal more effectively with local problems, the commission will establish branch offices in Boston, Chicago, Fort Worth, Denver, Atlanta, and San Francisco, in addition to New York." Kennedy said. "Trained inves-tigators will be assigned to each of those branch offices in the belief that quicker action can be had through decentralization of effort. The field investigators will work under the supervision of the Commission in Washington. The knowl-edge that the Federal authorities in each area are ready to proceed against those who violate the law will, I hope, be itself a deterrent."[96]

Kennedy hired James A. Fayne, a partner in the Boston law firm of Hornblower and Weeks, to open and staff the regional offices. John T. Calla-han, another Boston Irishman, was chosen to head the new Federal Securi-ties Investigation Corp. Callahan, a childhood friend of Rose Kennedy, was a graduate of Phillips Andover Academy and Yale University, where he was also captain of the football team and a 1920 Consensus All American Center. Fayne and Callahan generally succeeded in hiring the men they wanted for the regional office senior positions. One exception was the man they wanted to run the Chicago office, a bright young lawyer named Adlai Stevenson who turned them down.[97]

On January 25, Kennedy delivered to Speaker of the House of Representa-tives the commission's report on stock exchange governance, together with its recommendations as required under Section 19(c) of the Securities Exchange Act. The report contained eleven recommendations: there should be better numerical representation of commission brokers on governing committees; all partners should be eligible for membership on governing committees; nomination to governing committees should be by petition and not by a nominating committee; at least one third of the membership of governing committees should be elected annually; presidents of exchanges should be elected by the full membership; non-members should be allowed to be officers; membership on standing committees should be open to all members; arbitration costs for customers should be reduced; arbitration panels should have fair representation of customers; appeals of business conduct committee decisions to the governing committees should be allowed; and customers should be entitled to appear before conduct committees and appeal decisions to the governing committee.[98]

The "recommendations"—in reality the dictated terms of surrender imposed upon Whitney and the specialists and dealers—could well have upset the delicate diplomacy Kennedy was working on Wall Street. But Kennedy shrewdly recommended that Congress not enact legislation to bring about these recommendations. So as not to appear heavy-handed to the adversely affected members of the exchanges, he instead proposed that time be granted for exchanges to voluntarily accept these reforms without resorting to legislation.

In early February, a minor controversy erupted in connection with the reporting of stock ownership by insiders. It was revealed that approximately 40 percent of the reports from 1,300 officers, directors, and principal stockholders filed with the New York Stock Exchange were obviously inaccurate, and many were materially misleading. One particular area of confusion was the reporting of securities held by holding companies. Many took the position that only the holding company needed to report the stock ownership, not the individual who owned the holding company; this despite a ruling issued publicly by John Burns on January 13 "that in addition to the report required by a holding company itself, persons in control of a holding company which is owned by a small group primarily as a medium for investment or trading in securities should report to the extent of their respective interests the securities owned by the holding company."[99]

So concerned was the New York Stock Exchange that it refused to release copies of the ownership reports to the public or press unless the recipient agreed to release the exchange from all liability for errors in the reports. Kennedy notified the New York Stock Exchange that the refusal to release the Section 16 reports was in violation of Commission Rule UB-1, which stated that "the Exchange shall make available to public inspection at its offices during reasonable hours a copy of the statement and exhibits filed with the Commission." With the help of John Burns, who encouraged the seeking of advisory opinions on issues arising in the ownership reports, the inaccuracies were substantially eliminated and Kennedy indicated that no one would be punished for honest mistakes in reporting.[100]

At a speech to the Union League Club of Chicago on February 8, 1935, Kennedy set out the commission's plans for the regulation of the over-the-counter market. The plan had two essential elements—the registration of brokers and dealers and the registration of securities that were widely held but not listed on a national securities exchange. Congress intended that no undue regulatory advantage be given to trading in the over-the-counter market (as compared with trading on exchanges) and foresaw that the act could be defeated if effective regulation of over-the-counter markets was not provided for. "We are alive to this problem," said Kennedy. "We are considering the registration (or licensing, if you will) of the dealers and brokers of the country whose business involves interstate commerce. We are considering registering the securities of large corporations similarly involved whose securities are widely distributed and requiring reports of officials of such companies in order that delisting will not be an attractive process. We shall seek to place at the disposal of investors substantially the same information concerning issues of securities trading in over-the-counter as that required of listed companies. I would ask you in simple fairness: Why shouldn't each form of trading be subject to regulations substantially the same?"[101]

On February 15, Kennedy met with representatives of the New York Stock Exchange in Washington to discuss the commission's eleven recommendations for governance reform. The meeting was constructive, and Kennedy felt optimistic that voluntary adherence to the commission's recommendations was achievable. "The Exchange has presented a program for cooperation," Kennedy told reporters after the meeting. "It has shown evidence of good will and I am hopeful that agreement will be reached."[102]

He was less hopeful about the immediate prospects of his second child, seventeen-year-old John Fitzgerald Kennedy. Despite his obvious intelligence and charm, John was always an academic underachiever and was, at times, a discipline problem. Winter 1935 was one of those times. On February 17, Joe Kennedy was summoned to the Choate School by Headmaster George St. John. John Kennedy and his best friend, LeMoyne Billings, had formed a secret society called the "Muckers Club," named after the headmaster's term for boys who underperformed. St. John learned of the club when he intercepted a telegram from John Kennedy's fifteen-year-old sister, Kathleen, known to all as "Kick," congratulating John and Lem on the launch of their club. On February 20, after convincing St. John not to expel his son, Kennedy sent a letter to his eldest daughter:

> Dear Kick:
>
> I know you want to do all you can for Jack, but I think I should tell you that one of the serious difficulties he found himself in was his characterization of "public enemy" and that group with the frightful name "Muckers". I really don't think there is anything smart about it and I hope it won't be the cause of having him expelled from school. Therefore, I want to urge you to stop all this talk [in] letters and telegrams to him and LeMoyne, so that we can dismiss the whole matter. The Headmaster told me of the wire you sent him last Sunday and it merely added fuel to the fire. It has all been smoothed out temporarily, but have this in mind.[103]

By March, Kennedy's efforts to simplify the public offering registration process and his tireless cheerleading for new capital raising were beginning to produce results. The "capital strike" was broken on March 7, 1935, when Swift and Company, the Chicago packing company, filed a registration statement for an offering of $43,000,000 of 3¾ percent First Mortgage Sinking Fund Bonds. It was the largest single issue registered since the Securities Act became effective. Swift sought to use the proceeds from the offering to refinance notes bearing interest at 5 percent, producing an annual interest expense savings of approximately $500,000.[104]

In discussing the new registration, Kennedy said: "I think this is very significant. If we get a few big ones coming in others will feel they can do the same thing. Certainly there is a demand for such securities today and when corporations feel they can do refunding on a sound basis they will do it."[105]

William B. Traynor, the treasurer of Swift, said it had taken the company only one month to prepare the registration statement for filing. Kennedy proudly displayed a copy of the fifty-nine-page-long registration statement.[106]

Another noteworthy term of the offering was the low underwriting spread—a mere 0.40 percent for the "best efforts" (i.e., no underwriting commitment) offering as compared with the customary 2 to 3 percent fee. Underwriter Salomon Brothers was given 100 percent of the offering economics.[107]

The Swift deal was applauded in Washington and on Wall Street. Allan M. Pope, president of the First Boston Corporation and the former president of the Investment Bankers Association, noted that the "intelligent and cooperative attitude of the Securities and Exchange Commission toward potential legitimate borrowers is doing much to facilitate the re-entrance into the capital markets of many large companies."[108]

Arthur Krock's March 8 column in *The New York Times* was dedicated to trumpeting the Swift offering as a Kennedy triumph:

"Mr. Kennedy and his Commission, having made good his purpose, they expect that 'old and going' industry will now follow Swift & Co. and begin the financing of many projects which have been held up because of statement requirements under the old form. Capitalists who fear to expand or make necessary arrangements because of their distrust of the economic policies of the administration will not, of course, be affected by the reforms in regulations achieved by Mr. Kennedy. But he believes he has answered, by the experience of Swift & Co., the arguments of financial lawyers and accountants to their clients that Commission forms are so expensive, burdensome and hazardous that refinancing should not be attempted. He believes he has provided an effective reply also to lawyers who have advised capitalists that only through Congressional action could form requirements be made reasonable.[...]

"The President has had many disappointments in laws endorsed by him and administrators chosen by him since he took office more than two years ago. But from the SEC, since he selected Mr. Kennedy to be the chairman, he has had nothing but satisfactory and constructive labor, unmarred by blunders, unstained by accusations of venality, bureaucracy or business-baiting."[109]

The day after the Swift filing, Pacific Gas and Electric Company filed a registration statement for a $45,000,000 bond issue. On March 29, the commission was informed by telephone that Southern California Edison Company would be filing a registration statement for a $73,000,000 bond offering. The caller was Sullivan & Cromwell's Arthur Dean, who sent his messenger by plane from Los Angeles with the filing and requested that the commission stay open after 5:00 p.m. on Saturday, in case the plane was delayed.[110]

On March 19, 1935, Kennedy was honored by the American Arbitration Association at the Hotel Astor in New York City. The address to the more than 1,100 financial and industry leaders was broadcast live on the NBC Radio Network. Rather than the normal boosterism expected at this type of luncheon, Kennedy took the occasion to build on the momentum generated by the Swift, Pacific Gas and Electric, and Southern California Edison offerings by chiding New York's business leaders for not more aggressively accessing capital markets:

"Gentlemen, I am deeply concerned about the low state to which courage and confidence among businessmen has fallen. Moreover, because the rest of the country has a high estimate of the prophetic value of New York's opinion, you should be satisfied that your pessimistic frame of mind has a reasonable basis before you allow its influence to infect other communities. This industrial machine of ours is so delicate an instrument that opinion everywhere else is sensitive to its fluctuations here. And we must admit that today at least New York registers gloom and not sunshine; discouraging prophecies, not hopeful suggestions. Let us see if this brooding is worthy of us, whether the 'jitters' we talk about today isn't merely a manifestation of temporary ailments common to every generation in our history. Is there really any justification for the universal lament that things are worse today than ever before because today, in contrast to other periods, there is 'too much government in business'?"[111]

Referring to the recent registrations, Kennedy said:

"These, I am hopeful enough to believe, mark a turn in the road. Only a trickling little stream of private corporation finance as yet, where before there was a flood tide. But the stream is large enough and representative enough to justify the statement that there is no longer any excuse left to the corporation which has hitherto hesitated to go forth with such confidence. Can any reasonable man say that the control of those great corporations is in the hands of men recklessly imprudent about the management of their affairs? And if these men, after careful consideration of all the problems involved, have concluded that there is no unreasonable liability, burden or responsibility imposed by the new securities laws, who dares assert any longer that the government has made corporate financing legally impossible? Let me re-iterate to emphasize. Can these men, representing some of the best minds and hearts in American business, be entirely wrong, and the hesitant majority who carpingly criticize the existing law, without taking the trouble to become informed concerning it, be correct? We know better. Let us accept today's promise on its face. I am rash enough to believe that these recent registrations are harbingers of a real upward trend. Do not be disappointed if new financing is not a daily occurrence and business does not boom immediately. There will be lapses of course. A snowstorm in March cannot delay the advent of Spring. It is enough if the turn has been reached."[112]

A turn in the road had been reached. Kennedy's changes to simplify securities registration and his ceaseless effort to promote those changes were convincing Wall Street and corporate America to access the public markets. In 1935, $2,700,000,000 of securities would be registered with the SEC, more than four times the 1934 total of $641,000,000.[113]

Throughout March, the commission continued its negotiations with the New York Stock Exchange regarding implementation of its eleven recommended governance changes. Initially, Richard Whitney was inclined to resist the suggested changes. He hired attorney John W. Davis to prepare a constitutional challenge to the Securities Exchange Act. But when the commission brokers, led by E.A. Pierce and Paul V. Shields, endorsed the recommendations, he had no choice but to capitulate and began negotiations with the commission. On March 14, Whitney met again with Joe Kennedy in Washington to discuss their implementation.[114] On March 21, Kennedy sent Whitney a memorandum setting forth the current positions of the exchange and the commission regarding each of the recommendations. The memorandum revealed substantial progress—the two sides weren't very far apart. Kennedy was satisfied that Whitney's proposed responses constituted substantial compliance.[115]

On March 16, David Saperstein of the SEC's Trading and Exchange Division distributed a draft of the proposed over-the-counter market regulations to George Whitney of J.P. Morgan & Co. Two weeks later, the company provided four pages of comments. As a general matter, J.P. Morgan & Co. was not opposed to broker-dealer registration.[116]

The smaller broker-dealers, however, were opposed to the requirements. In a letter to the SEC dated April 9, 1935, the Bond Club of New Jersey wrote:

> "The so-called registration of brokers and dealers is a feature which goes further than anything yet undertaken by the government in relation to the securities market. A reading of the text shows that it provides for what in reality is a licensing instead of registration. This means that the Securities and Exchange Commission will be saddled with the tremendous responsibility of selecting those who will be allowed to engage in the securities selling business. There is no assurance that anything of value will be accomplished thereby, and past experience with legislation of this type indicates definitely that great harm to prospective investors may result."[117]

The opposition to broker-dealer registration was not convincing. It would be implemented. Likewise, issuers of securities widely traded on the over-the-counter markets would be subject to periodic reporting like listed companies.

As the 1935 baseball season approached, Babe Ruth let it be known that he wanted—and thought he deserved—to be manager of the New York Yankees. But the Yankees had Joe McCarthy as skipper, and he was widely considered the best manager in the game. And owner Jacob Ruppert had no intention of cutting loose McCarthy for the undisciplined, grandiose Babe. "How could Babe manage the team if he couldn't even manage himself?"[118]

There was one team interested in Ruth for the 1935 season. The Boston Braves were willing to promise him a managerial position, provided he agreed to put in another year as a player. The Braves were owned by Emil Fuchs, a barely reputable character who'd bought the team in 1923 and quickly run it into the ground. Things had gotten so bad for Fuchs that he petitioned the

National League to use Braves Field as a dog-racing track on off nights. He was denied. Ruth was to be his next gimmick.[119]

Fuchs offered Ruth a $25,000 contract, a percentage of (non-existent) profits, and gave him the title of vice president and assistant manager. He also promised Babe the manager's job at an undetermined future date. On February 29, at a press conference at Yankee Stadium, Colonel Ruppert, with Ruth and Fuchs beside him, announced he was releasing Ruth to play with the Braves.[120]

On Opening Day, Ruth hit a 430-foot home run off Giants pitcher and future hall-of-famer Carl Hubell, propelling the Braves to a four-to-two win. It was an auspicious start, but Ruth would quickly collapse. And he would soon realize that "assistant manager" meant nothing. He was little more than a gate attraction. Ruth would have one last moment of glory, though, on May 25, 1935, when he belted three home runs—the 712th, 713th, and 714th (and last) of his career—with six runs batted in. But the slump quickly returned. The Babe announced his retirement, effective immediately, on June 2, 1935. His batting average for the season to date was .181.[121]

On April 16, the SEC asked the New York Stock Exchange and twenty other national securities exchanges to adopt sixteen trading rules designed to eliminate manipulative practices and "even the playing field" for the small investor. These rules took direct aim at pools, bear raids, and the other dirty tricks that provided the shock-and-awe moments of the Pecora Hearings. Rather than require immediate adoption by exchanges, Kennedy decided that they should be tried on an experimental basis "voluntarily." Again, Kennedy exercised diplomacy by allowing the exchanges the opportunity to adopt the rules voluntarily. The new rules imposed limitations on trading off the exchange floor; participation in joint accounts; handling of customers' discretionary accounts and discretionary orders; the use of puts, calls, and straddles by members; members acting in the dual capacity of brokers and dealers; excessive trading; activities of specialists and odd-lot dealers; and short selling, by way of the "uptick rule."[122]

At a press conference announcing the new rules, Kennedy said:

"The commission has requested the Exchanges for the immediate present to adopt these rules as the rules of the Exchanges. This course will allow greater flexibility of administration to attend these rules—a desirable attribute inasmuch as these rules must still be regarded to a large extent as experimental. Furthermore, minor adaptation of the rules to the varying agencies of the many Exchanges can also readily be accomplished by this method. The enforcement of these rules will thus lie with the Exchanges, the Commission, however, being able to observe both their enforcement and effect.

"If we knew what the effect of these rules would be, we would be promulgating them. We started to study the matter four or five months ago because of the provision of the statute. One reason why there is no good way to judge their effect is because of the dull market. It is a very bad laboratory. If the market started to whirl, conditions might change overnight."[123]

Richard Whitney deferred formal action on the proposed rules by the governing committee of the New York Stock Exchange until after its annual meeting on May 13. Kennedy had no objection to the delay, given the internal political turmoil at the NYSE. The commission brokers had risen up against Whitney in the skirmish over Kennedy's exchange governance reform proposal. Whitney, they decided, had to go. Led by E.A. Pierce, Paul V. Shields, and Grayson M-P. Murphy, the commission brokers threw their weight behind John Wesley Haynes, whose family had been the original owner of the Reynolds Tobacco Company, for the presidency of the Exchange. The nominating committee had planned to duck the fight by proposing three names for president and letting the membership decide. The three proposed were Whitney, Haynes, and Charles R. Gay, a mild-mannered sixty-year-old self-made broker from Brooklyn who was well liked by both factions. In March, Haynes disappointed supporters by announcing that he would no longer pursue the presidency. Gay, the compromise candidate, also wavered, making it likely that Whitney would be reelected without opposition. The members of the nominating committee, however, wanted the controversial Whitney removed—even if they didn't have the guts to get rid of him themselves.[124]

On April 8, though, the nominating committee found its nerve, informing Whitney that he would not be nominated for reelection as president but would be nominated for another term on the governing committee. Charles Gay would be the nominee for president. Furious, Whitney vowed to get more votes as a governor than Gay as president, to demonstrate that he was still the real power behind the scenes.[125]

By mid-April, with the "capital strike" broken and basic organizational structure of the commission established, Kennedy, who had initially told President Roosevelt that he intended to stay in the chairmanship for no more than one year, was seriously considering quitting. He was thinking of announcing his resignation on April 23, following his keynote speech at the 300th Anniversary Dinner of the Boston Latin School, his alma mater. In an April 12 telegram to Felix Frankfurter asking for his input on a draft of the speech, Kennedy wrote "hate to trouble you, but it is my swan song. Therefore, must be good."[126]

In a sentimental speech, almost completely devoid of policy, Kennedy praised those members of Congress who had assisted him during his SEC chairmanship:

> "I have been greatly inspired, contrary to the general belief and my own expectations. The sincere purpose and earnest endeavors of the vast majority of men in the Congress of the United States and I have disabused my mind of the specter of constant political interference in the conduct of the Government business. Direct firsthand experience shows that those officials appear to great advantage when compared to the average businessmen I have known in twenty years of business life."[127]

Kennedy also praised the young people who had come to Washington to serve the New Deal:

> "In the case of the Securities and Exchange Commission and in the case of many Government agencies, responsible posts will be held by comparatively young men. The important position of General Counsel to our Commission is held by a young Boston attorney, Judge John J. Burns, who brings to his work the experience of attorney and judge, the research of a Harvard Law School professor and the philosophy of a reasoning student of public opinion. The only 'out' about Judge Burns is that he didn't prepare for college at Latin School."[128]

On May 2, the SEC continued its effort to simplify the public-offering process by streamlining requirements for advertising securities offerings in newspapers and magazines. Detailed financial information and descriptions of securities would no longer be required. Copies of advertisements could be filed with the commission as long as seven days after the advertisement was published. The American Newspaper Publishers Association, which had worked with the SEC on liberalizing the prior requirements, praised the SEC's revised rules: "In the opinion of the ANPA special committee, which has been at work upon the problem with the Securities and Exchange Commission, the regulation will be an important factor in stimulating the flow of investment funds into the industry. It is a logical step forward in the program of the Commission headed by Joseph P. Kennedy, which has already resulted within the last few weeks in greatly increased volume of private financing."[129]

In early May, Kennedy worked to buttress the effectiveness of his regional office operations. He contacted state officials to request sharing of information concerning firms and individuals convicted of crimes in the securities business. Kennedy believed only a federal agency with nationwide reach could effectively police brokers and dealers. "Most states have blue sky laws," Kennedy told *The New York Times*. "But even those with the best laws can't always reach these fellows because they operate over state lines and move so quickly that they often are gone before state officials know they have been working. Then it is too late for state officers to reach them. We have the equipment and the authority to jump state lines and follow them anywhere."[130]

On May 13, the New York Stock Exchange held its annual election. The turnout was very large—twice the usual number of members cast votes. Charles Gay won the presidency with 1,131 votes, but Whitney was elected to the governing committee with 1,146 votes, along with three of his allies. John Haynes, the rebel, received the lowest vote tally (371). Whitney made his statement.[131] Nonetheless, the governance reforms recommended by Kennedy would be implemented, and the balance of power at the exchange between the specialists and the dealers and the brokers would be realigned to better represent the Exchange membership.

On May 26, *The New York Times* ran another article on Joe Kennedy—again, likely orchestrated by Kennedy himself—in anticipation of his planned resignation. He triumphantly announced the end of the financial logjam. "I think there is five hundred million, possibly a billion dollars of new financing in the offices of lawyers and accountants today," he said. "There is so much demand by the big investors that the small investors, if unprotected, may be driven into dangerous fields. If we permitted that to happen it would nullify much of the work we have done in other directions. The Securities Act has been a great boon, however, instead of hindrance, to the securities business, by restoring public confidence. History has simply repeated itself again. Most banks opposed the establishment of the Federal Reserve System, but see what would happen if the government were to try now to abolish the Federal Reserve Board. Now that confidence is being established, there is cheap money in abundance and people always want to invest their funds. Every condition exists to aid a normal flow of capital, and if we get rid of the crooked and the grafters, we can go so much further."[132]

The *Times* article expressed Kennedy's desire to return to private life:

"Mr. Kennedy is rumored to dine at the White House three or four evenings weekly and he is the last man before whom proposals are laid by Mr. Roosevelt after the President has discussed them with the specialists. Outside his work there is only one interest in his life—his family. And he makes no secret of his desire to get out of public office as soon as possible in order to devote his attention to it. Circumstances make it impossible for all of the Kennedys to live in Washington, and upon Mrs. Kennedy falls the brunt of caring for the schooling, training and direction of the children."[133]

The day after *The New York Times* article appeared, Kennedy had scheduled a meeting with President Roosevelt. Walking to the White House with his resignation letter in his pocket, he saw an early edition of the *Washington Star*, its front page emblazoned with a large headline announcing that the Supreme Court had unanimously invalidated the National Industrial Recovery Act. The delegation of authority to the National Recovery Administration, the court ruled, both violated the separation of powers under the Constitution (as an improper delegation of legislative power to the executive branch) and exceeded congressional authority under the Commerce Clause by granting rulemaking authority to the NRA over matters of health and safety that were issues of state law. The decision called into question the validity of both the Securities Act and the Securities Exchange Act—and the legality of the commission and its rule making. It was not the day to resign. Kennedy tore up the resignation letter and went back to work.[134]

On June 19, Charles Gay traveled to Washington to meet with Joe Kennedy at the SEC. To demonstrate a return to normalcy and a spirit of coopera-tion with the commission, Gay announced that the New York Stock Exchange was closing its "Washington Embassy" in Georgetown, where his predecessor had waged combat against the Securities Exchange Act.[135] The sixteen trad-ing rules recommended by Kennedy were adopted by the Exchange, and equally important, would be enforced in good faith.

On July 1, 1935, Kennedy was reelected for another year as chairman of the commission with no opposition.[136] The principal job before him that sum-mer was one for which he had little enthusiasm—preparing the commission for its role as administrator of the Public Utility Holding Company Act.

The Public Utility Holding Company Act, signed into law by Roosevelt on August 26, 1935, limited each utility holding company to owning one in-tegrated utility system and required the approval of the SEC before entering into a non-utility business. The act also limited transactions between regulated utilities and their unregulated affiliates. The first order of business would be overseeing a massive divestiture program by the utility holding companies, a program that would take more than a decade to complete. Kennedy had no desire to preside over the breakup of the utility industry.

On July 22, Kennedy achieved a hallmark of star status when he made the cover of *Time* magazine. "The Securities and Exchange Commission, now just one year old has 659 employees, occupying most of the old Interstate Com-merce Building and has won the distinction of being the most ably adminis-tered New Deal agency in Washington," the article began. The magazine recited the commission's many first-year achievements, praising Kennedy's hands-on management style:

"Over all these SEC activities Chairman Kennedy keeps a sharp blue eye. In the Commission's Division of Labor, he personally reviews each and every appointment. But he drops into hearings, does liaison work with other gov-ernment agencies, sees the President frequently, confers with his colleagues twice each day. No federal official rides the airlines more than SEC Chair-man Kennedy. In the last year he has flown more than 65,000 miles. Lately, in one week he flew to San Francisco for the opening of a regional branch office, on to Los Angeles (with a stop-over at San Simeon to chat with

William Randolph Hearst) and back to Washington via Pittsburgh. At the week's end, he hopped to Manhattan. About once a fortnight, he manages to weekend with his wife and as many of his nine children as he can collect—in the winter at Palm Beach, in the summer at Hyannis Port on Cape Cod."[137]

The article concluded with talk of resignation: "Having set up the SEC machine and got it running smoothly, Chairman Kennedy wanted to return to private life last spring. But on the very day that he planned to take his resignation to the While House, the Supreme Court revoked the New Deal with the NRA decision. Loyally pocketing his resignation, Mr. Kennedy went back to work because he was too good a public man to desert his post when the sky seemed to be falling on the White House."[138]

After the *Time* cover story, Washington and Wall Street were preparing for Kennedy's imminent resignation. On August 16, *The New York Times* speculated that he might resign in early September after his August holiday in Hyannis Port, prior to setting sail for England where he was to enroll his son John at the London School of Economics to study under economist Harold Laski. Kennedy declined to comment on the rumors.[139]

Despite the many accomplishments of his tenure at the SEC, Kennedy had not yet brought an enforcement action against a major Wall Street player. That changed in August when he authorized commission staff to institute proceedings against Michael J. Meehan for alleged manipulations of Bellanca Aircraft Corporation stock. Meehan, the famous operator of the RCA pool, was accused of using matched orders—buying and selling at the same time in different markets—to boost the price of the Bellanca. The scheme doubled the stock price and Meehan quickly dumped hundreds of thousands of shares.[140]

Approving the SEC staff's recommendation of proceeding against Meehan must have brought Kennedy some measure of personal satisfaction (he is, after all, credited with coining the phrase, "Don't get mad, get even."). The commission would be extraordinarily harsh in dealing with Meehan, and that suited Kennedy. Even putting aside any lingering hurt feelings from Meehan's rejection six years earlier, nothing would better help Kennedy to transcend the ethnic tribalism of his Boston origins, to separate from the pack of Irish Wall Streeters more, than allowing one of his own to be the first casualty of the Kennedy SEC.

When Meehan caught wind of the SEC investigation, he decided to take a long vacation, as Ben Smith and Thomas Bragg had done when Pecora investigated the alcohol pools. Meehan stayed closer to home, though, checking into Bloomingdale, a posh private hospital in Westchester County, New York, where he stayed until June 1937, after the SEC had concluded its proceedings against him. His partner at M.J. Meehan & Co., James F. McConnochie, told reporters that "Meehan is taking a rest cure at a private sanitarium. He is not under restraint. He has been sick about a year and has paid no attention to business during that period. His condition is a matter of concern to his family and friends, but we are confident that under the expert care and attention which he is now receiving he will soon work his way back to good health."[141] Meehan entertained a large number of visitors at Bloomingdale and was seen happily strolling the grounds, cigar in hand, and was allowed to host posh catered picnics with dozens of guests on its well-manicured lawns. He was clearly thriving under excellent care.[142]

Commission lawyers played hardball with Meehan, going so far as to argue that they were not obligated to disclose to Meehan the details of his alleged misconduct or its witnesses against him because the SEC, as an administrative agency, was not bound by the principles of due process of judicial proceedings.[143]

On October 26, 1935, the SEC officially brought charges against him and ordered that hearings be held to determine whether the commission would recommend his suspension or expulsion under the Securities Exchange Act.[144] Commission hearing officer William Green opened hearings on December 10, 1935. Fourteen hundred trades were investigated and forty brokers were subpoenaed, producing over 70,000 pieces of evidence.[145]

On August 2, 1937, the commission announced its verdict: Meehan was to be expelled from the exchanges.[146] Its final order, dated August 19, 1937, gave him until October 14 to dispose of his seats on the exchanges.[147] Meehan decided not to appeal and never sought reinstatement. On October 14, he resigned from M.J. Meehan & Co. and never returned to its offices at 30 Broad Street. "The transactions in Bellanca stock for which he was prosecuted by the SEC were the kind that made him the toast of the trading circles in the Coolidge era," The New York Times noted.[148]

Kennedy returned from his summer vacation in Hyannis Port after Labor Day for a short four-day work week ending on September 6, 1935, his

birthday, when he was to return again to Hyannis Port. After a short celebra-
tion of his forty-seventh birthday with a cake sent by Rose and the children,
Kennedy sat down and wrote his second resignation letter to the president.
This time he delivered the letter.

> "My decision to ask to go at this time is made easier by the realization that
> the Commission is now strongly established as a going concern and that
> the lines of policy for the administration of those two great measures, the
> Securities Act and the Securities Exchange Act, have been firmly laid. There
> remain a few major problems in this first phase of the work of the Commission,
> but as to these also general principles have been agreed upon as the Com-
> mission is working toward an early announcement of conclusions, with which
> I am in agreement."[149]

Kennedy indicated in his letter that his lack of desire to administer the
Public Utility Holding Company Act precipitated his resignation.

> "The Public Utility Act of 1935 (which you have just signed) places additional
> large responsibilities upon the Commission. For quite some time, the ener-
> gies of the Commission in this field will be devoted largely to studies of the
> various holding company systems. Many of the most vital problems arising
> out of this legislation will not be imminent for a year and beyond. It seems
> most important that in working out the policies of the New Act, there should
> be a continuity of administration. Therefore, the present exigencies which
> compel me to ask you to relieve me coincide with the Commission's require-
> ments for administrative direction of long duration."[150]

Kennedy chose September 23 as the effective date of his resignation. "I suggested this particular date . . . because, as you know, Mrs. Kennedy and I plan
to go abroad with the children the latter part of the month and it seems wise
for me to terminate my official relations prior to leaving."[151]

Kennedy wrote another letter that day—to George Steele, the assistant
headmaster of the Choate School, from where John Kennedy had graduated
three months before. "Jack has really demonstrated more this summer than
ever before. Of course, as I have always told you, I would place a bet that he

has everything to go a long distance, and I am convinced now that he is on his way," Kennedy wrote. "My kindest regards to you and my appreciation for all the Choate School has done for Jack."[152]

President Roosevelt took two weeks to accept Kennedy's resignation:

"You undertook a pioneer piece of administration, the successful achievement of which was difficult as it was important for the country. Under your leadership, the Securities Exchange Commission took two of the most important regulatory mandates ever passed by Congress—the Securities Act and the Stock Exchange Act—and administered them so effectively as to win the confidence of the general investing public and of the financial community, for the protection of both of which these statutes was designed. You have every right to feel that the Securities Exchange Commission is now a going concern and that the major lines of policy for the administration of the Securities Act and the Stock Exchange Act have been firmly laid. Such a result never just happens. It comes to pass only through skill, resourcefulness, good sense, and devotion to the public interest. All your colleagues, I know, have contributed in full measure to the fine results that the Commission has accomplished. But every group, no matter how able, requires leadership. In you, your colleagues have had an able leader."[153]

At a press conference after his resignation was publicly announced, Kennedy declared: "I'm going to feel that I'm out of politics—if this is politics—for the rest of my natural life. I'm all through with public life."[154] He also took the opportunity to announce a new marquee public offering. Illinois Bell Telephone Company announced the filing of a bond offering underwritten by a new investment bank, Morgan Stanley & Co., formed by former partners of J.P. Morgan after its Glass-Steagall breakup. Harold Stanley came to Washington to discuss the offering with Kennedy; it would be the first offering to utilize the new newspaper advertising prospectus. "You can feel it in the air that the new kind of financing is coming along," said Kennedy.[155]

There was immediate speculation that Kennedy was not, in fact, done with public life and his resignation was just the first of a high-level shake-up in the Roosevelt administration. It was widely rumored that James Farley would be resigning as postmaster general to run the 1936 reelection campaign, and

Secretary of Commerce Roper would resign and take over as postmaster general, with Kennedy to become the new secretary of commerce.[156]

Most assumed that James Landis would be named as Kennedy's successor, but the names of John Burns, James Ross, and Ferdinand Pecora were also floated. Kennedy stated that he had not made a recommendation to President Roosevelt, nor had the president requested one.

The press reaction to Kennedy's resignation was near universal praise for his stewardship. According to *The New York Times*, "Brokers expressed regret at his retirement but said that men of his executive ability could not be expected to sacrifice their personal affairs in the public welfare for an indefinite period of time. The financial community is sincerely thankful to Mr. Kennedy for his constructive administration of the Securities Exchange Act. It is felt that the policies that he laid down were so sound that whoever succeeds him will not go wrong following the trail that he blazed."[157]

Even John T. Flynn, the sharpest critic of Kennedy's appointment, praised his tenure on the commission:

"When Joseph P. Kennedy was named by President Roosevelt as a member of the Securities and Exchange Commission and, in effect, made its chairman, I expressed in this department a sharp criticism of the appointment. I believed then, as I believe now, that no man should be named to such regulatory commission from among the groups that are to be regulated. And in the case of Mr. Kennedy, I verbalized some criticisms of his record in business which I thought made his appointment unwise. Now Mr. Kennedy has resigned as Chairman of the Commission. And I think it but fair to him to say that he disappointed the expectations of his critics. He was, I firmly believe, the most useful member of the Commission."[158]

Among the numerous personal letters Kennedy received was one from New York Stock Exchange president Charles R. Gay: "I hope that at the time of our conversation a day or so ago I made clear to you how much I regret that you are leaving the Commission. You have been so cordially cooperative that I shall always remember our meetings with great pleasure. I sincerely hope that the coming journey may be all that you anticipate in enjoyment and benefit. May I also venture to hope that upon your return I may have the pleasure of seeing you often here in New York?"[159]

On Kennedy's last day in office, the commission elected James Landis as the second chairman of the SEC. Both Roosevelt and Kennedy endorsed the selection. At a press conference announcing Landis's election, Kennedy stated: "After fifteen months of living with Jim Landis I see no reason in the world why any business interests need have the slightest misgiving that he will not give them the fairest and squarest deal a man can get. I would deem it an honor to have him a trustee of anything I owned. He is thoroughly cognizant of the importance of the successful administration of these acts in helping to revive the business of the country."[160]

Two days later Kennedy was sailing for England on the French liner *Normandie* with his wife, Rose, son John, and daughter Kick.

Kennedy's record of accomplishment at the Securities and Exchange Commission was indeed remarkable. The most pressing task he faced was gaining acceptance of the commission's regulatory authority by Wall Street. Kennedy's efforts to simplify registration under the Securities Act (through the adoption of Form A-2), the new prospectus advertising rules, and his tireless advocacy for capital raising succeeded in breaking the "capital strike." But more than that, he succeeded in convincing Wall Street that the commission need not be viewed as an adversary. It was more a policeman than an occupying army, more a referee than an opposing player.

Kennedy registered the nation's securities exchanges with forms and rules that resulted in a barely noticeable loss of liquidity or issuer delistings. He regulated the over-the-counter market through the registration of brokers and dealers, and formulated rules resulting in registration of over-the-counter securities issues. He succeeded in having exchanges voluntarily adopt the trading rules promulgated under the Securities Exchange Act. Despite initial glitches, stock ownership reporting rules and forms also gained adherence. The commission completed the study of exchange governance required under the Securities Exchange Act and saw its eleven recommendations adopted by the nation's major securities exchanges. The three other mandated studies—broker-dealer segregation, trading of unlisted securities on exchanges, and protective committees—were well under way, on track to be finished by January 1936.

Kennedy also assembled an initial structure and a roster of first-rate personnel. The Legal Division under John Burns, Administrative Division under Baldwin Bane, Registration Division under Donald Montgomery, and Trading and Exchange Division under David Saperstein represented perhaps the most talented senior staff of any regulatory agency of any era. And that's before considering the staff of the protective committee study, which was headed by two future U.S. Supreme Court justices. The decision to establish the eight regional offices and the speed and efficiency with which this was accomplished by James Fayne and John Callahan was also extraordinary. The list of what Kennedy did not accomplish is comparatively short. The commission under Kennedy did not adopt a net capital rule for brokers under Section 8 of the Securities Exchange Act nor proxy rules under Section 14.

A LEFT-HANDED FIRST BASEMAN'S MITT

Babe Ruth never did manage a major league team. The closest he came was a brief stint as an assistant coach for the Brooklyn Dodgers in 1938. After his retirement from baseball, his drinking and smoking—always legendary—only increased. He golfed and bowled, hunted and fished, but it was always leavened with heavy alcohol and tobacco use. On November 29, 1946, Ruth checked into French Hospital in Manhattan complaining of headaches. The source of his pain was quickly located: Ruth had a large cancerous tumor behind his nose and growing into his neck. He would remain in French Hospital for the next three months.[1]

On April 27, 1947, the Yankees held Babe Ruth Day at the stadium. Ruth's physical appearance was frightening—he had lost a considerable amount of weight and his voice was left faint and hoarse by radiation treatments. On August 16, 1948, Ruth died. He lay in state for two days at Yankee Stadium where nearly 80,000 fans came to pay their respects. Three days later, an almost equal number gathered outside Manhattan's St. Patrick's Cathedral for the Babe's funeral.[2]

The Banking Act of 1933's restructuring of the banking system by segregating deposits from riskier capital markets activities like securities trading and underwriting, while also restricting their use to the funding of traditional, more conservative (typically secured) lending and insuring those deposits through the FDIC, formed a stable foundation for America's banks for the next half-century. In the early 1980s, in response to interest rate hikes caused by Paul Volcker's inflation-fighting Federal Reserve, regulators and politicians began allowing banks and thrifts to make risky, higher-yielding loans. The result was a classic mismatch of short-term bank borrowing for long-term risky lending and an inevitable banking crisis—the savings and loan crisis. Thousands of mostly small financial institutions failed between 1982 and 1992 (2,808). In 1989 alone, more insured financial institutions failed (534) than during the 2008 financial crisis and its aftermath (478 failures in the four years following the crisis). There was even a bank holiday declared during this period. With echoes of Inauguration Day 1933, on New Year's Day 1991, moments after Rhode Island's new governor Bruce Sundlun took the oath of office, he ordered closed all forty-five banks and other financial institutions that were members of the state's deposit insurance plan. Sundlun's legal counsel, future U.S. senator Sheldon Whitehouse, had been up all night trying to avoid a bank holiday, but the deposit insurance fund had gone insolvent as a result of shocking corruption and mismanagement. Miraculously, Sundlun eventually managed to make nearly all depositors whole. Nevertheless, the record compares favorably with the fifty years prior to Glass-Steagall, which experienced four major financial panics: the Panic of 1873 and the subsequent Long Depression; the Gold Panic of 1893; the Panic of 1907; and the Crash and Great Depression. To the present day, federal deposit insurance and FDIC oversight remain a cornerstone of our banking system. Few seriously propose a banking system without them.

The "mission creep" of the Federal Reserve in the decades following enactment of Glass-Steagall would have had Carter Glass aghast. The Fed's expansion into the financing of the national debt continued well after World War II. From LBJ's "guns and butter" policies through the Reagan tax cut and bloated Pentagon budgets, up to George W. Bush's wars without taxes and his and Obama's bailouts, the Federal Reserve Board has been the loyal agent of the U.S. Treasury. And more—the Federal Reserve Board chairman has become our national economic Merlin, expected to work monetary magic by manipulating interests rates and money supply through gargantuan bond purchases to prop up equity markets, goose economic growth, and achieve "optimal" levels of employment, as he (and now she) sees fit. The Federal Reserve's "lender of last resort" function has also expanded far beyond its member commercial banks. It is expected to play matchmaker for failing Wall Street investment banks and insurance companies, using its balance sheet as dowry. Carter Glass would have railed against all of this.

This wall of separation between commercial and investment banking remained nearly undisturbed by regulators and lawmakers for over fifty years. Beginning in December 1986, however, the Federal Reserve Board reinterpreted Section 20 of the Glass-Steagall Banking Act of 1933 to allow banks to generate up to 5 percent of their total revenues from securities operations involving less risky debt securities. In 1989, the Federal Reserve Board raised the portion of gross revenues that may be derived from securities operations from 5 percent to 10 percent of total revenues while expanding the types of securities that could be underwritten by banks to include all debt and equity securities. In December 1996, the Federal Reserve Board permitted bank holding companies to have up to 25 percent of their gross revenues from the securities business. In 1997, Bankers Trust became the first modern commercial bank to purchase an investment bank when it acquired Alex Brown & Co.[3]

On April 7, 1998, Travelers Insurance Company (which owned the investment bank Salomon Smith Barney) announced a $70,000,000,000 stock-for-stock merger with Citicorp, which under then-existing law would have required the disposal of the Travelers Insurance business. The merger was subject to Federal Reserve Board approval.[4] On September 23, 1998, the Federal Reserve Board approved the merger, provided the two companies took all necessary actions to conform the activities of Travelers and its subsidiaries to the requirements of law within two years after consummation of the merger.[5] On November 4, 1999, after an intensive lobbying campaign by Wall Street, the Senate and the House of Representatives passed the Financial Services Modernization Act of 1999, eliminating the restrictions on commercial banks engaging in securities and insurance operations.[6] President Bill Clinton signed the act into law on November 12, 1999.[7] The wall of separation between commercial banking and investment banking had been torn down.

The 2008 financial crisis saw renewed calls for the separation of insured deposits from activities perceived to be riskier than traditional secured commercial lending. Title VI of the Dodd-Frank Wall Street Reform and Consumer Protection Act, signed into law by President Barack Obama on July 21, 2010 (and referred to as the Volcker Rule), generally prohibits deposit-taking financial institutions from engaging in proprietary trading of securities and limits the amount that those institutions may invest in hedge funds or private equity funds. Most of the substantive provisions of the Volcker Rule were left to the federal banking regulatory agencies to determine through rulemaking.

William Woodin's throat never got better. During the summer of 1933, doctors finally diagnosed the problem—and it was far worse than strep throat. While Woodin did his best to beat the metastasizing cancer, Dean Acheson ran the Treasury Department in his absence until he resigned over FDR's gold-buying policy. In November 1933, Woodin offered his resignation because of his illness. Roosevelt refused, but named Henry Morgenthau Jr. acting secretary of the Treasury in his absence. Woodin died on May 3, 1934.[8]

Carter Glass's disenchantment with the New Deal only grew over time. He parted ways early with FDR over a number of fiscal issues he thought irresponsibly inflationary. When Roosevelt introduced the Judicial Procedures Reform bill of 1937—commonly known as his "court-packing" plan—Glass led the revolt among conservative Democrats in the Senate. Glass also openly opposed a third term for Roosevelt. When FDR's long-feared Irish rebellion came, it wasn't an allied effort with the rural populists, as he initially feared. Huey Long was dead. Father Coughlin, at his best always near the edge of nutty, had gone off the rails into anti-Semitic conspiracy theories. Populism's new leader, Henry Wallace, would be co-opted by Roosevelt as his running mate for the third term. The attack came from the right, with James Farley, backed by Carter Glass and other conservatives, challenging Roosevelt in 1940.

Glass travelled from his sickbed in Washington to Chicago to place Farley's name in nomination at the convention. He might as well have stayed in bed, as Roosevelt masterfully divided his opposition, all the while disingenuously claiming he did not want to break the two-term tradition and would only run for third term if drafted at the convention. The convention in Chicago, with the outcome preordained and known to all, had a comedic lack of drama. At the appointed hour on the first day of the convention, when the signal was given, Thomas D. Garry, superintendent of the Department of Streets & Sanitation of the City of Chicago, stationed in the basement of Chicago Stadium, flipped a switch that activated the stadium's speaker system and began chanting "We want Roosevelt." Chicago mayor and Roosevelt backer Ed Kelly had stationed hundreds of city workers throughout the stadium to join in the chant. Within minutes, Roosevelt acceded to the "will of the convention." Newsmen cynically joked that in accepting a nomination for a third term, Roosevelt answered the call of the "Voice from the Sewers."

Carter Glass died in office on May 28, 1946, at the age of 88. Stubborn until the end, he refused to resign from the Senate, even though he had been confined to bed in his apartment at the Mayflower hotel in Washington and hadn't answered a roll call vote in over two years.[9]

By February 1935, Huey Long had decided he would run for president. He began promoting his Share the Wealth clubs nationwide to cultivate a grassroots base of power from which to launch his campaign. Despite his national ambitions, Long never lost his grip on local Louisiana politics. On September 8, 1935, Long was in the State Capitol in Baton Rouge for a special session of the legislature overseeing a number of bills, including one gerrymandering Judge Benjamin Pavy, a political opponent, out of a job. Earlier, Long had arranged for Paul Pavy, the judge's brother, to be removed from his job as a high school principal, and for Marie Pavy, the judge's daughter, to be fired from her job as a third-grade teacher. Dr. Carl Weiss, Judge Pavy's son-in-law, confronted Long in the State House corridor that day and shot him once in the stomach. Long's bodyguards opened fire, shooting Weiss sixty-two times, killing him instantly. Long also died, two days later.[10]

More than eighty years after the enactment of the Securities Act of 1933, the registration process and disclosure requirements currently applicable today would be easily navigable by Corcoran, Landis, Cohen, and Dean. It has proven to be a durable, elegant, and precise piece of statutory work, perhaps Middleton Beaman's best. After Kennedy's successful efforts to simplify the registration process and gain market acceptance, fundamental dismantling of the Securities Act was never again seriously considered.

Tommy Corcoran was one of Roosevelt's hatchet men in Congress during the court-packing fight and the subsequent purge of "disloyal" congressional Democrats in the 1938 midterm election, and he paid a personal price for his loyalty to the president. Because of the heavy-handed nature of those measures, neither of which Corcoran enthusiastically supported, he became persona non grata to many Democrats in Congress and stood no chance of being appointed to any office requiring Senate confirmation.

After the 1940 election, Corcoran left government but always maintained his old friendships with those in power in Washington and collected new ones. He became the prototype for the lawyer-lobbyist, the fixer, and influence peddler. When Joe Kennedy wanted to replace low-rent federal government tenants with high-rent private sector tenants in the Merchandise Mart in Chicago after he bought it in 1945, he hired Corcoran to pull strings with the Treasury Department to get it to let Kennedy out of the long-term leases. Corcoran made a few phone calls and saved Kennedy millions. When he sent Kennedy a bill for $75,000 (nearly $1,000,000 in today's dollars), Kennedy sent back a more than generous check for $25,000. Despite his complaining that Joe was "a cheap son of a bitch,"[11] Corcoran continued to work for Joe Kennedy, and once tried to sell him the *Washington Times-Herald*.[12]

In October 1969, Corcoran's lobbying went a bit too far when he tried to persuade Supreme Court justices Hugo Black and William Brennan to rehear a case involving the El Paso Natural Gas Company. Both Black and Brennan were outraged by Corcoran's unethical attempt to influence a case before the court, but the new chief justice Warren Burger wanted the case reheard and the court's earlier decision overturned and thought he had the votes to do so. This would have required Burger to change the court's rules to permit the case to be reheard despite Black's and Brennan's recusals on the rehearing vote, necessitated by Corcoran having tainted them with his improper lobbying. Brennan told Burger that if he pushed the issue and got the case reheard, Brennan would write a dissent disclosing both Corcoran's misdeeds and Burger's willingness to change the court's rules to suit his whim. Luckily for Corcoran, Burger backed down and Corcoran's ethics violation was never disclosed until after his death.[13]

Corcoran maintained a thriving practice at his firm, Corcoran, Foley, Youngman and Rowe, through the 1970s and into the 1980s. Just after Thanksgiving 1981, Corcoran entered the hospital to have his gall bladder removed. On December 6, 1981, while recovering from the surgery, Tommy Corcoran suffered an embolism and died. He was eighty years old.[14]

Sam Rayburn never remarried. His legislative accomplishments, though, made him a legend in the House of the Representatives. He co-sponsored five of the most important pieces of New Deal legislation: the Securities Act of 1933; the Securities Exchange Act of 1934; the Public Utilities Holding Company Act of 1935; the Federal Communications Act of 1934; and the Emergency Railroad Transportation Act of 1933.

On June 4, 1936, Joseph Byrns, the sixty-six-year-old Speaker of the House, died suddenly. Within hours, the Democratic caucus chose Majority Leader William Bankhead of Alabama as the new Speaker. The choice of a new majority leader, always important, was even more so given Bankhead's precarious health. He had had a massive heart attack the year before and been unable to attend a single session of the House in 1935.[15]

The two men vying for majority leader were Rayburn and Representative John J. O'Connor of New York, chairman of the powerful Rules Committee. While O'Connor's brother, Basil, was President Roosevelt's law partner, the president had never particularly liked John O'Connor, and liked him less when he conspired with the utility companies to weaken the Public Utility Holding Company Act against the president's wishes. Roosevelt wanted Rayburn.[16]

Winning over the New York congressional delegation would be critical to Roosevelt's plan to get Rayburn in as majority leader. If O'Connor couldn't hold his home delegation, it would be fatal to his candidacy. It came down to Tammany Hall, which meant it came down to James Farley, who was not only chairman of the National Democratic Party but also chairman of the New York State Democratic Party. Farley was on an ocean liner coming back from Europe. Frantic that he would not get to him before the Tammany Hall gang— who might convince him to make a public endorsement supporting the local boy O'Connor—Roosevelt instructed Tommy Corcoran to go to New York and wait on the dock, if he had to, to get to Farley before O'Connor's Tammany cronies did. Tommy Corcoran did one better. He had a friend who was an officer in the Coast Guard, and Corcoran convinced his friend to provide him with a fast boat and crew to speed out to Farley's ocean liner in the Atlantic. Corcoran literally climbed up the ship's ladder and searched the large ship until he found Farley. "Rayburn's our man," he breathlessly told Farley. Corcoran then climbed back down the ladder onto the Coast Guard boat and beat the liner to shore, smiling and waving to the Tammany hacks at the pier, who knew that they had been outfoxed by "Tommy the Cork."[17]

Rayburn was elected majority leader on January 4, 1937, by a vote of 184 to 127.[18] When William Bankhead died on September 15, 1940, Rayburn was elected the forty-eighth Speaker of the House of Representatives.[19]

During the 1940s, Rayburn became the most powerful Speaker in the history of the House. In 1942, President Roosevelt summoned the senior congressional leadership to a secret meeting at Blair House. With Roosevelt at the meeting was Albert Einstein, who explained to the leadership what an atom bomb was and where Hitler's scientists likely were in building one. Roosevelt then stated the obvious: whoever got the bomb first would win World War II. The president called the group together to brainstorm about how they could quickly and secretly fund the Manhattan Project, which would cost around $2,000,000,000. Rayburn spoke next. "Leave it to me" was all he said.[20]

Rayburn asked each of the subcommittee chairmen to put an extra $100,000,000 in their budget requests. Each chairman complied, and none dared to ask Rayburn why. And that was how the atomic bomb program was funded.[21]

In his later years as Speaker, Rayburn became more isolated, knowing few of the younger members and interacting primarily with the committee chairmen, which the press called his "College of Cardinals." "If you want to get along, go along," he would tell freshmen congressmen. "Don't open your mouth until you know what you're talking about."[22] He liked the old ways. For example, he never had a press secretary. When reporters would gather outside his office before he made his way to the floor of the House, his only comment was often: "You remember how things were yesterday? Well they're the same today."[23]

One day in 1960, Rayburn went up to a young-looking man on the House floor and asked: "New member, son?" It was Edward Boland, representative from Massachusetts. He had been in the House for seven years.[24] Boland's roommate in Washington and fellow Massachusetts congressman and future Speaker, Tip O'Neill, overheard this conversation and would tease Boland about it for the rest of his life. Around the same time, O'Neill was chatting with Daniel Inouye of Hawaii, a World War II hero who lost an arm fighting in Italy and who had been elected to Congress only a few months before. Rayburn passed by and warmly said, "Hello, Dan!" Later, O'Neill, amazed and somewhat jealous that Rayburn knew the brand-new congressman, convinced Inouye to ask Rayburn how it was he knew him by name. "Come on," said Rayburn, "How many one-armed Japs do we have around here?"[25]

Sam Rayburn died, still Speaker of the House, on November 16, 1961.[26]

Decades after Mr. Sam's death, a different, more plausible narrative of his romantic life would emerge. It would have been impossible in the 1930s—and for many decades thereafter— for an openly gay man to ascend the treacherous slope of leadership in Congress, where, it is said, advancement is most often predicated on the death, defeat, or disgrace of one's colleagues. A brief marriage to the sister of the fellow Texas Congressman would certainly provide the cover for a touching romantic tale of lost love and heartbreak. But our hearts are frankly more durable than that, and Sam Rayburn had a great deal more heart than most. Members of the Texas delegation would recall many years later hints at Rayburn's homosexuality by Lyndon Johnson, his protégé.[27]

Arthur Dean's relationship with the Securities and Exchange Commission grew closer over the years. He even had a hand in drafting the Trust Indenture Act of 1939 and the Investment Company Act of 1940, assisting SEC counsel.

On September 15, 1953, a tent was placed across the thirty-eighth parallel in the mountains of central Korea. In the tent there was a table. On one side sat Chinese communists and on the other side sat Arthur Dean. At the request of President Dwight Eisenhower and Dean's old mentor at Sullivan & Cromwell, Secretary of State John Foster Dulles, in that freezing cold tent, Arthur Dean negotiated the end of the Korean War.[28]

In the early 1960s, President John F. Kennedy called on Arthur Dean to serve as chief negotiator with the Soviets for the Nuclear Test Ban Treaty of 1963. President Lyndon Johnson also called upon Dean to be the co-chairman of the body overseeing compliance with the Civil Rights Act of 1965. After the disastrous Tet Offensive in 1968, Dean helped to persuade LBJ to stop the bombing of North Vietnam and not seek reelection. Dean retired as partner from Sullivan & Cromwell in 1976. He died in 1987 at age eighty-eight.[29]

Senator Key Pittman's career suffered no adverse consequences as a result of his outrageous misbehavior at the London Economic Conference. Whatever his character defects may have been, he was a man of supreme self-awareness and foresight. He insisted that his prenuptial agreement contain a clause providing that habitual drunkenness would *not* be grounds for divorce. His wife, whose name was actually Mimosa, consented.[30] Pittman remained Chairman of the Senate Foreign Relations Committee until the day he died, which fittingly was shrouded in controversy and outrageous misbehavior. While campaigning for reelection in 1940, Pittman, to the surprise of no one, went on another bender. While boozing it up in Reno at the Riverside Hotel bar a couple of days before the election, Pittman suffered a heart attack. A local physician, Dr. A.J. "Bart" Hood, was summoned immediately to examine the senator. He told Pittman's cronies (Pittman by then had lost consciousness) that the senator's condition was critical. Quietly, Pittman was admitted to Washoe General Hospital. A specialist who examined him at the hospital confirmed the worst: nothing could be done for the senator, he could die at any moment.

This left the Nevada Democratic leadership with a moral dilemma. If they told the truth about Pittman's condition, his Republican opponent, Samuel Platt, might win the election. If they lied, and Pittman hung on until after Election Day, his successor would be appointed by Democratic governor Edward Carville. After briefly considering the matter, the Nevada Democrats decided to lie. Dr. Hood was convinced (and the means used to convince him are lost to history, but one can speculate) to put out an entirely fictitious statement from the hospital: "The Senator was suffering from sheer exhaustion and fatigue, and the strain of the campaign through the state has been too much for an already overworked condition. The Senator's condition is not critical, but he will be kept in the hospital several days, principally for the rest."

On November 5, Pittman won reelection with over 60 percent of the vote. He died no later than November 10, 1940—his official listed date of demise. For years, it was claimed he died on November 4—before the election—but was kept on ice in a bathtub at the Riverside Hotel until after he could be fraudulently reelected in order to deny the Republicans the seat. In any event, Governor Carville appointed a Democrat, Berkeley L. Bunker, to succeed him.[31]

Like the Securities Act, the Securities Exchange Act of 1934 has also withstood the test of time. All of the principal provisions of the Securities Exchange Act remain operative today: registration of exchanges; registration of listed securities; ownership reports of equity securities of listed companies; regulation of the over-the-counter market; anti-manipulation provisions; annual and quarterly reporting; and proxy regulation. Today, the relationship between the SEC and the stock exchanges is nearly always harmonious, and the notion of the president of the New York Stock Exchange arguing repeal of any of these provisions—or openly expressing hostility toward the SEC—would be unthinkable.

Notwithstanding his position and status, Richard Whitney had terrible business judgment. He had a weakness for get-rich-quick investment schemes, including land deals in Florida, risky start-ups, and whatever happened to be in vogue. During the run-up of the Repeal stocks, Whitney began investing his and his firm's money in the stock of Distilled Liquors Corporation, whose principal product was a hard cider called Jersey Lightning.[32] Always in debt, he had yet to repay the $100,000 he borrowed from E.A. Pierce in 1934, which was but one of many loans to Whitney by New York Stock Exchange members. And he was beginning to borrow outside his inner circle, soliciting loans even from those who wouldn't feel constrained from embarrassing him. Whitney had approached Ben Smith seeking a $250,000 loan. "I told him that he had a lot of nerve to ask me for $250,000 when he didn't even bid me the time of day. I told him, I frankly didn't like him—that I wouldn't loan him a dime," Smith later recalled. The first outward sign that Richard Whitney's debts had gotten away from him was Christmastime 1935. Two of his friends, Herbert Wellington and George H. Bull, were talking at the Racquet and Tennis Club on Park Avenue in midtown Manhattan. Bull casually mentioned to Wellington that Richard Whitney had asked him for a $100,000 loan. Wellington, who had himself lent Whitney over $100,000, didn't tell his friend not to loan Whitney the money but said that Bull should make sure he had his lawyer involved. Between the two polite gentlemen, the remark was taken as it was intended, as a bright red flag as to Whitney's creditworthiness.[33]

On Valentine's Day 1936, Whitney crossed the line from bad businessman to felon. He took $150,000 of bonds entrusted to him by the New York Yacht Club, where he served as treasurer, and used them as part of the collateral for a $200,000 personal loan from the Public National Bank & Trust Company. He also took bonds belonging to the estate of his deceased father-in-law, George R. Sheldon, and used them as collateral for a personal loan as well.[34]

By July 1937, things had gotten so desperate that Whitney had asked his brother, George, to arrange a personal loan to clear up his affairs. He thought

$650,000 would do it. George, of course, lent him the money with very few questions asked. George Whitney was an extraordinarily loyal brother. He already had loans outstanding to his brother in excess of $1,000,000.[35]

But George's new loan wasn't anywhere near enough. In February 1937, the accountant of the New York Stock Exchange Gratuity Fund, of which Richard Whitney was trustee, noticed that $657,000 of its bonds entrusted to Whitney's care had gone missing. For months, Whitney promised they would be returned. By Thanksgiving, Exchange officials were forcing the issue. With nowhere else to turn, Whitney again went to his brother. It was worse even than it appeared. Richard Whitney had also taken $221,000 in cash from the Gratuity Fund, which assisted widows and orphans of Exchange members. A back-of-the-envelope accounting of Richard Whitney's liabilities revealed that a loan of more than $1,000,000 would be required to keep him and his company afloat. George Whitney did not have that much money to lend, so he turned to J.P. Morgan & Co. Thomas Lamont was assigned to diligence the sensitive matter and reported to J.P. Morgan Jr., who gave his approval. As displeased as Morgan was about the loan and its circumstances, the alternative—public disgrace of Richard Whitney and by association J.P. Morgan & Co.—was worse. Lamont and George Whitney were then charged with running the sale process for assets of Richard Whitney & Co. sufficient to repay the loan.[36]

Richard Whitney & Co.'s largest holding was its shares in Distilled Liquors Corporation. The stock had tanked along with most other Repeal stocks, and there was no buyer for Whitney's stake. Besides, all the company's assets were already hocked to banks for the nearly $30,000,000 of secured loans to the company.[37] The Morgan partners then tried selling the company as a whole. There were no takers for it either. Word was out. Richard Whitney & Co. was teetering.

On February 21, 1938, Richard Whitney & Co. filed with the Securities and Exchange Commission and the New York Stock Exchange a statement of its net capital as required by Securities Exchange Act of 1934.[38] The filing, it was later learned, fraudulently misstated the company's assets and liabilities, but not enough to show sufficient capital. As was customary when reports showed insufficient capital, an Exchange audit team was sent in to investigate the books. By month's end, the audit team had discovered misappropriation of customer securities to support loans to the company and to Whitney personally.[39]

On Tuesday March 1, New York Stock Exchange President Charles Gay was informed of what the audit team had found. By Friday, the audit team had also found clear evidence of embezzlement and had concluded that Richard Whitney & Co. was insolvent. On Sunday, a delegation of the old guard from the Exchange confronted Whitney, and he essentially confessed to everything, wagering that the Exchange would rather find a way to fix the problem and make it go away than explain it to the SEC.[40]

Whitney guessed wrong this time. The Exchange would not lift a finger for him, although they gave him the weekend to arrange a bailout, which, if successful, might have permitted him to resign from the Exchange voluntarily. Again, Whitney reached out to J.P. Morgan & Co. At a summit at J.P. Morgan Jr.'s Glen Cove, New York, estate on Sunday, March 6, Morgan, advised by John Davis of the Davis Polk law firm, came to a fast decision: do nothing more for Richard Whitney.[41]

Word was relayed immediately to the NYSE's lawyers to proceed with formal charges against Richard Whitney and his firm. The charges were prepared by Roland Redmond, Whitney's close friend and long-term consigliere, who had tears literally streaming down his face as he drafted the documentation.[42]

On Monday, first the business conduct committee and then the governing committee voted unanimously to expel Whitney from the Exchange.[43] As mandated by law, the SEC was notified immediately. Chairman William O. Douglas briefed President Roosevelt who gasped: "Not Dick Whitney!"[44] Douglas also sent his personal envoy, John Wesley Hames, to New York to deal with the fallout once the word about Whitney became public.

On Tuesday, Hames arrived on the floor of the Exchange to find it aflame with rumors about Whitney, many worse than the actual truth. He instructed Exchange president Gay to make a public announcement about the charges that morning to quell the rumors. Shortly after 10:00 a.m., Gay stepped up to the rostrum on the Exchange floor and announced that Richard Whitney & Co. was insolvent and had been shut down.[45] The company filed for bankruptcy the following Monday.[46]

Two days later, New York County Prosecutor Thomas Dewey indicted Whitney for embezzlement from his father-in-law's estate.[47] The next day, the New York State attorney general indicted him for stealing from the New York Yacht Club.[48]

On March 14, Whitney pleaded guilty to the charges—while pleading for his partners to not be charged as all wrongdoing was his alone.[49] On March 25, he filed for personal bankruptcy.[50] On April 15, Judge Owen H. Bohan sentenced Whitney to five to ten years' imprisonment at Ossining State Prison.[51]

In May, the personal property of Richard Whitney & Co. was sold at auction. One of the items sold was "Post No. 2" from the floor of the New York Stock Exchange, where on Black Thursday, October 24, 1929, Richard Whitney had made his famous bid of $205 for U.S. Steel shares. It was "retired" from the floor and given to Whitney in honor of his heroic conduct that day. The high bidder acquired it for $5.[52]

Whitney was a model prisoner. He mopped floors without complaining. He was popular with both the guards and his fellow inmates. He even played a respectable first base on the prison baseball team.

During his first summer in Sing Sing, a heartbroken but still staunchly loyal Reverend Endicott Peabody visited his former favorite student. Peabody asked Whitney whether there was anything he could do for him. "Yes," said Whitney, former captain of the Groton baseball team, "I need a left-handed first baseman's mitt."[53]

Whitney was paroled in August 1941. For a while he managed a dairy farm owned by George's wife's family in Barnstable on Cape Cod. In 1946, he went back into business, becoming the president of a small textile company in Florida. It failed three years later. In 1955, he worked as an executive at Jersey Mills Dairy in Raritan, New Jersey, which was owned by Clarence Dillon of Dillon, Read & Co. With the help of his brother, he made restitution in full to all who suffered losses as a result of his wrongdoing. He avoided media attention and lived a quiet life in Far Hills, New Jersey, where he died on December 5, 1974.[54]

The SEC was the model federal regulatory agency during the twentieth century—efficient, professional, effective, and without scandal. The twenty-first century has so far been less kind to the agency. The commission was harshly criticized for failure to address investment-banking conflicts that came to light after the Internet-telecom bubble burst in 2000. It was also accused of abdicating its role as chief securities regulator when New York State attorney general Elliott Spitzer took the lead with a global settlement among the investment banks that required the banks to implement stronger protections against conflicts of interest. At the same time, the commission failed to prevent the massive accounting frauds at Enron and WorldComm.

Two thousand and eight would prove to be the worst year for the SEC. First, it was unable to prevent the Bear Stearns collapse and was essentially a spectator as the Treasury and the Fed arranged the bailout merger with J.P. Morgan. Next came the Lehman Brothers collapse and even greater impotence, and some say incompetence, during the subsequent meltdown. And lastly, the worst moment in its history was on December 11, 2008, when Bernie Madoff, former chairman of the NASDAQ stock market, was arrested, and it was revealed that a $65,000,000,000 fraud had been committed right under the nose of the SEC and that reputable whistle-blowers had been warning the commission about Madoff for more than eight years.

Michael J. Meehan had purchased 75 percent of the stock of the Good Humor ice cream company in 1930 for $500,000. After he was barred from the securities business by the SEC, Meehan focused on the ice cream business. Ice cream was an inexpensive diversion during the Great Depression, and with innovations Meehan developed, like making ice cream on a stick and selling it from trucks and boats, the business grew to be worth tens of millions of dollars. After World War II, the company became many times more valuable when it expanded into the suburbs, its ever-present fleet of trucks bringing smiles to baby boomers across the nation. In 1961, the Meehan family sold its stock to a subsidiary of Unilever.[55]

In 1939, Meehan's twenty-one-year-old son, Joseph, became the senior partner of M.J. Meehan & Co. and took a seat on the New York Stock Exchange while he was a senior at Fordham University.[56] Joseph Meehan became a specialist in RCA stock—the same stock that made his father rich and famous in the great pool of 1928. Joseph Meehan would go on to become a member of the governing committee of the New York Stock Exchange in 1962.[57]

Notwithstanding the issues between the fathers, the Meehan children and the Kennedy children were on friendly terms,[58] and they, along with the grandchildren of Thomas Murray, would form the upper crust of young Irish society in New York. (Future president John F. Kennedy would have his heart broken by a young Charlotte McDonnell, who rebuffed his talk of marriage.)

Michael Meehan did not seem to miss Wall Street and divided his time between his apartment at 770 Park Avenue and his country home upstate at Mahopac. He continued to be one of the leading benefactors of Catholic charities and a leading philanthropist in New York, generously supporting St. Vincent's Hospital and other institutions. Michael Meehan died of pneumonia at the Waldorf hotel on January 2, 1948, at age fifty-six.[59]

Joe Kennedy strongly backed FDR's reelection campaign in 1936, even writing a book, *I'm for Roosevelt,* making Roosevelt's case for a second term to the business community. In 1937, Roosevelt appointed Kennedy as the first chairman of the U. S. Maritime Commission. His record of accomplishments there did not quite compare to his time at the SEC, but he was widely praised for his hard work and his standing up to the longshoreman's union. On December 9, 1937, Arthur Krock broke the news that Kennedy was to be appointed U.S. ambassador to the Court of St. James.

Kennedy served as ambassador to Great Britain during a perilous time, with Europe engulfed in another brutal world war. His loftiest accomplishment was his development of a plan to save the Jews of Europe in 1938, after Kristallnacht. Benjamin Cohen visited him in London, convincing him of the need to intervene on behalf of European Jews. Kennedy's plan, which would have saved millions of lives, required a number of nations, including the United States, to allow in Jewish immigrants from Europe. Roosevelt's State Department sabotaged the plan, the best opportunity America would have to prevent the Holocaust.[60]

Kennedy never really forgave Roosevelt for allowing the State Department to bypass him and publicly undermine him. By 1940, with the continent at war, Kennedy was eager to keep America out of another European conflict and equally eager to return home. His isolationist views were increasingly at odds with Roosevelt's policies. His son Joe Jr. was a delegate to the 1940 Democratic Convention, and despite the fact that his father was Roosevelt's sitting ambassador in London, Joe Jr. cast his roll call vote loudly for "James A. Farley." When furious Roosevelt backers called him in London, Kennedy told them he supported his son's decision.[61] Kennedy resigned his ambassadorship shortly after the 1940 election.

During Kennedy's last federal government position as a member of the Hoover Commission in 1947, he and fellow commission member James

Farley executed a little posthumous revenge on FDR when the commission recommended an amendment to the Constitution limiting presidents to two terms. The Twenty-second Amendment passed Congress on March 21, 1947, and was ratified on February 27, 1951.

Kennedy continued to employ his SEC associates throughout his life. John Burns was particularly close, until the two parted ways after a money dispute. James Landis and James Fayne were hired to help John F. Kennedy research his Pulitzer Prize–winning book, *Profiles in Courage,* while he was confined to a hospital bed in New York City after back surgery.[62]

After his Hoover Commission service, most of Kennedy's time was spent managing his business investments and directing his sons' careers. The war he never wanted took from him his oldest son, Joe Jr., who died in a bombing mission over the English Channel, and nearly took his second son, John, who gravely wounded his back when his boat was sunk by the Japanese in the Solomon Islands. In 1946, John was elected a congressman from Boston, and in 1952 he was elected senator from Massachusetts. In 1960, he was elected president. His brother Robert was appointed attorney general of the United States in 1961, and the following year, Kennedy's youngest son, Edward, was elected senator from Massachusetts.

On December 19, 1961, after playing golf at the Palm Beach Country Club, Joseph Kennedy suffered a devastating stroke, robbing him of mobility and speech. Doctors assured his family that his mind was unaffected. It is probable that he fully comprehended the losses in Dallas and Los Angeles.

He died on November 17, 1969.[63]

NOTES

PROLOGUE

1. Irving Bernstein, "Americans in Depression and War," History, Chap. 5, www.dol.gov.
2. U.S. Department of Commerce, Bureau of Economic Analysis, *GDP of Other Major NIPA Services, 1929–2012: II*, August 2012.
3. S&P Dow Jones Indices website.
4. Alexis Coe, "When Sheep Ruled Central Park," *Modern Farmer*, February 10, 2014.
5. Lionel Robbins, *The Great Depression*, (Freeport, NY: Books for Libraries Press, 1934.)
6. Jack Yellen and Milton Ager, "Happy Days Are Here Again," from the movie *Chasing Rainbows*, MGM, 1929. Published by Ager, Yellen & Bornstein, Inc., New York.
7. Yip Harburg (lyrics) and Jay Gorney (music), "Brother, Can You Spare a Dime," 1931.

CHAPTER ONE

1. S&P Dow Jones Indices, www.spindices.com.
2. John Brooks, *Once in Golconda* (New York: Allworth Press,1969), 111.
3. S&P Dow Jones Indices, www.spindices.com.
4. Brooks, *Once in Golconda*, p. 124.
5. Ibid., pp. 61–62.
6. Ibid., pp. 126–127.
7. S&P Dow Jones Indices, www.spindices.com.
8. Ibid.
9. Ibid.
10. Ron Chernow, *The House of Morgan* (New York: Grove Press,1990).
11. Gilbert King, "The Copper King's Precipitous Fall," *Smithsonian*, September 20, 2012, www.smithsonianmag.com/history.
12. Chernow, *The House of Morgan*, Chap. 7.
13. Allan H. Meltzer, *A History of the Federal Reserve, Volume I, 1913–1951* (Chicago: University of Chicago Press, 2003), Chap. 3.

14. Neil Irwin, *The Alchemists* (New York: Penguin Press, 2013), Chap. 3.
15. Chernow, *The House of Morgan,* Chap. 8.
16. Meltzer, *A History of the Federal Reserve, Volume 1,* Chap. 3.
17. John R. Walter, "Depression-Era Bank Failures: The Great Contagion or the Great Shake-out?" *Federal Reserve Bank of Richmond Economic Quarterly,* 91, no. 1 (Winter 2005).
18. Federal Deposit Insurance Corporation (FDIC), *Federal Deposit Insurance Corporation: The First Fifty Years* (Federal Deposit Insurance Corporation, Washington, D.C., 1984), p. 36.
19. Susan Easterbrook Kennedy, *The Banking Crisis of 1933* (Lexington, Kentucky: University Press of Kentucky, 1973), Chap. 1.
20. Meltzer, *A History of the Federal Reserve, Volume I,* Chap. 5.
21. Ibid.
22. Kennedy, *The Banking Crisis of 1933,* p. 40.
23. Richard D. White Jr., *Kingfish* (New York: Random House, 2006), Chap. 1–3.
24. Ibid., Chap. 3.
25. Ibid., Chap. 1.
26. Ibid., Chap. 3.
27. Ibid.
28. Ibid., Chap. 6.
29. Kennedy, *The Banking Crisis of 1933,* pp. 40–43.
30. Ibid., p. 108.
31. FDIC, *Federal Deposit Insurance Corporation: The First Fifty Years,* p. 36.
32. David McKean, *Peddling Influence* (Hanover, NH: Steerforth Press, 2004), Chap. 1–3.
33. Ibid.
34. Meltzer, *A History of the Federal Reserve, Volume I,* Chap. 4.
35. Kennedy, *The Banking Crisis of 1933,* p. 45.
36. Meltzer, *A History of the Federal Reserve, Volume I,* Chap. 5.
37. Ibid.
38. Kennedy, *The Banking Crisis of 1933,* p. 47.
39. Ibid.
40. Marcus Nadler and Jules I. Bogen, *The Banking Crisis* (London: George Allen & Unwin Ltd., 1934), pp. 112–113.
41. Ibid., p. 116.
42. Doris Kearns Goodwin (speech, 2004 Annual Meeting of the Securities and Exchange Commission Historical Society, June 3, 2004), available at www.sechistorical.org.
43. Leigh Montville, *The Big Bam* (New York: Doubleday, 2006), Chap. 21.
44. The American Presidency Project, Elections, 1932, available at www.presidency.ucsb.edu.
45. Kennedy, *The Banking Crisis of 1933,* pp. 61–67.
46. Ibid.
47. Ibid., p. 74.
48. Nadler and Bogen, *The Banking Crisis,* pp. 134–140.
49. Kennedy, *The Banking Crisis of 1933,* pp. 75–76.

50. Ibid.
51. Kennedy, *The Banking Crisis of 1933*, Chap. 4.
52. Barrie A. Wigmore, *The Crash and Its Aftermath* (Westport, CT: Greenwood Press, 1985), p. 537.
53. Bernhard Ostrolenk, "Workings of the Federal Reserve System," *The New York Times*, March 19, 1933.
54. Jonathan Alter, *The Defining Moment* (New York: Simon & Schuster Paperbacks, 2006), p. 158.
55. Ibid., p. 159.
56. James E. Palmer Jr. and Jesse H. Jones, *Carter Glass: Unreconstructed Rebel: A Biography* (Daleville, VA: Southeastern Press, Inc., 1938), p. 14.
57. Ibid., p. 46.
58. Alter, *The Defining Moment*, p. 159.
59. Ibid., p. 158.
60. Ibid., p. 159.
61. James A. Farley, *Behind the Ballots* (New York: Harcourt, Brace and Company, 1938), p. 181.
62. Q. David Bowers, "Remembering William H. Woodin—Part One," Stack's–Bowers Numismatics News, June 10, 2010.
63. "William H. Woodin's Political Journey and Musical Talent," The E-Sylum, Volume 10, Number 51, Article 16, December 16, 2007.
64. "James P. Warburg to Be Woodin's Aide," *The New York Times*, March 18, 1933.
65. Arthur Krock, "'New Deal' Praise Shared by Woodin," *The New York Times*, March 19, 1933.
66. Alter, *The Defining Moment*, pp. 178–183.

CHAPTER TWO

1. Michael Perino, *The Hellhound of Wall Street* (New York: Penguin Press, 2010), p. 57.
2. Ibid., p. 48.
3. Ibid., pp. 50–51.
4. Ibid., p. 61.
5. "Pecora Appointed for Stock Inquiry," *The New York Times*, January 25, 1933.
6. Perino, *The Hellhound of Wall Street*, Chap. 2.
7. Frank Freidel, *Franklin D. Roosevelt—Launching the New Deal* (Boston: Little, Brown and Company, 1973), pp. 175–176.
8. Perino, *The Hellhound of Wall Street*, p. 132.
9. Ibid., Chap. 5.
10. Ibid., p. 82.
11. Charles D. Ellis with James R. Vertin, *Wall Street People, Volume 2* (Hoboken, NJ: John Wiley & Sons, 2003), p. 193.
12. "Mitchell Avoided Income Tax in 1929 by $2,800,000 Loss," *The New York Times*, February 22, 1933; Perino, *The Hellhound of Wall Street*, pp. 153–154.

13. Alter, *The Defining Moment*, p. 150.
14. Perino, *The Hellhound of Wall Street*, pp. 247–248.
15. Ferdinand Pecora, *Wall Street Under Oath* (New York: Simon and Schuster, 1939), p. 121.
16. Ibid., pp. 122–123.
17. Ibid., p. 127.
18. Ibid., pp. 128–129.
19. "National City Lent $2,400,000 to Save Stock of Officers," *The New York Times*, February 23, 1933; Perino, *The Hellhound of Wall Street*, pp. 168–169.
20. Ibid.
21. Ibid., pp. 169–170.
22. Ibid., pp. 181–182.
23. "National City Sold Bank Stock Short During 1929 Boom," *The New York Times*, February 24, 1933; "Report of the Senate Committee on Banking and Currency on Stock Exchange Practices," dated June 16, 1934, pp. 172–173.
24. Senate Committee on Banking and Currency, *Hearings on Stock Exchange Practices*, 72d Cong., February 23, 1933, p. 1924.
25. Kennedy, *The Banking Crisis of 1933*, p. 134.
26. "Report of the Senate Committee on Banking and Currency on Stock Exchange Practices," pp. 156–157.
27. Senate Committee on Banking and Currency, *Hearings on Stock Exchange Practices*, 72d Cong., February 24, 1933, pp. 2030–2042.
28. Report of the Committee Appointed Pursuant to H.R. 429 and 504 to Investigate Concentration of Control of Money and Credit, February 28, 1913, pp. 155–156; "Federal Inquiry on National City and Insul Starts," *The New York Times*, February 25, 1933.
29. Ibid., p. 171.
30. Kennedy, *The Banking Crisis of 1933*, p. 134.
31. Perino, *The Hellhound of Wall Street*, p. 229.
32. "National City Sold Peru Bond Issues in 'Honest Mistake,'" *The New York Times*, February 28, 1933; "Report of the Senate Committee on Banking and Currency on Stock Exchange Practices," pp. 126–131.
33. Ibid., p. 129.
34. Ibid., p. 130.
35. Ibid.
36. Ibid., p. 131
37. Ibid., p. 215.
38. Kennedy, *The Banking Crisis of 1933*, p. 134.
39. "'Shorn Lamb' Tells Senators of Loss," *The New York Times*, March 1, 1933; "Report of the Senate Committee on Banking and Currency on Stock Exchange Practices," pp. 131–133.
40. Ibid., p. 131.
41. Ibid., p. 132.
42. Ibid.
43. Ibid., p. 133.

44. Perino, *The Hellhound of Wall Street*, p. 253

45. "Report of the Senate Committee on Banking and Currency on Stock Exchange Practices," p. 133.

46. Kennedy, *The Banking Crisis of 1933*, p. 139.

47. "Report of the Senate Committee on Banking and Currency on Stock Exchange Practices," p. 214; "City Bank Officer Bares Ramsey Loan," *The New York Times*, March 2, 1933.

48. Perino, *The Hellhound of Wall Street*, pp. 262–263.

49. Kennedy, *The Banking Crisis of 1933*, p. 144.

50. "Profit in Mergers Told to Senators," *The New York Times*, March 3, 1933; "Report of the Senate Committee on Banking and Currency on Stock Exchange Practices," p. 107.

51. Ibid., pp. 107–108.

52. Alter, *The Defining Moment*, p. 188.

53. Kennedy, *The Banking Crisis of 1933*, p. 144.

54. Ibid., p. 146.

55. Ibid., p. 147.

56. Ibid., p. 144.

CHAPTER THREE

1. Nadler and Bogen, *The Banking Crisis*, p. 160.

2. Freidel, *Franklin D. Roosevelt—Launching the New Deal*, pp. 197–198.

3. Alter, *The Defining Moment*, p. 212; "Roosevelt Busy from Dawn to Night," *The New York Times*, March 5, 1933.

4. Freidel, *Franklin D. Roosevelt—Launching the New Deal*, p. 198.

5. Francis Gloyd Awalt, "Recollections of the Banking Crisis in 1933," *Business History Review*, XLIII, no. 3 (Autumn 1969), pp. 358–363.

6. James A. Hagerty, "Roosevelt Address Stirs Great Crowd," *The New York Times*, March 5, 1933.

7. Ibid.

8. "Ready to Call Congress," *The New York Times*, March 5, 1933; "Roosevelt Proclamation Calling Congress to Meet in Extra Session Thursday Noon," *The New York Times*, March 6, 1933.

9. *Documents and Statements Pertaining to the Banking Emergency, Part I, February 25–March 31, 1933*, (Washington, D.C.: U.S. Government Printing Office, 1933), pp. 1–2.

10. "Big Plant Speeds Printing of Scrip," *The New York Times*, March 7, 1933.

11. Freidel, *Franklin D. Roosevelt—Launching the New Deal*, p. 218.

12. Kennedy, *The Banking Crisis of 1933*, p. 173.

13. Raymond Moley, *After Seven Years* (New York: Harper & Brothers Publishers, 1989), p. 150.

14. "City Awaits Scrip as Cash Dwindles," *The New York Times*, March 7, 1933.

15. Kennedy, *The Banking Crisis of 1933*, p. 161.

16. Alexander D. Noyes, "Financial Markets," *The New York Times*, March 6, 1933.

17. James P. Dawson, "Ruth Unrelenting on $25,000 Slash," *The New York Times*, March 6, 1933.
18. "National City to Drop Affiliate," *The New York Times*, March 8, 1933.
19. Moley, *After Seven Years*, p. 152.
20. Awalt, *Recollections of the Banking Crisis in 1933*, p. 358.
21. "The Cabinet: The Cabinet Off Bottom," *Time*, March 20, 1933.
22. The American Presidency Project, Franklin D. Roosevelt, Press Conference, Transcript of March 8, 1933, Press Conference, available at www.presidency.ucsb.edu.
23. *Documents and Statements Pertaining to the Banking Emergency, Part I, February 25–March 31, 1933*, pp. 2–3.
24. Ibid.
25. Ibid.
26. FDIC, *Federal Deposit Insurance Corporation: The First Fifty Years*, p. 38.
27. Ibid.
28. Ibid.
29. Kennedy, *The Banking Crisis of 1933*, p. 176.
30. Ibid.
31. White, *Kingfish*, Chap.s 8–10.
32. Farley, *Behind the Ballots*, pp. 170–171.
33. Ibid., p. 171.
34. Freidel, *Franklin D. Roosevelt—Launching the New Deal*, p. 227.
35. 73d Cong., 1st sess., *Congressional Record* (March 9, 1933): S.
36. Kennedy, *The Banking Crisis of 1933*, pp. 176–177.
37. *Documents and Statements Pertaining to the Banking Emergency, Part I, February 25–March 31, 1933*, pp. 3–6.
38. "The Cabinet: The Cabinet Off Bottom," *Time*, March 20, 1933.
39. Ibid.
40. "Woodin Prepares Steps for Reopenings," *The New York Times*, March 10, 1933.
41. Arthur Krock, "Roosevelt Gets Power of 'Dictator,'" *The New York Times*, March 11, 1933.
42. *Documents and Statements Pertaining to the Banking Crisis, Part I, February 25–March 31, 1933*, p. 7.
43. Ibid., pp. 7–8.
44. William L. Silber, "Why Did FDR's Bank Holiday Succeed?" *FRBNY Economic Policy Review* (July 2009), p. 26.
45. *Documents and Statements Pertaining to the Banking Crisis, Part I, February 25–March 31, 1933*, pp. 8–9.
46. Ibid.
47. U.S. Treasury, *Regulation No. 23*, March 11, 1933.
48. Moley, *After Seven Years*, p. 154.
49. Awalt, *Recollections of the Banking Crisis*, p. 370.
50. *Documents and Statements Pertaining to the Banking Crisis, Part I, February 25–March 31, 1933*, p. 9.
51. Ibid.

52. Ibid.
53. Ibid., p. 10.
54. Ibid., pp. 10–11.
55. Ibid.
56. "Bank Rushes Out Notices," *The New York Times*, March 13, 1933.
57. "Sound Banks Classified," *The New York Times*, March 13, 1933.
58. "Banks Over Nation Set for Reopening," *The New York Times*, March 13, 1933.
59. "The Cabinet: The Cabinet Off Bottom," *Time*, March 20, 1933.
60. "New Bills Copies of 1929 Banknotes," *The New York Times*, March 14, 1933.
61. "Chicago Gold Flow Rises," *The New York Times*, March 14, 1933.
62. "White House Hails Bank Reopenings," *The New York Times*, March 14, 1933.
63. *Documents and Statements Pertaining to the Banking Crisis, February 25–March 31, 1933*, p. 6; "State Acts to Aid Non-Member Banks," *The New York Times*, March 15, 1933.
64. James P. Dawson, "Ruth and Ruppert Clash on Salary," *The New York Times*, March 14, 1933.
65. "Stock Exchanges Resume Today; More Banks Open," *The New York Times*, March 15, 1933.
66. "Huge Deposits Mark Newark Reopenings," *The New York Times*, March 15, 1923.
67. "798 Banks in State Reopened in Full," *The New York Times*, March 16, 1933.
68. S&P Dow Jones Indices, www.spindices.com; Silber, "Why Did FDR's Bank Holiday Succeed?" p. 28.
69. Kennedy, *The Banking Crisis of 1933*, p. 142.
70. "Banking Solution in the Nation," *The New York Times*, March 19, 1933.
71. "Ends Life So $50,000 Policy Will Help His Bank Reopen," *The New York Times*, May 18, 1933; *20th Century History of New Castle and Lawrence County*, 1908, pp. 370–371.
72. Montville, *The Big Bam*, Chap. 22.

CHAPTER FOUR

1. Franklin D. Roosevelt (campaign address, Columbus, Ohio, August 20, 1932), The American Presidency Project, available at www.presidency.ucsb.edu.
2. *Legislative History of the Banking Act of 1933 (Glass-Steagall Act)*, compiled by Robert A. Fink of O'Melveny & Myers (Los Angeles, 1937), pp. 7-8.
3. Ibid., pp. 25–46.
4. Ibid., pp. 8–9.
5. Ibid., p.10.
6. Ibid., pp. 11–12.
7. White, *Kingfish*, p. 172.
8. Fink, *Legislative History of the Banking Act of 1933 (Glass-Steagall Act)*, p. 111.
9. Ibid., p. 114.
10. Ibid., pp. 11–13.
11. Ibid.
12. Ibid.

13. Franklin D. Roosevelt, *Looking Forward* (New York: John Day Company Inc., 1933), p. 189.
14. FDIC, *Federal Deposit Insurance Corporation: The First Fifty Years,* p. 13–30.
15. "Bill to Unify Deposit Banks," William H. Grimes, *The Wall Street Journal,* April 3, 1933.
16. "Altered Glass Bill Submission Nears," *The Wall Street Journal,* April 5, 1933.
17. *Banks Under Roosevelt,* J.F.T. O'Connor, Callaghan and Company (Chicago 1938), p. 105–107.
18. "Three-Way Split Over Glass Bill," *The Wall Street Journal,* April 12, 1933.
19. "Roosevelt Delays Bank Bill Action," *The Wall Street Journal,* April 13, 1933.
20. "Bank Reform Bill Backed Unchanged," *The New York Times,* April 14, 1933.
21. "Woodin Sees Flaws in Bank Reform Bill," *The New York Times,* April 22, 1933.
22. "Roosevelt Ends Stalemate Over Bank Bill; Asks $10,000 Limit on Deposit Guarantee," *The New York Times,* April 25, 1933.
23. "Banking Bill Completed," *The New York Times,* May 2, 1933.
24. "Bank Bill Taken Up with President," *The New York Times,* May 5, 1933.
25. "Roosevelt Favors Pushing Bank Bill," *The New York Times,* May 5, 1933.
26. "Deposit Insurance to Be in Banking Bill," *The Wall Street Journal,* May 6, 1933.
27. "Glass Bill Likely to Wait," *The Wall Street Journal,* May 11, 1933.
28. "Glass Bill Ready for Senate," *The New York Times,* May 14, 1933.
29. "Steagall Bank Bill," *The Wall Street Journal,* May 17, 1933.
30. "Sisson Opposes Bank Guaranty," *The Wall Street Journal,* May 20, 1933.
31. "The Banking Bill," *The New York Times,* May 25, 1933.
32. "Bank Bills Pushed in Both Chambers; Glass Hits Woodin," *The New York Times,* May 20, 1933.
33. Ibid.
34. Ibid.
35. "Glass Bill Passed by Senate," *The New York Times,* May 26, 1933; Bernard Kilgore, "Bank Insurance," *The Wall Street Journal,* May 27, 1933.
36. "Deposit Insurance Stirs New Dispute," *The New York Times,* June 2, 1933.
37. Brooks, *Once in Golconda,* p. 184.
38. Ferdinand Pecora, *Wall Street Under Oath: The Story of Our Modern Money Changers* (New York: Simon and Schuster, 1939), p. 5.
39. "Report of the Committee on Banking and Currency on Stock Exchange Practices," pp. 101–108.
40. Ibid., p. 102.
41. Pecora, *Wall Street Under Oath,* pp. 36–37.
42. Brooks, *Once in Golconda,* pp. 180–182.
43. Kennedy, *The Banking Crisis of 1933,* p. 219.
44. "Deposit Insurance Stirs New Dispute," *The New York Times,* June 2, 1933.
45. "Roosevelt Warns of Bank Bill Veto," *The New York Times,* June 6, 1933.
46. "Conferees Split on Banking Bill," *The New York Times,* June 7, 1933.
47. "Bank Bill Delay Looms," *The New York Times,* June 9, 1933.
48. "Conferees Agree on Banking Bill," *The New York Times,* June 13, 1933; "Final Drive for Bank Insurance," *The Wall Street Journal,* June 13, 1933.

49. "Both Houses Pass Glass Banking Bill," *The Wall Street Journal*, June 14, 1933; "Bank Reform Bill Swiftly Approved," *The New York Times*, June 14, 1933.

50. Fink, *Legislative History of the Banking Act of 1933 (Glass-Steagall Act)*, p. 14.

51. *Banking Act of 1933*, Public Law No. 66, 73d Cong., H.R. 5661.

52. Ibid.

53. Ibid.

54. Ibid.

55. "The Great Deposit Insurance Debate," Mark D. Flood, *Journal of the Federal Reserve of St. Louis* (July–August 1992), p. 72.

56. *Banking Act of 1933*, Public Law No. 66, 73d Cong., H.R. 5661.

57. Ibid.

58. Ibid.

59. Ibid.

60. Ibid.

61. Ibid.

62. FDIC, *Federal Deposit Insurance Corporation: The First Fifty Years*, p. 46.

63. Ibid., pp. 46–48.

64. Antony C. Sutton, *Wall Street and FDR* (New York: Arlington House, 1975), p. 23.

CHAPTER FIVE

1. The American Presidency Project, Political Party Platforms, 1932, available at www.presidency.ucsb.edu.

2. Joel Seligman, Wolters Kluwer Law & Business, *The Transformation of Wall Street*, 3rd ed., (Aspen Publishers, 2003), p. 51.

3. Ibid., p. 52.

4. Report of the Committee Appointed Pursuant to H.R. 429 and 504 to Investigate the Concentration of Control of Money and Credit, Submitted by Rep. Pujo, February 28, 1913, (Washington, D.C.: U.S. Government Printing Office, 1913), pp. 170–173.

5. Ibid., pp. 166–173.

6. Ibid., p. 171.

7. Samuel Untermyer, "Speculation on the Stock Exchanges and Public Regulation of the Exchanges" (address, American Economic Association, Princeton, N.J., December 29, 1914).

8. Senate Committee on Banking and Currency, *Hearings on S.R. 3895, a Bill to Prevent the Use of the Mails and of the Telegraph and Telephone in Furtherance of Fraudulent and Harmful Transactions on Stock Exchanges*, 63rd Cong., 2d sess., 1914, pp. 819–822.

9. Ibid., pp. 710–711; Julia Ott, *The 'Free and Open' People's Market: Public Relations at the New York Stock Exchange, 1915–1929*, Business History Conference (2004), p. 8.

10. Report of the Governor's Committee on Speculation in Securities and Commodities, 1909, New York, June 7, 1909.

11. Ibid.

12. Senate Committee on Banking and Currency, *Hearings on S.R. 3895*, 63rd Cong., 2d sess., p. 712.

13. Ibid., pp. 712–713.
14. Seligman, *The Transformation of Wall Street*, p. 44.
15. Ibid.; Sean M. O'Connor, "Be Careful What You Wish For: How Accountants and Congress Created the Problem of Auditor Independence," *Boston College Law Review*, 45, Issue 4 (2004), p. 795.
16. Senate Committee on Banking and Currency, *Hearings on S.R. 3895*, 63rd Cong., 2d Session, p. 367.
17. War Finance Corporation Act, Approved April 5, 1918 (Booklet Printed by Guaranty Trust Company of New York, 140 Broadway, New York, NY).
18. Ibid.
19. Federal Reserve, *Federal Reserve Bulletin, January 1919* (Washington, D.C.: U.S. Government Printing Office, 1919), p. 18.
20. Ibid.
21. Ibid., pp. 18–19.
22. House Capital Issues Committee, *Final Report of the House Capital Issues Committee, February 19, 1919*, 65th Cong., 3d sess., 1919, H. Rep. 1836.
23. Michael E. Parrish, *Securities Regulation and the New Deal* (New Haven, CT: Yale University Press, 1970), pp. 17–18.
24. Isaiah Leo Sharfman, *The American Railroad Problem* (New York: The New Century Co., 1921), p. 420.
25. Seligman, *The Transformation of Wall Street*, p. 50.
26. Parrish, *Securities Regulation and the New Deal*, p. 20.
27. Seligman, *The Transformation of Wall Street*, p. 52.
28. "Stock Regulation May Be Albany Topic," *The New York Times*, January 2, 1933.
29. "Untermyer Urges Stock Regulation," *The New York Times*, January 9, 1933.
30. Huston Thompson, Commissioner, Federal Trade Commission, letter to Justice Louis D. Brandeis, May 20, 1919.
31. Donald A. Ritchie, *James M. Landis* (Cambridge, MA: Harvard University Press, 1980), p. 46; Dan Ernst, "Felix Frankfurter, Eustace Seligman, and the Securities Act of 1933," Legal History Blog, December 14, 2009.
32. The American Presidency Project, Political Party Platforms, 1932, available at www.presidency.ucsb.edu.
33. Seligman, *The Transformation of Wall Street*, pp. 52–53.
34. Friedel, *Franklin D. Roosevelt—Launching the New Deal*, pp. 342–343.
35. Seligman, *The Transformation of Wall Street*, p. 52.
36. Franklin D. Roosevelt, "Message from the President—Regulation of Securities Issues," presented to the Senate, on March 29, 1933, 77th Cong., *Cong. Rec.* 937.
37. Friedel, *Franklin D. Roosevelt—Launching the New Deal*, p. 344.
38. H.R. 5480 (as introduced), 73d Cong., 1st sess. (1933); "Both Houses Gut Securities Bill," *The Wall Street Journal*, March 30, 1933.
39. Ibid.
40. Ibid.
41. Ibid.
42. Ibid.

43. Ibid.
44. Donald C. Bacon, *Rayburn, A Biography* (Austin, TX: Texas Monthly Press Inc., 1987), pp. 11–59.
45. Robert A. Caro, *The Years of Lyndon Johnson, Volume I, The Path to Power* (New York: Vintage Books, 1990), pp. 330–331.
46. 77th Cong., *Cong. Rec.* 1018 (1933).
47. 77th Cong., *Cong. Rec.* 1020 (1933).
48. Ibid.
49. "Wall Street Cool to Securities Bill," *The New York Times*, March 30, 1933.
50. Eustace Seligman, "Securities Bill Held Too Strict," *The New York Times*, April 1, 1933.
51. Ibid.
52. Ibid.
53. "Securities Hearing Divides Leaders; Measure Is Rushed," *The New York Times*, April 1, 1933.
54. "Investment Heads Back Security Bill," *The New York Times*, April 2, 1933.
55. Ibid.
56. Seligman, *The Transformation of Wall Street*, p. 56.
57. "Securities Bill Held Inadequate," *The New York Times*, April 5, 1933.
58. Freidel, *Franklin D. Roosevelt—Launching the New Deal*, p. 344.
59. Lia Barker, *Felix Frankfurter* (New York: Coward-McCann, Inc., 1969), p. 155.
60. "Securities Bill Being Revised," *The Wall Street Journal*, April 6, 1933.
61. "Securities Bill to Be Revised," *The New York Times*, April 6, 1933.
62. "New Attacks Made on Securities Bill," *The New York Times*, April 8, 1933.
63. McKean, *Peddling Influence*, p. 38.
64. Arthur M. Schlessinger Jr., *The Age of Roosevelt: The Coming of the New Deal, 1933–1935* (New York: First Mariner Books, 2003), p. 441.
65. James M. Landis, 28, "The Legislative History of the Securities Act of 1933," *Geo. Wash. L. Rev.*, 29 (1959), p. 33.
66. Ritchie, *James M. Landis*, pp. 1–28.
67. McKean, *Peddling Influence*, p. 38.
68. Landis, *The Legislative History of the Securities Act of 1933*, p. 34.
69. Felix Frankfurter, *Felix Frankfurter Reminisces*, recorded talks with Dr. Harlan B. Phillips (New York: Reynal & Company, 1960), p. 235.
70. H.N. Hirsch, *The Enigma of Felix Frankfurter* (New York: Basic Books, Inc., 1981), p. 100.
72. Ibid., p. 148–149.
73. Hirsch, *The Enigma of Felix Frankfurter*, p. 103.
74. Freidel, *Franklin D. Roosevelt, Launching of the New Deal*, pp. 346–347.
75. Ibid., pp. 34–35.
76. Ibid., p. 36.
77. Freidel, *Franklin D. Roosevelt—Launching the New Deal*, p. 347.
78. Landis, *The Legislative History of the Securities Act of 1933*, pp. 36–37.
79. Thomas Eliot, "The Social Security Bill 25 Years After" (originally published in *Atlantic Monthly* and reprinted by permission), available at www.ssa.gov/history.

80. John M. Kernochan, "A University Service to Legislation: Columbia's Legislative Drafting Research Fund," 16, *Louisiana Law Review,* p. 623 (June 1956).

81. Landis, *The Legislative History of the Securities Act of 1933,* p. 37.

82. Ibid., p. 38.

83. William Lysser, *Benjamin V. Cohen, Architect of the New Deal* (New Haven, CT: Yale University Press, 2002), pp. 77–79.

84. Ibid.

85. Landis, *The Legislative History of the Securities Act of 1933,* p. 29.

86. Ibid.

87. Lasser, *Benjamin V. Cohen, Architect of the New Deal,* p. 77.

88. Freidel, *Franklin D. Roosevelt—Launching the New Deal,* p. 348.

89. Landis, *The Legislative History of the Securities Act of 1933,* p. 40.

90. Ritchie, *James M. Landis,* p. 48.

91. Caro, *The Years of Lyndon Johnson, The Path to Power,* p. 323.

92. H.R. 5480, 73d Cong., 1st sess. (1933).

93. Seligman, *The Transformation of Wall Street,* p. 66.

94. H.R. Rep. No. 85 (accompanying H.R. 5480), 73d Cong., 1st sess. (1933).

95. "Securities Bill Today," *The Wall Street Journal,* May 5, 1933.

96. 77th Cong., *Cong. Rec.* 2910 (1933).

97. "Securities Bill Passed by House; Vote Unanimous," *The New York Times,* May 6, 1933.

98. Benjamin V. Cohen, letter to James M. Landis, May 5, 1933.

99. "Attacks Securities Bill," *The New York Times,* May 8, 1933.

100. Ibid.

101. "National Affairs: Glass's Stand," *Time,* May 8, 1933.

102. "Senators Revise Securities Bill," *The New York Times,* April 9, 1933.

103. "Securities Bill in Third Print," *The Wall Street Journal,* April 14, 1933.

104. Seligman, *The Transformation of Wall Street,* pp. 67–68.

105. Ibid., p. 68.

106. Landis, *The Legislative History of the Securities Act of 1933,* pp. 42–43.

107. H.R. Rep. No. 152, 73d Cong., 1st sess. (1933).

108. Caro, *The Years of Lyndon Johnson, The Path to Power,* p. 325.

109. Landis, *The Legislative History of the Securities Act of 1933,* p. 45.

110. Ibid., pp. 45–46.

111. Ibid., pp. 44–47.

112. Ibid., p. 48.

113. Ibid., pp. 48–49.

114. H.R. Rep. No. 152, 73d Cong., 1st sess. (1933).

115. "House Repasses Securities Bill," *The Wall Street Journal,* May 23, 1933.

116. "Truth in Securities Bill Repassed by House, Senate," *The Wall Street Journal,* May 25, 1933.

117. "Roosevelt Signs the Securities Bill," *The New York Times,* May 28, 1933.

118. "Roosevelt Approves Securities Measures," *The Wall Street Journal,* May 29, 1933.

119. "Roosevelt Signs the Securities Bill," *The New York Times,* May 28, 1933.

120. Benjamin V. Cohen, letter to James M. Landis, June 7, 1933.
121. Montville, *The Big Bam,* Chap. 22.
122. Joseph H. Baird, "Key Pittman: Frontier Statesman," *The American Mercury,* July 1940, p. 313.
123. Brooks, *Once in Golconda,* p. 158.
124. Ibid.
125. Betty Glad, *Key Pittman* (New York: Columbia University Press, 1986), p. 199.
126. Ibid.

CHAPTER SIX

1. Brooks, *Once in Golconda,* p. 211.
2. Seligman, *The Transformation of Wall Street,* p. 73.
3. "Whitney Confers with Roosevelt," *The New York Times,* April 6, 1933.
4. Parrish, *Securities Regulation and the New Deal,* p. 108.
5. "Kuhn, Loeb Inquiry to Sift Rail Deals," *The New York Times,* June 27, 1933; "Then a Private Citizen," *The New York Times,* June 28, 1933.
6. Michael Kilian, "All for Sport," *Chicago Tribune,* March 2, 1988.
7. Chernow, *The House of Morgan,* p. 197.
8. Parrish, *Securities Regulation and the New Deal,* p. 110.
9. Arthur Dean, "The Federal Securities Act," *Fortune,* August 1933, p. 30.
10. Ibid., p. 106.
11. Ibid.
12. "Securities Law Changes Urged," *The Wall Street Journal,* September 13, 1933.
13. Ibid.
14. Montville, *The Big Bam,* Chap. 22.
15. "Business: Dillon's Pyramid," *Time,* October 16, 1933.
16. Ibid.
17. Report of the Committee on Banking and Currency, 73d Cong., 2d sess., Rep. 1455, pp. 145–148.
18. Senate Committee on Banking and Currency, *Hearings on Stock Exchange Practices,* 73d Cong., 2d sess., p. 2109.
19. Brooks, *Once in Golconda,* p. 198.
20. Ibid., pp. 198–199
21. "Exchange Rejects Pecora's Demands," *The New York Times,* October 17, 1933.
22. "Protest Pecora Order," *The New York Times,* October 18, 1933.
23. "Chase Bank Voted Salary of $100,000 to Wiggin for Life," *The New York Times,* October 18, 1933; "Business: Senate Revelations 5:1," *Time,* October 30, 1933.
24. Ibid.
25. "Chase Securities Since 1929 Set Aside $119,000,000 to Loss," *The New York Times,* October 19, 1933.
26. "Wiggin Pools Sold Chase Bank Stock," *The New York Times,* October 20, 1933.
27. Pecora, *Wall Street Under Oath,* p. 152.

28. Senate Committee on Banking and Currency, *Hearings on Stock Market Practices*, 73d Congress, 1st sess., p. 2432.

29. "Chase Stock Sold Short by Wiggin Before 1929 Crash," *The New York Times*, November 1, 1933; Pecora, *Wall Street Under Oath*, pp. 154–161.

30. "Operations of Pool Are Told," *The New York Times*, November 2, 1933; Pecora, *Wall Street Under Oath*, pp. 154–161.

31. Pecora, *Wall Street Under Oath*, p. 168.

32. Senate Committee on Banking and Currency, 73d Cong., 2d sess. S. Rep. 1455, pp. 63–66.

33. Ibid., pp. 215–220; "Rockefeller Part in Pool Gift Denied," *The New York Times*, November 16, 1933.

34. Ibid.; "Business & Finance: Senate Revelations, 5:4," *Time*, November 20, 1933.

35. Parrish, *Securities Regulation and the New Deal*, pp. 113–114.

36. Seligman, *The Transformation of Wall Street*, p. 81.

37. Ibid., pp. 81–82.

38. Ibid.

39. Parrish, *Securities Regulation and the New Deal*, p. 115.

40. Herbert Levy, *Henry Morgenthau Jr.* (New York: Skyhorse Press, 2010), Chap. 2.

41. Levy, *Henry Morgenthau Jr.*, Chap. 3.

42. Ibid., Chap. 5.

43. Ibid.

44. Ibid.

45. David Nasaw, *The Chief* (New York: Houghton Mifflin Company, 2000), Chap. 32 (Citing Morgenthau Diaries, September 11, 1934).

46. Seligman, *The Transformation of Wall Street*, p. 85.

47. "Reporters Advise Bankers on Policy," *The New York Times*, October 30, 1933.

48. "IBA Asks Change in Security Law," *The Wall Street Journal*, October 31, 1933.

49. "Exchange Control Studied in Capital," *The New York Times*, December 5, 1933.

50. "Whitney Denies Exchange Plans a Drive for Public Aid to Combat Regulation," *The New York Times*, December 6, 1933.

51. "Business: Ganged," *Time*, December 4, 1933.

52. "Business & Finance: First Plunge," *Time*, December 25, 1933.

53. "Survey of Markets by Filene Near End," *The New York Times*, January 1, 1934.

54. Ibid.

55. Montville, *The Big Bam*, Chap. 23.

56. Stock Exchange Regulation—Letter for Mr. President of the United States to the Chairman of the Committee on Banking and Currency with an Accompanying Report Relative to Stock Exchange Regulation, 73d Cong., 2d sess., (Washington, D.C.: U.S. Government Printing Office, 1934).

57. Ibid.; "Advise Control of Stock Market," *The New York Times*, January 27, 1934.

58. Seligman, *The Transformation of Wall Street*, p. 85.

59. "Senators to Rush Exchange Control," *The New York Times*, January 31, 1934.

60. "Whitney Plan Is Rejected," *The New York Times*, January 31, 1934.

61. "Pecora Demands Exchange Control," *The New York Times*, February 4, 1934.

62. Ibid.

63. "Roosevelt Speeds Bill on Exchanges," *The New York Times,* February 8, 1934.

64. "Filene Fund Urges Curb on Exchanges," *The New York Times,* February 9, 1934.

65. Seligman, *The Transformation of Wall Street,* p. 85.

66. Message from the President of the United States Recommending Enactment of Legislation Providing for the Regulation by the Federal Government of the Operations of Exchanges Dealing in Securities and Commodities for the Protection of Investors, 73d Cong., 2d Session, S. Doc. 132.

67. H.R. 7852, 73d Cong., 2d sess.; S.R. 2693, 73d Cong, 2d sess.

68. Ibid.

69. Ibid.

70. Ibid.

71. Ibid.

72. Ibid.

73. Ibid.

74. Ibid.

75. Ibid.

76. Ibid.

77. Ibid.

78. Ibid.

79. Ibid.

80. "Fletcher's Statement on Stock Market Bill," *The New York Times,* February 10, 1934.

81. "Drastic Stock Market Bill Provides Federal Control; Outlaws 9 Types of Deals," *The New York Times,* February 10, 1934.

82. Thomas Corcoran, telegram to Felix Frankfurter, February 13, 1934.

83. "Wide Drive Begins on Exchange Bill," *The New York Times,* February 15, 1934.

84. "Whitney Extends Market Bill Fight," *The New York Times,* February 16, 1934.

85. "Three Tight Rules Added by Exchange," *The New York Times,* February 14, 1934.

86. Ibid.

87. Ibid.

88. Ibid.

89. Ibid.

90. Ibid.

91. Ibid.

92. "Whitney Extends Market Bill Fight," *The New York Times,* February 16, 1934.

93. "Wide Drive Begins on Exchange Bill," *The New York Times,* February 15, 1934.

94. "Whitney Extends Market Bill Fight," *The New York Times,* February 16, 1934.

95. Brooks, *Once in Golconda,* pp. 200–202.

96. "Flexibility Urged in Exchange Bill," *The New York Times,* February 15, 1934.

97. "Calls Floor Trades Chiselers," *The New York Times,* February 22, 1934.

98. "Whitney Proposes a Federal Board on Stock Trading," *The New York Times,* February 23, 1934.

99. Ibid.

100. S.R. 2642, 73d Cong., 2d sess.
101. Senate Committee on Banking and Currency, 73d Cong., 2d sess., S. Rep. 1455, p. 55–62; Pecora, *Wall Street Under Oath*, p. 270.
102. Senate Committee on Banking and Currency, 73d Cong., 2d sess., S. Rep. 1455, p. 61.
103. "Wall Street to the Last Drop," *Time*, September 30, 1966.
104. Brooks, *Once in Golconda*, p. 79.
105. Ibid., p. 78.
106. Ibid.
107. Ibid.
108. Herb Greenberg, "Business Insider—The Mailbag—That Quote about Shoeshine Boys and Stocks, Also Why Doesn't the SEC Find Fraud as It Reviews IPO?" *SFGate*, September 27, 1997.
109. Ronald Kessler, *The Sins of the Father* (New York: Warner Books, Inc., 1996), p. 82.
110. Richard J. Whalen, *The Founding Father* (Washington, D.C.: Regnery Gateway, 1964, 1995), p. 107.
111. Whalen, *The Founding Father*, p. 113.
112. Ibid., pp. 119–125.
113. Steven Birmingham, *Real Lace* (New York: Syracuse University Press, 1978), p. 56.
114. Birmingham, *Real Lace*, pp. 45–48.
115. Ibid., p. 52.
116. Ibid.
117. Senate Committee on Banking and Currency, 73d Cong., 2d sess., S. Rep. 1455, p. 70.
118. Ibid., p. 59.
119. Ibid., p. 61.
120. Ibid., pp. 61–62.
121. Pecora, *Wall Street Under Oath*, pp. 272–273.
122. Senate Committee of Banking and Currency, Hearings on Stock Exchange Practices, 73d Cong., 2d sess., pp. 6221–6222.
123. Ibid., p. 6223.
124. Ibid., p. 6222.
125. Ibid., p. 6229.
126. "Whitney Assails Charges of 'Propaganda' Defends Letter Warning on Exchange Curb," *The New York Times*, February 24, 1934.
127. Senate Committee on Banking and Currency, *Hearings on Stock Exchange Practices*, 73d Cong. 2d Session, pp. 6463–6581.
128. "Arbitrage Firms Protest," *The New York Times*, February 28, 1934; "Protest Control of Stock Markets," *The New York Times*, February 28, 1934; Seligman, *The Transformation of Wall Street*, p. 92.
129. "Whitney Sees Curb as Nationalization," *The New York Times*, March 1, 1934.
130. "Dickinson Opposes 'Change Curb Bill'; Fears Liquidation," *The New York Times*, March 7, 1934.
131. "Rayburn Expects Revision," *The New York Times*, March 1, 1934.
132. Seligman, *The Transformation of Wall Street*, p. 93.

133. Ibid.
134. Parrish, *Securities Regulation and the New Deal*, p. 125; Seligman, *The Transformation of Wall Street*, p. 94.
135. H.R. 8720, 73d Cong., 2d sess.
136. Ibid.
137. Ibid.
138. Ibid.
139. Ibid.
140. Ibid.
141. Ibid.
142. "Exchange Renews Its Attack on Bill," *The New York Times*, March 21, 1934.
143. Ibid.
144. Ibid.
145. Ibid.
146. "Exchange Control Strikes New Snag," *The New York Times*, March 22, 1934.
147. "Exchanges United in Attack on Bill," *The New York Times*, March 23, 1934.
148. Paul V. Shields, letter to James A. Farley, March 22, 1934.
149. Parrish, *Securities Regulation and the New Deal*, p. 140.
150. "Federal Reserve for Exchange Curb as in Pending Bill," *The New York Times*, March 24, 1934.
151. Ibid.
152. Ibid.
153. Ibid.
154. Ibid.
155. "'Brain Trust' Faces Inquiry by House on Alleged Aims," *The New York Times*, March 25, 1934.
156. "Roosevelt Wants 'Teeth' in Stock Exchange Bill; Seeks Speculation Limit," *The New York Times*, March 27, 1934.
157. "Final Pleas Heard on Exchange Curbs," *The New York Times*, March 28, 1934.
158. "New House Group to Study Changes in Exchange Bill," *The New York Times*, April 5, 1934.
159. "Untermyer Urges Exchange Control; Finds Bill Faulty," *The New York Times*, April 8, 1934.
160. "Committee Trims the Exchange Bill," *The New York Times*, April 10, 1934; "New Leeway Put in Exchange Bill," *The New York Times*, April 11, 1934; "Senators Approve New Margin Rules," *The New York Times*, April 12, 1934.
161. "Committee Trims the Exchange Bill," *The New York Times*, April 10, 1934.
162. "Senators Approve New Margin Rules," *The New York Times*, April 12, 1934.
163. Richard Whitney, letter to Franklin D. Roosevelt, April 12, 1934.
164. "New Path Charted on Exchange Bill," *The New York Times*, April 13, 1934.
165. "Further Revisions on Exchange Bill," *The New York Times*, April 14, 1934.
166. "Exchange Control Goes to Senate," *The New York Times*, April 21, 1934.
167. "House Group Backs the Exchange Bill," *The New York Times*, April 26, 1934.

168. "Charges Exchange Rules Lobby," *The New York Times*, April 24, 1934.
169. "Attack Is Opened on Exchange Bill," *The New York Times*, May 1, 1934.
170. 78th Cong., *Cong. Rec.* 7944.
171. 78th Cong., *Cong. Rec.* 7941–7943.
172. 78th Cong., *Cong. Rec.* 7948.
173. 78th Cong., *Cong. Rec.* 7960.
174. 78th Cong., *Cong. Rec.* 8007–8040.
175. 78th Cong., *Cong. Rec.* 8086–8117.
176. 78th Cong., *Cong. Rec.* 8048.
177. "Bill Would Ease the Security Act," *The New York Times,* April 6, 1934.
178. 78th Cong., *Cong. Rec.* 8160–8203, 8270–8287, 8298–8301.
179. "Senate Rejects Ban on Margins," *The New York Times*, May 10, 1934.
180. 78th Cong., *Cong. Rec.* 8714.
181. "House Stands Fast on Exchange Bill," *The New York Times,* May 15, 1934.
182. "Exchange Bill Tilt Stirs Ire of Glass," *The New York Times,* May 16, 1934.
183. "President Favors House Bill Terms on Exchange Curb," *The New York Times*, May 17, 1934.
184. "Exchange Bill Conferees Defer Disputes to Cool Down Revolt Over Control Board," *The New York Times*, May 18, 1934.
185. "One Change Halted in Securities Act," *The New York Times*, May 25, 1934.
186. "Talk Compromise on Exchange Bill," *The New York Times*, May 26, 1934.
187. "Exchange Bill Agreement Provides New 5-Man Board, Flexible Curb on Margins," *The New York Times,* May 27, 1934.
188. Seligman, *The Transformation of Wall Street*, p. 99.
189. "Stock Exchange Pledges Cooperation in Act; Whitney 'Hopeful' Law Will Be 'Constructive,'" *The New York Times*, June 2, 1934.
190. Richard Whitney, letter to Franklin D. Roosevelt, May 30, 1934.

CHAPTER SEVEN

1. *Hostage to Fortune, the Letters of Joseph P. Kennedy*, ed. Amanda Smith (New York: Viking, Penguin Putnam Inc., 2001), p. 107.
2. Ibid.
3. Joseph P. Kennedy, memorandum, *Hostage to Fortune*, pp. 127–129.
4. Ibid.
5. Ibid.
6. Joseph P. Kennedy to Joseph P. Kennedy Jr., May 4, 1934, *Hostage to Fortune*, pp. 133–136.
7. Thomas Corcoran, letter to Felix Frankfurter, May 11, 1934.
8. Moley, *After Seven Years*, pp. 286–287.
9. "Brokers Discuss New Control Body," *The New York Times*, June 22, 1934.
10. Joseph P. Kennedy, memorandum, *Hostage to Fortune*, pp. 136–139.
11. "Naming of Securities Commission Likely Early This Week; J.M. Landis Seen as Head," *The New York Times*, June 25, 1934.

12. Joseph P. Kennedy, memorandum, *Hostage to Fortune*, pp. 136–139.
13. Ibid.
14. Ibid.
15. Joseph P. Kennedy, memorandum, *Hostage to Fortune*, pp. 136–139.
16. Ibid.
17. Ibid.
18. Ibid.
19. Seligman, *The Transformation of Wall Street*, p. 105.
20. Whalen, *The Founding Father*, p. 144.
21. Moley, *After Seven Years*, p. 289.
22. "Kennedy in Chair After Long Parley by Exchange Board," *The New York Times*, July 3, 1934.
23. Seligman, *The Transformation of Wall Street*, p. 108.
24. "Kennedy in Chair After Long Parley By Exchange Board," *The New York Times*, July 3, 1934.
25. "Kennedy Declares Speculation War," *The New York Times*, July 4, 1934.
26. Ibid.
27. Whalen, *The Founding Father*, p. 145.
28. Doris Kearns Goodwin, *The Fitzgeralds and the Kennedys* (New York: St. Martin's Press, 1987), p. 448.
29. Harold L. Ickes, *The Secret Diary of Harold L. Ickes, The First Thousand Days, 1933–1936* (New York: Simon and Schuster, 1953), p. 172.
30. Seligman, *The Transformation of Wall Street*, p. 107.
31. Moley, *After Seven Years*, p. 284.
32. Seligman, *The Transformation of Wall Street*, p. 106.
33. Whalen, *The Founding Father*, p. 131.
34. Ibid., p. 103.
35. Ibid., p. 210.
36. Interview with Michael J. Meehan II, November 4, 2014, at the Brook Club, New York City.
37. Geoffrey Perret, *Jack, A Life Like No Other* (New York: Random House, Inc., 2001), p. 188.
38. Arthur Krock, "In Washington," *The New York Times*, July 4, 1934.
39. "Kennedy Started as Candy Vendor," *The New York Times*, July 3, 1934.
40. "'Change Board Bans Staff Speculator," *The New York Times*, July 7, 1934.
41. Securities and Exchange Commission, Telephone Directory, July 1, 1935.
42. Seligman, *The Transformation of Wall Street*, p. 110.
43. Charles R. Geisst, *Wall Street: A History*, (New York: Oxford University Press, 1997), p. 231.
44. Peter Collier and David Horowitz, *The Kennedys* (San Francisco: Encounter Books, 1984), p. 7.
45. Franklin & Eleanor Roosevelt Institute Website, Biographies, Judge John Burns (available at newdeal.feri.org).
46. Joseph P. Kennedy, letter to Bart A. Brickley, July 14, 1934; "Kennedy Appoints a Judge Counsel," *The New York Times*, July 17, 1934.

47. Interview with Milton V. Freeman, *The Making of the New Deal, the Insiders Speak,* ed. Katie Louchheim, (Cambridge, MA: Harvard University Press, 1983), pp. 141–142.

48. Ibid.

49. Whalen, *The Founding Father,* p. 154.

50. John T. Flynn, "Other People's Money," *The New Republic,* July 18, 1934, pp. 264–265.

51. Ibid.

52. Ibid.

53. *Financial Statements Under the Securities Act and the Securities Exchange Act Report,* submitted to the Securities and Exchange Commission by a Joint Committee representing the American Institute of Accountants and the American Society of Certified Public Accountants, August 3, 1934, p. 1.

54. "Discuss Workings of Exchange Law," *The New York Times,* July 25, 1934.

55. Joseph P. Kennedy, (address, National Press Club, July 25, 1934).

56. Ibid.

57. "Whitney, Exchange Head, Approves Stand of Kennedy of Securities Commission," *The New York Times,* July 27, 1934.

58. A.M. Berle Jr., letter to Joseph P. Kennedy, July 30, 1934.

59. "Kennedy Sees End of 'Shoestring Era,'" *The New York Times,* August 12, 1934.

60. Ibid.

61. Ibid.

62. Ibid.

63. "Board Issues First Rules on Control of Exchanges; Wall Street Fears Allayed," *The New York Times,* August 14, 1934.

64. Ibid.

65. "Rules Set for Sale of Unlisted Shares," *The New York Times,* August 30, 1934.

66. "Sees No Upheaval in Exchange Rules," *The New York Times,* September 15, 1934.

67. "Kennedy and Aides Inspect Exchange," *The New York Times,* September 19, 1934.

68. Ibid.

69. Ibid.

70. Montville, *The Big Bam,* Chap. 22.

71. "Exchange Board Halts B.M.T. Action," *The New York Times,* September 27, 1934.

72. Securities and Exchange Commission, *First Annual Report of the Securities Exchange Commission, Fiscal Year Ended June 30, 1935,* pp. 11–13.

73. Ibid.

74. Ibid., p. 20.

75. Joseph P. Kennedy, memorandum to the Executive Director of the National Emergency Council, November 23, 1934.

76. Joseph P. Kennedy (address, Boston Chamber of Commerce, November 15, 1934), Washington, D.C.: U.S. Government Printing Office, 1934.

77. Ibid., p. 5.

78. Ibid., p. 6.

79. Ibid., p. 7.

80. Ibid.

81. Securities and Exchange Commission, *Release No. 66,* December 21, 1934.
82. Seligman, *The Transformation of Wall Street,* pp. 109–110; "Topics in Wall Street," *The New York Times,* January 11, 1935.
83. "New SEC Rules Monday in Move to Free Capital," January 11, 1935.
84. "Securities Filing Simplified by SEC to Loosen Capital," *The New York Times,* January 14, 1935.
85. Ibid.
86. Ibid.
87. Ibid.
88. James M. Landis, "Interpretations of Rules and Regulations of the Securities and Exchange Commission," (address, New York State Society of Certified Public Accountants, Waldorf-Astoria Hotel, January 14, 1935.
89. George C. Mathews, (address, Illinois Society of Certified Public Accountants, January 18, 1935).
90. Judge John J. Burns, (address, delivered to the chairman of the Investment Bankers Regional Code Committees, Washington, D.C., January 15, 1935).
91. "SEC Names Confirmed," *The New York Times,* January 17, 1935.
92. Ferdinand Pecora, letter to Franklin D. Roosevelt, January 18, 1935.
93. Seligman, *The Transformation of Wall Street,* p. 123.
94. "First SEC Chairman Works Long Hours," *The New York Times,* January 20, 1935.
95. Ibid.
96. Whalen, *"The Founding Father,"* p. 154.
97. Ibid.
98. "Stock Racketeers Face Heavy Drive," *The New York Times,* January 20, 1935.
99. Kessler, *The Sins of the Father,* p. 121.
100. Report on the Government of Securities Exchanges, 79th Cong., 1st sess., Document No. 85, p. 17.
101. Eugene Lokey, "Along the Highways of Finance," *The New York Times,* February 10, 1935.
102. "Stock Exchange to Take No Liability for Reports," *The New York Times,* January 31, 1935.
103. Joseph P. Kennedy (address, Union League of Chicago, Illinois, February 8, 1935) Washington, D.C.: U.S. Government Printing Office, 1935.
104. "Kennedy Hails Cooperation," *The New York Times,* February 16, 1935.
105. Joseph P. Kennedy to Kathleen Kennedy, February 20, 1935, *Hostage to Fortune,* p. 151.
106. Registration on Form A-2 of Swift and Company With Respect to $43,000,000, 3¾% First Mortgage Sinking Fund Bonds, as filed with the Securities and Exchange Commission on March 7, 1935.
107. "Swift's Bond Issue Ends Security Jam," *The New York Times,* March 8, 1935.
108. Ibid.
109. Ibid.
110. Eugene Lokey, "Along the Highways of Finance," *The New York Times,* March 10, 1935.
111. Arthur Krock, "In Washington," *The New York Times,* March 8, 1935.
112. Robert H. Gerdes, telegram to the Securities and Exchange Commission, March 8, 1935.

113. Joseph P. Kennedy (address, American Arbitration Association, New York City, March 19, 1935) Washington, D.C.: United States Government Printing Office, 1935.
114. Ibid.
115. Seligman, *The Transformation of Wall Street*, p 116.
116. "Whitney Confers With Kennedy," *The New York Times*, March 14, 1935.
117. Joseph P. Kennedy, memorandum to Richard Whitney, March 21, 1935.
118. J.P. Morgan & Co., memorandum to David Saperstein, March 30, 1935.
119. Bond Club of New Jersey, memorandum to the Securities and Exchange Commission, April 9, 1935.
120. Montville, *The Big Bam*, Chap. 23.
121. Ibid.
122. Ibid.
123. Ibid.
124. "SEC Offers Rules to Check 'Abuses,'" *The New York Times*, April 17, 1935.
125. Ibid.
126. Brooks, *Once in Golconda*, pp. 225–229.
127. Ibid., pp. 226–227; Seligman, *The Transformation of Wall Street*, p. 120.
128. Joseph P. Kennedy, telegram to Felix Frankfurter, April 12, 1935.
129. Joseph P. Kennedy (address, Tercentenary Dinner, 1635–1935, Boston Latin School, The Copley Plaza, Boston, April 23, 1935).
130. Ibid.
131. "Advertising Rules Are Eased by SEC," *The New York Times*, May 3, 1935.
132. "Insuring an 'Even Break' for Investors," by Charles W. B. Hurd, *The New York Times*, May 26, 1935.
133. Brooks, *Once in Golconda*, p. 227.
134. Charles W.B. Hurd, "Insuring an 'Even Break' for Investors," *The New York Times*, May 26, 1935.
135. Ibid.
136. Whalen, *The Founding Father*, pp. 174–175.
137. "Business & Finance: Personnel: June 24, 1935," *Time*, June 29, 1935.
138. "Kennedy in Office a Year," *The New York Times*, July 1, 1935.
139. "Business: Reform & Realism," *Time*, July 22, 1935.
140. Ibid.
141. "Kennedy May Quit as SEC Chairman," *The New York Times*, August 16, 1935.
142. Securities and Exchange Commission, Staff Memorandum, September 1935; "SEC Calls Meehan for Stock Inquiry," *The New York Times*, October 27, 1935.
143. "Meehan, Broker, Ill in Sanatorium," *The New York Times*, November 25, 1936.
144. Brooks, *Once in Golconda*, pp. 278–279.
145. Ritchie, *James M. Landis*, p. 71.
146. "Text of SEC Order Against Meehan," *The New York Times*, October 27, 1935.
147. "Meehan Is Guilty, SEC Agent Finds," *The New York Times*, December 16, 1936.
148. "SEC Expels Meehan on Rigging Charge," *The New York Times*, August 3, 1937.
149. "Meehan Expelled from 3 Exchanges," *The New York Times*, August 20, 1937.

150. "SEC Expels Meehan on Rigging Charge," *The New York Times*, August 3, 1937.
151. Joseph P. Kennedy, letter to President Roosevelt, September 6, 1935; "Kennedy Observes Birthday," *The New York Times*, September 7, 1935.
152. Ibid.
153. Ibid.
154. Joseph P. Kennedy to George Steele, September 6, 1935, *Hostage to Fortune*, p. 160.
155. Franklin D. Roosevelt, letter to Joseph P. Kennedy, September 20, 1935.
156. "Kennedy Predicts Big Capital Issues," *The New York Times*, September 21, 1935.
157. Ibid.
158. Ibid.
159. "Topics in Wall Street," *The New York Times*, September 21, 1935.
160. John T. Flynn, "Other People's Money," *The New Republic*, October 9, 1935, p. 244.
161. Charles Gay, letter to Joseph P. Kennedy, September 21, 1935.
162. "Landis Heads SEC; Succeeds Kennedy," *The New York Times*, September 24, 1935.

EPILOGUE

1. Montville, *The Big Bam*, Chap. 25.
2. Ibid.
3. Elizabeth Owen, "Bankers Trust Acquires Alex. Brown," *Time*, April 7, 1997.
4. Mitchell Martin, "Citicorp and Travelers Plan to Merge in Record $70 Billion Deal," *The New York Times*, April 7, 1998.
5. Ibid.
6. H.R. 10, 106th Cong.
7. Bill Clinton (statement, signing of the Financial Modernization Bill, November 12, 1999).
8. "W.H. Woodin Dies Here at Age 65," *The New York Times*, May 4, 1934.
9. Daniel Scroop, *Mr. Democrat* (Ann Arbor, MI: The University of Michigan Press, 2006), p. 189; "Carter Glass, 88, Dies in Capital," *The New York Times*, May 30, 1946.
10. White, *Kingfish*, Chap. 16.
11. McKean, *Peddling Influence*, p. 197.
12. Ibid., pp. 197–198.
13. Ibid., pp. 267–271.
14. "Thomas G. Corcoran, Aide to Roosevelt, Dies," *The New York Times*, December 7, 1981.
15. D.B. Hardeman and Donald C. Bacon, *Rayburn* (Austin, TX: Texas Monthly Press, Inc., 1987), p 207.
16. Ibid., pp. 207–208.
17. Ibid., pp. 212–213; McKean; *Peddling Influence*, p. 74.
18. Hardeman and Bacon, *Rayburn*, p. 213.
19. Ibid., p. 243.
20. Speaker Tip O'Neill (with William Novak), *Man of the House*, (New York: Random House, Inc., 1987), pp. 128–129.
21. Ibid.
22. Ibid., p. 130.

23. Ibid.

24. Ibid., p. 131.

25. Ibid.

26. "Rayburn Is Dead ; Served 17 Years as House Speaker," *The New York Times*, November 17, 1961.

27. Telephone interview with the Hon. Barney Frank, December 2, 2014.

28. "Arthur H. Dean, Envoy to Korea Talks, Dies at 89," *The New York Times*, December 1, 1987.

29. Ibid.

30. "Young Key Pittman Waits to be Resurrected," *Henderson Home News and Boulder City News*, February 18, 1991

31. "The Mysterious Demise of Key Pittman," *Nevada Magazine* (October 1996), pp. 80–83.

32. Brooks, *Once in Golconda*, p. 206.

33. Ibid., p. 233; Malcom MacKay, *Impeccable Connections* (New York: Black Tower Press, 2011), pp. 82–83.

34. Ibid., pp. 234–235.

35. Ibid., pp. 228–239.

36. Ibid., pp. 246–248.

37. Ibid., p. 244.

38. Ibid., p. 256.

39. Ibid., p. 257.

40. Ibid., p. 258.

41. Ibid., p. 264.

42. Ibid., p. 267.

43. Ibid., pp. 266–267.

44. Chernow, *House of Morgan*, Chap. 21.

45. Brooks, *Once in Golconda*, pp. 268–269.

46. Ibid., p. 270.

47. Ibid., p. 271.

48. Ibid., p. 272.

49. Ibid., p. 274.

50. Ibid., p. 275.

51. Ibid., p. 277.

52. Ibid., p. 286.

53. Ibid., p. 287.

54. MacKay, *Impeccable Connections*, pp. 103–104.

55. "Good Humor in Sedate Company; Purchase by Lipton Adds Ice Cream to Tea Line," *The New York Times*, April 27, 1961.

56. "Meehan's Son Buys Stock Exchange Seat," *The New York Times*, March 25, 1939.

57. "New York Stock Exchange Nominates Henry Walker, Jr. as Chairman," *The New York Times*, April 10, 1962.

58. Interview with Michael J. Meehan II, November 4, 2014, at the Brook Club, New York City.

59. "M.J. Meehan Dies, Once Stockbroker," *The New York Times*, January 3, 1948.

60. David Nasaw, *The Patriarch* (New York: Penguin Press, 2012), Chap. 18.

61. Whalen, *The Founding Father*, p. 305.

62. Whalen, *The Founding Father*, p. 495.

63. Kessler, *The Sins of the Father*, p. 348.

ACKNOWLEDGMENTS

The great fun of writing this book was made possible by a number of people to whom I need to express my gratitude, but none more supporting, encouraging, smarter, or better looking than my wife, Chele Upton Farley.

Literally every word of this book was written out longhand on yellow legal pads in my shockingly illegible handwriting. The task of deciphering it all (and running my life generally) fell on Arlene Colon, my always unflappable, entirely loyal and multitalented executive assistant at Paul Hastings LLP. We are lucky at Paul Hastings to have the most extraordinary leadership team. I am grateful for the support throughout of our chairman, Seth Zachary, and managing partner, Greg Nitzkowski.

Judith Regan is a legend. And she's back! She is also the most compassionate and loyal friend (when you're down even more than when you're up). She's assembled an all-star team at Regan Arts, and they are a joy to work with. Lucas Wittmann endured too many emails, phone calls, and practical jokes while working tirelessly, as did Michael Moynihan, my editor. Richard Ljoenes, who designed the cover, is a true artist. I also want to thank Lynne Ciccaglione, Emi Battaglia, and Lara Kleinschmidt at Regan Arts. Last, but certainly not least, thanks must go out to Leon and Debra Black.

I am lucky to have a great publicist to promote this book. Dini von Mueffling and her team are stars. I also must thank my attorney, Ed Hayes. It's true—he really can get you out of anything. Ann Caruso was always available to vet ideas—and stopped a few bad ones! Gladys Hernandez held down the

ACKNOWLEDGMENTS   283

fort at Sutton Place while Antonia Carmona kept the four Farley boys from hurting each other! We are so fortunate to have them in our family.

A number of people kindly took the time to talk with me about family members, colleagues, and other matters of critical importance in writing this book. Barney Frank read every word and made me defend any he couldn't agree with. He, of course, was right, and the final product reflects his generous input. Congressman Joseph P. Kennedy III and Amanda Kennedy Smith were very helpful on matters relating to their grandfather. And, special thanks must be given to Max Kennedy and his wife, Vicki, who enthusiastically encouraged this project and were unconditionally supportive. Michael J. Meehan II graciously endured my questions, corrected my errors, and told me wonderful stories about his incredibly talented and colorful grandfather. (I must also thank Bill Detwiler for encouraging Mungo to speak with me.) Senator Christopher Dodd and his former top economic aide, Aaron Klein, were both generous with their time in reading the manuscript and making improvements. Sheila Bair, who knows more about this subject matter than anyone alive, was incredibly helpful. Jonathan Alter, the leading historian on FDR's Hundred Days and an expert on the presidency, agreed to read the galley after my wife charmed him at a dinner party. He was incredibly kind to blurb the book.

IMAGE CREDITS

PHOTO INSERT

1   © Bettmann/CORBIS (top); © Corbis (bottom)
2   © Bettmann/Corbis (top); © Bettmann/CORBIS (bottom)
3   © Condé Nast Archive/CORBIS (top); © Corbis (bottom)
4   Keystone/Getty Images (top); © Bettmann/CORBIS (bottom)
5   © Bettmann/CORBIS (top left); © Bettmann/CORBIS (top right); © Bettmann/CORBIS (bottom)
6   © Corbis (top); © Bettmann/CORBIS (bottom left); © Corbis (bottom right)
7   © Bettmann/CORBIS
8   © Corbis (top); © Bettmann/CORBIS (bottom)
9   © Bettmann/CORBIS (left); © Bettmann/CORBIS (right)
10 © Bettmann/CORBIS
11 © Corbis (top); © Bettmann/CORBIS (bottom)
12 © Bettmann/CORBIS (top); © Bettmann/CORBIS (bottom left); © Bettmann/CORBIS (bottom right)
13 Underwood And Underwood/The LIFE Images Collection/Getty Images (top); © Bettmann/CORBIS (bottom)
14 © Bettmann/CORBIS
15 © Bettmann/CORBIS (top); © Corbis (bottom)
16 © Bettmann/CORBIS

INDEX

Hartman, Sheridan & Tekulsky, 25
Hastings, Daniel, 186
Hastings bill, 186
Hayden, Stone & Co., 145
Haynes, John Wesley, 227
Healy, Robert E., 193, 194, 195, 196, 204, 217
Hearst, William Randolph, 142, 165, 194, 203
Heinze, Augustus, 4
Heinze, Otto, 4
Henderson, Alexander, 114
Hibernia Bank and Trust Company of New
    Orleans, 17
Hitler, Adolf, 47, 246
hoarding, 49, 76; currency hoarding, 14–15,
    20, 45–46, 49, 53–54, 56–57, 76, 77; of
    food, 46; of gold, 77
holding companies, 97, 219; bank holding
    companies, 71, 87; utility holding
    companies, 231
Holmes, Oliver Wendell, 12
Holocaust, 254
Home Owners' Loan Act, 15
Home Owners' Loan Corporation, 15
Hood, A.J. "Bart," 248
Hoover, Herbert, 8, 10–11, 14–16, 20, 23, 26,
    42, 44, 49, 109
Hoover Commission, 254–255
Hornblower and Weeks, 218
housing bubbles, 15
Howard, Roy, 194, 198
Howe, Louis M., 20, 21, 57–58, 199
Hoxsey, J.M.B., 205
H.R. 5480, 115–116
Hubell, Carl, 226
Huddleston, George, 107, 118, 179, 186
Hughes, Charles Evans, 44, 92
Hughes Commission, 92
Hull, Cordell, 118, 123
Hyva Corporation, 169

Ickes, Harold, 197
Idaho, 41
Illinois, 42, 95–96

Illinois Bell Telephone Company, 235
Illinois Society of Certified Public
    Accountants, 216
I'm for Roosevelt (Joseph P. Kennedy),
    254
inflation, 46, 76, 77
inflationary policy, 21, 26, 76, 77, 123, 124,
    141, 179, 240
Inouye, Daniel, 246–247
Insull, Samuel, 11
insurance companies, 4
Internal Revenue Service, 29, 142
international trade, 8, 123
Internet-telecom bubble, 252
interstate commerce, 95–96, 97, 98–99
Interstate Commerce Commission, 95, 213
Investment Bankers Association of
    America, 105, 116, 143, 222
Investment Bankers Regional Code
    Committees, 216
investment banking: predecessors of, 81–83
    (see also private banks); separation
    from commercial banking, 67, 74,
    77–80, 86, 89, 124–125, 130, 202–203,
    240–242. See also specific banks
Investment Company Act of 1940, 247
investment trusts, 70, 132
Irish and Irish Americans, 128, 162–163,
    165–166, 200–201, 203, 218, 232–233,
    242, 253
Irish rebellion, 242
Irving Trust Company, 62
Italian Americans, 26

J&W Seligman & Co., 38–39
Jews, 8, 127–128, 175, 202; European, 254;
    German, 128; securities reform
    movement and, 202; WASP-Jewish
    relationship, 128
Johnson, Hiram, 117–118, 118, 120
Johnson, Lyndon Baines, 51, 132, 240, 247
Jones, Jesse, 11, 142–143
Jones, Metze, 101–102